You Can't Have My Daughter

You Can't Have My Daughter

*A true story of a mother's fight to save
her daughter from Oxford's sex traffickers*

ELIZABETH McDONNELL

PAN BOOKS

First published 2015 by Pan Books
an imprint of Pan Macmillan, a division of Macmillan Publishers Limited
Pan Macmillan, 20 New Wharf Road, London N1 9RR
Basingstoke and Oxford
Associated companies throughout the world
www.panmacmillan.com

ISBN 978-1-4472-7085-0

135798642

A CIP catalogue record for this book is available from the British Library.

Printed and bound by CPI Group (UK) Ltd, Croydon, CR0 4YY

Visit **www.panmacmillan.com** to read more about all our books
and to buy them. You will also find features, author interviews and
news of any author events, and you can sign up for e-newsletters
so that you're always first to hear about our new releases.

To Lara, Noah and Olivia,
the best is yet to be.

This book is also dedicated to the memory
of our dear friend 'Mary' who shared much of
the desperation of the times described here with us,
but who died before she could see us survive
and emerge the other side.

CONTENTS

INTRODUCTION

We are sitting at the back of court 12 in the Old Bailey under-neath the public gallery so we can't be seen. Four of the six victims are here, with either a family member or social worker or similar. Each of us has a police officer sitting with us, which makes us feel cared for and protected. We have come to court for the sentencing of the Oxford gang who groomed, trafficked and abused six girls for over eight years. One of those girls is sitting beside me, bolt upright, a terrified look in her eyes. She is my daughter, Lara. She is now nearly twenty-one, but was just twelve years old when she fell into their clutches. She is shaking like a leaf but determined to see this through. I am surprised to realize that I have never before met the three other victims who are here today. They are not girls Lara used to hang around with, although one of the two girls who have chosen not to be here was.

Stuck at the back of the court, it's really hard to hear the judge. Did he say, 'Life'? I turn to the police officer next to me and see she is grinning and giving the thumbs-up to a colleague. And then it keeps coming: 'Life . . . Life . . . Life . . . Life . . . Life . . .'

The court is quietly buzzing now. A couple of the journalists, including a familiar face, Naresh Puri from the BBC, leave the courtroom, presumably wanting to be the first to broadcast the news of the sentences to the outside world. The rest of the journalists are scribbling or texting furiously. The police are exchanging triumphant glances and discreet air punches. The jury, too, most of whom have returned for the sentencing, are looking jubilant. Sadly, from our position, all we can really see are the backs of the heads of the defence barristers, but one of the prosecution barristers is chuckling and keeps tipping his wig over his eyes.

Not all of the gang are in court for the sentencing, and it's hard to see them anyway because we are below the glass-fronted dock, but I need to try and get one good look at the men who blighted our lives for so long, so I stand up and stare into the dock. One of them is yawning, another smirking; the rest are staring into space. They look rather pathetic and insignificant with their masks of indifference. I want to look at them and feel full of hate and rage, but I don't. Contempt is about all I can muster.

Then the judge starts to catalogue some of the offences. The details are so awful they can't be reported in the media. I thought I pretty much knew everything that had happened, but I haven't been present for the entire trial, and some of the information being revealed now by the judge in his quiet, moderate, unemotional voice is beyond belief. Indescribable acts of sadistic depravity inflicted on children as young as eleven. Gradually my feelings of triumph and revenge evaporate, to be replaced by utter desolation and a grief far stronger than I have ever felt before. The distillation of eight years of abuse, suffering, pain, worry, shock and anger into a few minutes of judicial summing-up is so powerful, so potent that it's overwhelming. Suddenly I have a sense of the true awfulness of what happened to Lara and the other girls in a way I have never felt before. Stripped of the extraneous padding of our everyday life, which of course went on throughout the episodes of abuse, the sum total of the crimes themselves is too intense to bear. It's hard to breathe, and even though I feel a fool for crying when we have at last succeeded, the tears won't stop. Everywhere I look around the court – the press benches, the police, the jury, everywhere except the dock – I see people with tears streaming down their faces.

The judge praises the girls' bravery in giving evidence, thanks the police, and then, suddenly, it's all over and Lara and I leave the courtroom, ushered out in a protective huddle of police officers and witness support volunteers. Several of the journalists and reporters we have got to know over the last few months come up to us. There are smiles and handshakes, even kisses. 'Congratulations'; 'Fantastic result'; 'You must be so pleased'; 'How does it feel?'; 'Can you give us a reaction?'

Lara doesn't want to speak to anyone, but I agree to talk to a few reporters who by now feel like old friends. We have shared a lot with them, had some of them in our home to pre-record carefully anonymized interviews for radio, television and newspapers. The journalists we have chosen to give interviews to have, by and large, shown us great respect and empathy, and treated Lara's story with enormous sensitivity. Of course they want a final comment from us on this tumultuous day.

The problem is, I don't know how I feel . . . I do know that justice has been served and that life sentences show the world just how serious these crimes are, and I hope it will mark a turning point in how the courts treat child exploitation in the future. I hope, too, that it will demonstrate to Lara the true severity of what happened to her. But I can't dredge up any sound bites; I can't even articulate how I feel about the men. I feel absolutely nothing except overwhelming grief. Hollow, grey and bitter.

BBC News has booked a room in a pub over the road from the Old Bailey to record a quick interview. Lara and my brother Michael go over to wait for me, along with some of the police. We dodge the cameras on the pavement recording interviews with the Crown Prosecution Service and police. I mutter a few meaningless words to the BBC's social affairs correspondent, Alison Holt, while the cameraman carefully films just the back of my head to ensure my anonymity, and then I go to find Michael and Lara in the upstairs bar. There is a party going on.

It feels like being with a group of colleagues out in the pub on a Friday night to celebrate the end of a successful week at work. Most of these Thames Valley police officers I have never met before, but they have all worked on the case as part of Operation Bullfinch. Their sense of achievement, of a job well done, is very clear, as is the amount of personal commitment most of them have given.

After a few minutes a group of the Old Bailey's witness support volunteers who looked after us and the other witnesses in court come into the bar. They are warm and delightful women, mostly in their late sixties and seventies, and look as though they would be more at home at a coffee morning than supporting witnesses in a child exploitation and prostitution trial. They have shown great insight, understanding and compassion throughout. Now they, too, want to mark the end of a case, one that they say, even by Old Bailey standards, was complex and harrowing in the extreme. They don't join us, but we smile and wave across the bar, sharing a mutual sense of satisfaction and relief.

And then we are off, crawling through London's rush-hour traffic, back to Wales, driven by two personal protection police officers who have chauffeured us back and forth many times over the past four months. We talk and joke with the police about the traffic, the weather, other drivers on the road, anything but what we have all just witnessed. Emotionally drained, there are no words left to talk about that. No one even wants to try. We head back to the sanctuary we found when we fled Oxford and the gang three years earlier, with their threats to cut off our faces, slit our throats and behead us ringing in our ears.

Sitting in the back of the car staring out at the landmarks of the M4, a motorway that has played such a significant part in the journey Lara and I have been on since I decided to adopt a child eleven years ago, I realize that we are, for the first time, free of external interference in our lives. There are no social workers, no police, no gang members to change, distort or damage our relationship. It's up to us now. Can we go back to the beginning and rebuild something that came so close to being destroyed?

1

There Must Be More Than This

24 December 1999, 6 p.m. I was on the M4 on the way to Wales for the usual family Christmas, singing along to the radio as the Salvation Army played 'O Come, All Ye Faithful'. Late as usual. Why did I always leave wrapping presents until Christmas Eve? Truth was, I left it so late because I was always in denial about Christmas. I tried to ignore it until, like Canute, the waves broke over me.

I always had that Christmas Eve sense of 'There must be something more than this, something more I can do with my life', and this year it was even worse. The millennium was looming, along with my fiftieth birthday in six months' time. The problem with being childless, single and career-fixated was that however satisfying and stimulating and worthwhile my job was, on days like Christmas Eve, when there was no job to be done, I really didn't exist. My home life was pointless. Being the family's high-flying daughter, sister and aunt were reasonable roles to play at thirty or even forty, but at almost fifty, it had got to feel a bit inadequate. How many Christmases had I felt like this now, driving off to someone else's more meaningful, grounded and complete life and home?

Except for one year when I went trekking in East Africa and another I spent cross-country skiing in Norway, Christmas had always been a family affair, with my parents, my two younger brothers, Gerry and Michael, and, over time, their wives, in-laws and my two nieces. Originally from Merseyside, we had moved when I was a teenager to Surrey. When I left home, I went to live and work in London, where most of my work still was. However, wanting a house and garden, which were unaffordable in Central London, I had moved to Oxford ten years earlier.

Shut in the warm, dark bubble of the car on a motorway with the tumultuous music at almost full volume, it all seemed so clear: something had to change; I had to make a choice about what to do with the rest of my life.

Oh, I had recently been sounded out about a couple of prestigious end-of-career public appointments – very flattering, very exciting, and they would have been great work, but somehow this career thing was no longer enough. And time was running out to do anything but accept a few puffed-up sinecures. I didn't just want to slip into smug end-of-career mode and have nothing left to look forward to but retirement. I wanted life to be different and difficult and uncertain again.

Things had to change in 2000. But how often had I felt this on Christmas Eve only to find that the determination to make big changes slipped away with the activities, companionship and indulgences of Christmas?

Christmas Eve a year later, 3 p.m., on the M4 on the way to Wales again. I was singing the first verse of 'Once in Royal David's City' along with a chorister's treble.

The millennium and my fiftieth birthday had come and gone, and I had managed to make a few changes to my life. I'd quit my job. After over twenty years running national charities, I was now a freelance consultant working with a range of charities across the country. And I had got a dog, Meg, a West Highland terrier, and finally proved to myself I could look after something more demanding of attention and attachment than cats.

But I was still certain this was not all there could be to my life. I didn't like freelancing: the money was good, but you didn't really belong anywhere or feel truly part of anything. I so missed that. The pace and passion of running an organization gave such a sense of validation and identity and belonging.

I had got my presents wrapped a bit earlier this year, but I vowed to myself that I would make real changes to my life in 2001.

24 December 2001, noon, on the M4. I was listening to a talk on the radio about the work St Martin-in-the-Fields does at Christmas with homeless people. The sort of work I used to do and had felt engaged with and driven by since I was sixteen, until somehow career progression, complacency and middle age crept up and I rationalized away all that passion.

'Do They Know It's Christmas?' was coming out of the crackly tannoy as I filled up with petrol at Chippenham, juggling the petrol nozzle from one hand to the other because it was so cold to hold and I didn't have gloves. That's when it came to me. Right, that's it – I know what I'm going to do. I promised myself, I will never again spend a Christmas Eve feeling so superficial and unfulfilled and alone . . . I'm going to apply to foster young homeless people, perhaps care leavers. I have two spare rooms and over thirty years' professional experience helping vulnerable homeless people; now I'm going to make the professional personal. Why had I never thought of this before?

I knew there was one big thing left to do with my life – something amazing and really important. Things were truly going to change in 2002. I was determined.

I rang Oxfordshire County Council's social services department on the first working day of 2002 and spoke to someone in the Adoption and Fostering Section. I explained that I was enquiring about possibly fostering one or two young adults, that I had worked in the housing and support fields all my adult life and had two spare bedrooms. She asked me various questions about myself.

'Have you thought about adopting?' she asked.

She obviously hadn't been listening when I said I was fifty-one and single, so I repeated it.

'We no longer consider age or marital status to be an automatic barrier, especially when placing an older child. I'll send you some information about our adoption service.'

Adoption, having a child, becoming a parent . . . A shiver ran down my spine. Could that be possible?

A week later and the information hadn't come through, but there was a piece in the *Observer* about single people who adopt. It featured a first-person account by a woman in her forties who had just adopted two boys. Apparently the statistics showed that far fewer adoptions by single people break down compared to

those by married couples because the child didn't have to negotiate relationships with two parents, there could be no playing
one off against the other, and the parent had no responsibility to
a partner to factor in to how much time could be devoted to the
child. The child could have their parent's undivided time and
energy. The woman in question had adopted through NCH, a
national children's charity who act as an adoption agency, and
she rated them highly. I checked out their adoption work on the
internet and it certainly looked good, so I rang their national
office in London. Apparently Oxford wasn't covered by their
adoption service, but they said to ring their Midlands office and
ask.

I did and they said Oxford was really just outside their area,
but given the good motorway link with Birmingham, they
would stretch a point and come and visit me to have a preliminary chat.

I could hardly believe it. Was it really possible that, at the age
of fifty-one, after all those years of believing that parenthood
was for other people, I might become a mum? I walked Meg for
miles that afternoon on a cloud of incredulous, terrified excitement. Could it really happen?

Two weeks later Liz, an adoption social worker from NCH,
came to see me. I was excited and incredibly nervous all at once.
What if she thought I was totally unsuitable? Might this meeting be the end of it all?

Liz was about my age, clearly very experienced in childcare
and adoption, and in weighing up and assessing potential parents. She was warm, funny and very informal; she instantly put

me at my ease and we chatted away. She also loved dogs. Meg
jumped on her lap and didn't budge for the next two hours.

'Now, why would you want to give up this comfortable and
ordered life you have? Do you realize what a mess a child will
make of this house?'

'Yes. I think I can cope with that. Houses can always be
tidied up again.'

'And what about the loss of freedom? You won't be able to
call your life your own again for at least fifteen years.'

'But I'm tired of only having me in my life. I really feel I want
to share it. But am I too old?'

No, she said, it was perfectly possible for someone of my age
to adopt, especially an older child. A rough rule of thumb they
used was whether a child could have been the natural child of
the potential parent. So in your fifties, you might well have a
child of, say, eight or ten. She explained how NCH worked to
assess, train and approve prospective adoptive parents. Did that
sound OK? Of course it was OK. I was so fired up I would do
anything, go anywhere to become a mum.

After some preliminary paperwork and a medical check
were out of the way, Liz visited me nearly every week for ten
weeks. The assessment was nothing if not thorough. My childhood, every relationship I had ever had, my motivation for
wanting to adopt were all scrutinized in detail. I had to do
'homework', writing up a synopsis of my family, an exploration
of my reasons for wanting to adopt and an analysis of my support networks. References were taken not just in writing but by
face-to-face visits. I also attended a week-long training course
for prospective adopters in NCH's offices in Birmingham. It was
really quite rigorous and challenging, and they were very firm

about which attitudes and approaches to parenthood were and were not acceptable. I think it made one or two of those attending rethink whether adoption was for them. But I thought it was OK, just a pity that *all* parents – whether through birth or adoption – couldn't be made to go through the same process.

All the assessment and training seemed to have gone well because in the middle of June Liz visited to say everything was satisfactory and I would be 'going to panel' for approval on 10 August. I could choose to go to the meeting and talk to the panel if I wanted to. Oh yes, please! I couldn't imagine how the panel could make a decision about whether or not to approve someone as an adoptive parent without meeting them. I would definitely be there.

Hannah and Lottie, my teenage nieces, who lived in Wiltshire, came to stay and I got them to introduce me to McDonald's. All these years I had somehow managed to avoid going to one, but I couldn't be a McDonald's virgin when I finally adopted. Hannah and Lottie, and my parents, brothers and sister-in-law as well as most of my friends were, after some initial surprise at my plans, very supportive and enthusiastic about the proposed adoption. While we were out in town, I bought a child's duvet cover, and then wished I hadn't, because it might be tempting fate.

By July I was beginning to get pretty fed up with the process. It seemed to be going forward in such mini-bite-sized chunks, with huge gaps in between small bursts of activity. But by the end of the month I finally had my last assessment visit and celebrated by decorating the bedroom that the (my) child would have. I went for a gender-neutral yellow. Although I had always assumed I would adopt a girl, or girls, I supposed it could be a boy; I just felt I knew more about girls. I made a mental note to buy childproof window latches, and would I need to get a mattress protector?

And then, just two days after feeling everything was moving forward again, disaster: my application would not go to the August panel meeting after all. There had been some sort of muddle. The next panel meeting was on 24 September, when I was due to be leading a group of friends on a painting holiday in the South of France. It was all organized and couldn't go ahead without me, as I would be chauffeur, guide and cook, and we had borrowed my brother and sister-in-law's house. Liz assured me that not being there would not adversely affect my application, but I was concerned that it would make me look less than 100 per cent committed. Still, there was little I could do about it, and as the next panel might not be until November, with great regret, I decided to let my application go to the meeting on 24 September without me and hope for the best. I sent the panel a letter, which at least gave me some presence.

I had never wanted to go away on holiday less. Although the South of France wasn't the other side of the world, it seemed a long way from Birmingham, where the important decision was to be made. If that decision was to reject my application, that would probably be the end of any hopes of adopting a child.

It was a glorious early autumn day and we were sitting painting in a monastery cloister near Toulouse when Liz rang. Thank God I had managed to find somewhere with a phone signal for that afternoon's outing.

'Well, they liked you,' she said happily. 'Congratulations – you're approved! So now the real work starts. Ring me when you're back and we will begin to contact some local authorities to talk about children.'

Oh wow, oh yes, oh thank God! I wanted to jump on a plane and start ringing round local authorities myself. Instead, I had to drive everyone back to the house and cook a meal, but after that I jumped in the swimming pool and swam up and down for about an hour to try and get the adrenalin and excitement under control.

Adoption UK, a charity for adoptive parents, produce a monthly magazine called *Children Who Wait*, an Argos-style catalogue of children from tiny babies to almost teenagers. Children who, through no fault of their own, have no permanent family. They come singly, in twos or occasionally as whole family groups of four or five. There is every ethnic group; some have disabilities, physical or learning, or both; many clearly have emotional and behavioural issues. And there they were, page after heartbreaking page, every one crying out for a loving home and family. And one of them might become my child. For several weeks I couldn't bring myself to look at the magazine – it seemed wrong to be browsing through these bright little faces as though looking for a new vacuum cleaner – but after a bit I steeled myself, persuading myself that it was just a means to an end and the most effective way to start looking for a child.

I did try phoning round one or two local authorities' adoption teams, but if I got any response, it was, 'Don't call us – we'll call you.' One or two were quite hostile, particularly Birmingham, who responded to me as though I had said, 'I am ringing

to arrange to steal one of your children.' Most were simply disinterested, not even wanting to take a note of my name and
address. No wonder there were so many children stuck in care;
the inertia in the adoption system was staggering.

Liz sent me through forms on a few children for whom social
workers were looking for adoptive parents and I followed them
up, but they, too, came to nothing. In one case, the form painted
an incredibly gloomy picture of the child, not a single positive
word about her. Nothing on her interests or strengths or what
she was like to be with. Surprisingly the set form that is used to
give details of any child seeking adoption doesn't ask for that
information, so if the social worker doesn't think to put in some
positives, the form just reads like a catalogue of disasters. Some
of them almost seemed to blame the children for their predicament. They really sold some children short. So much potential
gone to waste.

So the Argos catalogue it had to be. And I must confess to a
feeling of excited anticipation each time a new edition flopped
through the letter box. This time could be the one.

And I became quite forensic in my reading of it. I was
approved to adopt one or two children from birth to age twelve
of either sex. Liz and I had talked through what sort of 'issues'
I felt I could cope with. At my age, a very small child or baby
was a non-starter, but in any case I felt I definitely wanted to
have an older child of perhaps up to age eight, one for whom
the likelihood of adoption was less. Given that my house was a
four-storey terrace with steps up to the front door and down to
the garden, it would not be sensible to consider a very severely
physically disabled child, but apart from that I was fairly open. I
certainly didn't think learning disabilities would be a particular

problem. The one area that I said I didn't think I was equipped to cope with was a child who had been severely sexually abused. I just didn't think I had the necessary knowledge or skills.

Of course, the information provided in *Children Who Wait* was limited, but most entries gave a feel for the difficulties the child was facing. Some authorities placing the entries seemed more forthcoming than others. I saw a very appealing little girl – Lauren, aged ten. She had such a sweet, slightly wistful smile and rather untidy hair. She had had huge disruptions, including a failed adoptive placement, but still believed there was a 'forever family' out there for her. I phoned the named social worker in Stoke-on-Trent and they said they would send me details via NCH.

After four weeks passed and I had heard nothing back from Stoke, I followed up on another couple of children mentioned to me by NCH. All three authorities were supposed to be interested in me, but none got back to me.

Then in mid-November a social worker from Stoke rang to say they would like to come to see me to talk about Lauren. Having heard nothing from Stoke for so long, I had rather put Lauren to the back of my mind. Though she did sound lovely, she was ten and a half, which was rather older than I had in mind, and they wanted her to have a lot of direct contact with her birth family – six times a year. Liz said that was far too much; she would never settle with me if she was going back to Stoke to meet her birth family every few weeks. We would see.

Anne Jenkins and Maureen Thompson from Stoke-on-Trent Social Services came to Oxford to see me and Liz. They asked a few questions about local schools and what my plans for work were and then told me a little more about Lauren.

'She is a very compliant child and extremely eager to please any adults in her life.'

'Is that because she is frightened about what will happen to her if she displeases someone?' I asked.

'Well, some of it is just her nature, but we do feel that one of the challenges for an adoptive parent will be to encourage her to be more independent-spirited and confident in forming her own opinions and standing up for herself.'

They went on to explain that she was taken away from her birth family just before her fifth birthday because of extreme abuse and neglect. After two years in foster care she was placed with a family with a view to adoption, along with her sister, who was a year older. Her sister ran away from the home fairly soon after and refused to go back, so was now living with another foster family. Lauren remained there for another two years, but Stoke became so concerned about the suitability of the family that they went to the high court last summer to get her removed and she was now back in foster care again. They didn't go into a lot of detail but said that the family was very dysfunctional. The two teenage birth children had fallen out with the mother and run away, and Lauren was clearly being subjected to a lot of emotional abuse and possibly worse. Poor little mite.

The high court judge had made it a condition of removing Lauren from her adoptive family that Stoke should urgently and as a matter of priority seek to find another, more suitable home for her. The social workers would go back to Stoke to discuss my suitability, and if they wanted to take it further, the next step would be for me to go up to Stoke to meet with people who knew Lauren, such as her foster carers and teachers.

We talked for a couple of hours and I gave them lunch. We became quite relaxed and informal, and they seemed to like me and the house. I felt sick with excitement. Totally stupid, but after they left, I went upstairs and put the duvet cover I'd bought on the bed in the newly yellow room, along with a beautiful silk butterfly mobile and some pictures of animals.

The social workers must have agreed that I might be suitable because they got back to me quite quickly, and on a cold, snowy day, 6 December 2002, I was off to Stoke-on-Trent to the social services offices. I stopped and bought a Stoke-on-Trent *A–Z* on the motorway because I knew it was not the easiest place to navigate. I arrived two hours early. I had planned that I would, if necessary, kill time looking around the nearby Spode pottery shop, but my heart wasn't in it, so I just sat in the car park looking at piles of frozen slush, feeling increasingly sick.

When it was time to go in and I saw the meeting room, I thought, Blimey, they must be quite keen, because they had laid on a really nice lunch with posh sandwiches and mince pies and fresh fruit juice. I was being wined and dined. This seemed a good sign, although I knew there could still be many a slip.

First they told me that there had been a bit of a development that they needed to share with me: Lauren had run away from the foster home a couple of days ago and had been missing for a whole night. A ten-year-old out all night in December just didn't bear thinking about. They had sent up a police helicopter to look for her but found nothing. Luckily the next morning a schoolteacher had seen her in a local park and taken her into school. It transpired that the foster parents had split up and the 'father', John Harris, had moved out of the home, which had further unsettled Lauren. What made it worse was that the foster mother had tried to hide his disappearance and had asked Lauren not to say anything to anyone.

All of this meant that social services wanted to move quite quickly to find Lauren a permanent home. Good news for me!

Lauren's head teacher joined the meeting and we talked about how she was coping at school. This was the fourth primary school she had attended, and although she had only been there three months, she had settled in reasonably well and made a few friends. It was clear, however, that the head teacher felt she was quite a troubled little girl.

Next I was taken to the foster home to meet the foster mother, Karen. She was supposed to be a 'super' foster parent, with special training to look after Lauren, but she seemed a cold fish. There was no warmth about the house either, and Lauren's bedroom was not much more than a cupboard. It was weird standing in Lauren's bedroom with her folded pyjamas on the tiny two-foot bed when I had still not met her. And she didn't even know of the existence of the woman who was looking at her books and toys, and thinking how few there were.

And I wouldn't be meeting her anytime soon, certainly not until after Christmas, as her social workers believed it would disturb her even to know about my existence before the end of the holidays. I supposed I could see it, but it would have been so unbelievably in keeping with the spirit of Christmas (certainly Hollywood style) for this little girl to hear that she was going to have a forever family after all, and for this big girl to be able to put a face to the name of the child she was fairly certain she was about to have and maybe buy her a tiny present and even chat with her on the phone on Christmas Day. But that was just silly sentiment, I told myself. Stop it. Be patient.

24 December 2002, 10 a.m., on the M4 on the way to Wales, listening to a programme on Radio 4 about Christmas kitchen disasters.

The presents were all wrapped the previous night. I was going to be a mother, so I had to be better organized domestically. It was so hard not to be wrapping presents for Lauren, but even so, what a different feel there was to Christmas that year.

Life would totally change in 2003. After twenty years of indecision, I was going to be a mum.

2

All Change

1 February 2003
Dear Ms McDonnell,
    I am pleased to inform you that Stoke-on-Trent
Adoption Agency is now able to offer you a child . . .
    I attach an envelope for your urgent reply.

The letter came just as I was leaving the house to meet, for the
first time, the child who was to become my daughter. Slightly
strange wording, I thought, but who cares – it's now in black
and white.

I spent the night with my friend Sue in Stourbridge before
going on to Stoke-on-Trent. Stoke is only 120 miles from
Oxford, but I didn't want to risk the chance of being late, especially as there was a fair amount of snow on the ground. It was
also nice to be around others that night and Sue was almost as
excited as me. Sue had been a close friend since we met on our
masters degree course in the 1970s. I was a godparent to her two
children, Ian and Zoe, who were by now teenagers. We spent the
evening talking and anticipating.

I didn't sleep very well, kept awake by alternating feelings of excitement and apprehension. The excitement was familiar – this was a pretty significant day, one that I had been looking forward to for months – but the apprehension was a new feeling. Suddenly the fantasy that I had nurtured for years really was going to become reality. What if she didn't like me? What if I didn't like her? What if this was a complete disaster? What if I wasn't up to the job?

Sue and Zoe waved me off, and as usual, in my nervousness, I had allowed far too much time. I was going to the foster father John's house, as Lauren had been living with him full-time since Christmas, despite the fact that his wife was the official foster carer.

There were not many people around in Burslem, a suburb of Stoke-on-Trent, at half past nine on a snowy Sunday morning – just a couple of joggers and someone collecting the newspaper – to notice a strange woman driving around peering at street names and house numbers, her dog in the car. I eventually spotted the grey pebble-dashed house, but was still an hour early, so Meg and I huddled down in the car trying to keep warm and not look too suspicious. I was so nervous, just like the feeling before a job interview. I kept rehearsing how I would knock on the door and what I would say first to Lauren.

Eventually it was 11 a.m., the appointed hour. I drove a bit closer to the house, walked up the path, took a deep breath and knocked on the door. I assumed John would answer, but it was a small girl who opened the door, smiled and said, 'Hello.' It took a moment for me to connect the picture in the Argos catalogue with the girl in front of me. She was smaller than I'd imagined, and her hair was shorter and lighter than it was in the photo I'd seen in the catalogue. But it was Lauren.

'Hello. I'm Elizabeth,' I said.

'Yes, I know,' she responded. 'Have you brought your dog?'

I dashed back to the car and a few moments later Meg bounded in and helped to break the ice, although she behaved very badly by chasing John's much larger dog out of the house and then jumping up at Lauren and licking her. Lauren squealed with delight.

'She adores dogs,' said John, coming into the hallway.

I was invited into the living room, where we sat down. The room was cosy and chaotic and still full of Christmas decorations. John was warm and welcoming and clearly very fond of Lauren.

Lauren asked what she should call me and I asked what she would feel comfortable with. 'Well, I think I'll call you "Mum", because that's what you're going to be. You are going to be my mum, aren't you?'

'Yes, I am going to be your mum, and it would be lovely if you want to call me that,' I responded, moved by her easy acceptance, although I knew I must be at least the fifth person she had called 'Mum' in her ten years. What could the word mean to her? It was clear Lauren was so much better at all this than I was, very matter-of-fact and wanting to get the basics clear from the start. I decided to let her set the tone and content of the conversation for a bit.

We chatted about Christmas presents, the snow and dogs, and then we went out for Sunday lunch at a carvery. Lauren was wearing a sparkly blouse with long cowl sleeves that dangled in the gravy. She clearly loved food, including vegetables, particularly sprouts! She seemed extremely relaxed in this strange situation and very open, friendly and down-to-earth. Back outside in the car park, John offered to take some photos of us. At first we stood side by side, not touching, but then I decided that although I had only known her for two hours, she was about to become my daughter so it was not inappropriate to put my arm around her shoulders. I breathed a sigh of relief when she did not flinch or pull away.

I drove back to Oxford in a daze. She was lovely, warm and funny, and the introduction had gone really well. But was I worthy of her and the role I was about to take on? She could not be let down again. Come what may, however tough it might get, I knew I was going to be Lauren's forever mum.

Two days later I was back in Stoke for an intensive three-week introduction programme. Though this was held mainly in Stoke, it also included three visits by Lauren to Oxford, one overnight. While in Stoke, I stayed in a hotel near the huge Britannia Football Stadium. Lauren had never been in a hotel before and she loved it, especially the little packs of coffee and milk and shampoo, and we passed several hours with her making tea and coffee, and having showers wearing the complimentary shower cap. As we therefore kept running out of supplies, she took it upon herself to go down to reception for replenishments. The first few times I went with her, but in the end I let her go on her own. After ten minutes, though, she had still not returned. Oh God, I thought, I've already let her come to harm and I've only been with her half a day! I went racing down to reception. She was sitting on a bar stool, fists and pockets full of supplies and a mouth full of sweets from the dish on the counter.

Once the delights of the freebies had worn off, it became quite hard to keep a child entertained in a hotel room, and Stoke-on-Trent in February had limited public attractions, but we went swimming, mooched around the museum and decorated crockery in one of the pottery shops. Lauren did a really nice bowl for me, painting 'Mum' on the bottom. I made a poor job of a mug with 'Lauren' emblazoned on the side. We still have them to this day.

For her first visit to Oxford, a social worker brought Lauren down on the train, another first for her, and I showed her the house and the local area. She met the cats as well as reacquainting herself with Meg. We also went to what would be her new school, met some of the staff and bought her the bright red school sweatshirt.

The next time she came down was the following week. She was allowed to stay overnight and said she liked the yellow walls and the duvet cover. She asked if she could have a hamster, but apart from that she had no special wishes or requests. After all, she had been through this new-home stuff so many times it was no big deal. But the deal for me was enormous. I actually had a child, my child, sleeping in my house, which would soon become our home.

Driving back up to Stoke the next day, we discovered a mutual love of Meatloaf played very loud with the car windows open, and she told me all about her horse, Silver Shadow, and how good she was at riding. I asked her what was going to happen to the horse when she left Stoke and she became a bit vague.

While in Stoke, I was asked to go to social services. They were concerned about Lauren being bounced between the homes of the now-separated foster carers for much longer, and as our 'introductions' had gone well, they wanted to bring forward the date for Lauren to move in with me. Did I mind?

Did I mind! Oh, bring it on.

There were, however, two very important parts of Lauren's life in Stoke that I hadn't been introduced to yet: her teachers and friends at school and her sister, Kirsten. And there would need to be a meeting with her birth mother, brother and grandparents. Those would be organized over the following couple of days.

The staff at school were all very welcoming when Lauren took me in and introduced me; they had been briefed as to who I was and clearly cared a lot for Lauren, even though she had only been with them a few months, and were very keen about the adoption. I attended a leaving assembly that had been organized in her honour, and she was presented with a pencil case, which was followed by lots of photos and hugs. And then we went off to meet Kirsten at a swimming pool.

Kirsten is just eleven months older than Lauren, and although they had been living separately since Kirsten ran away from the former adoptive placement nearly three years earlier, they had been through a lot together and were clearly very important to each other. They had been meeting up every week, but that obviously couldn't continue when Lauren moved to Oxford. Kirsten, who was with a support worker, was very pleased to see Lauren and offered to buy me a coffee in a very grown-up way. She was a little smaller than Lauren, very slight, with pretty red hair and animated speech and movements. I suddenly felt terrible. Was I splitting up these two little girls who were pretty much all each other had? Could I have offered to adopt Kirsten too? How could I possibly compensate for what Lauren was about to lose?

I asked these questions the next day in the social services offices as we were waiting for Lauren's birth family to arrive from the grandparents' home in North Wales. Liz and I sat in the meeting room at one end of a large table. The social workers were adamant that it was not in the best interests of either girl for them to be placed together. I was not sure why, other than the length of time they had been apart. They explained Kirsten had made it clear that she didn't want to be placed for adoption again. She was going to wait until she was sixteen, when she believed she could go back and live with her birth mother.

Even though I had been told that Lauren's birth family knew about me and supported the planned adoption, it felt uncomfortable to think that I was taking Lauren further away from them, especially as I already had Kirsten weighing on my mind. I was so glad I had Liz for moral support.

'Don't worry,' she said. 'I'm sure they're not going to hate you. This is just the last part of the process.' With her experience, empathy and humour, she managed to ease this awkward time for me.

The family finally arrived and I was introduced to Lauren's birth mother, Terri, Terri's parents, Malcolm and Anne, and Jayden, who was Lauren's fourteen-year-old half-brother. Lauren was on her way to join us with John. I saw where Kirsten got her hair colour from: Terri, too, had red hair, but there the similarity ended. In stark contrast to Kirsten's vitality, Terri seemed barely with it. I knew she was an alcoholic and struggled with drug addictions, but I was still shocked. She made some eye contact when we were first introduced, but then fell into a stupor. She was pale, overweight and looked a lot older than her thirty-five years.

It was quite hard to know what to talk about at first, but the weather was a good topic: it was snowing yet again. Malcolm and I came from Merseyside, and he too had a brother who lived near Oxford. Suddenly we were chatting away, everyone except poor Jayden, who looked bored stiff, and Terri, who was just staring into the middle distance. And then John brought Lauren in, who presented her mother with a single red rose. Terri just about managed a smile for her daughter and then lapsed back into her gloom and didn't say another word. Terri's indifference didn't seem to faze Lauren, who smiled at me and sat down beside John.

As she was on the other side of the large meeting-room table from me, physical contact, including a hug goodbye, wasn't possible. This was probably just as well, as it felt like this was meant to be time for Lauren to be with Terri and it might have been insensitive of me to have shown any interest, yet alone affection towards her/my daughter. We all shook hands, the grandparents thanked me for coming forward, and we arranged to meet at what social workers call a 'contact' in the summer, when all the children, including Lauren's two younger brothers, who had been adopted separately, would be there.

As I left, the social worker handed me a large photocopied document. It was the summing-up by the judge at the high court hearing the previous summer, giving the arguments for and against removing Lauren from her former adoptive family, the Spraggs. It detailed the judge's reasons for deciding that she should be taken away. Apparently he said in court that if Lauren was placed with another adoptive family, they should be given a copy of his judgment so that they understood the complexities of the issues and the problems they might encounter in the future.

That night back at home, I read the high court judge's ruling. Blimey, complex indeed. Truly awful, in fact. Wrapped up in very careful judicial language and without going into too many specifics was a catalogue of conflict within the family and with neighbours, often involving the police, and of emotional, psychological and, occasionally, physical abuse meted out by the so-called 'mother', who presumably would, only three years earlier, have been put through the same rigorous vetting and selection process for prospective adoptive parents as I'd been.

The ruling described how Lauren became the family's scapegoat, blamed for everything from Barbara Spragg's violent dispute with the neighbours to the delinquent behaviour of Ms Spragg's own teenage birth children, including the fact they ran away from home after falling out with their mother. It cited how Ms Spragg would deliberately set Kirsten and Lauren against each other, triggering violent fights between the girls and resulting in increasingly disturbed behaviour, which included gnawing furniture, ripping wallpaper and making attempts at self-harm. It described how Barbara and her son David both hit the little girls and how on one occasion he tried to smother Kirsten with a pillow. Shortly after that incident Kirsten had run away and refused to go back. Barbara blamed Lauren for that, too, and went on to tell a child psychiatrist who had got involved with the family that she could find nothing positive to say about Lauren, describing her as cruel, mean, secretive, dishonest and thoroughly unlikeable.

The judge described the huge emotional impact this had had on Lauren, causing her to swing from being a fairly happy and optimistic seven-year-old when she moved in with the Spraggs to being defiant and argumentative to overly compliant and appeasing, as she was said to be now, especially when in the company of the 'mother', who was described as very controlling and without any understanding or empathy. Meanwhile, at school, her teachers described Lauren as defiant and argumentative, and all the experts who gave evidence said that this was because she felt she had to walk on eggshells at home, while in the safer environment of school she could express some of her distress. They agreed that the effect of the emotional abuse and neglect Lauren had suffered could be disastrous.

The judgment ended with the judge speculating as to the effects all this would have on Lauren in adolescence and giving warnings of potentially stormy times ahead. This was obviously why the judge said that any adoptive parents should be given a copy of his summing-up.

I closed the file feeling shocked and incredibly sad at everything Lauren had been through. I also thought I should have been shown the ruling sooner. It wouldn't have affected my desire to go ahead, but I should have been told and I should have been warned earlier, as the judge had wanted, about what might be to come. I was gradually to learn that the judicial summing-up barely scratched the surface of the twisted and sadistic abuse Lauren had experienced in that home.

*

Two days later, on Saturday 15 February, Meg and I left Oxford at 6 a.m. – about three hours earlier than necessary. It was very silly, as I then had to entertain a dog in a motorway service station for hours before I could pick up Lauren and bring her home with me for good. But I couldn't bear to be late – what message would that send? And if I was up early, it seemed so was Lauren: she was waiting at the window when we drew up. I wondered if somewhere deep down she thought I might not turn up. She couldn't have had much faith in the reliability of adults.

John carried out her stuff, one small canvas sports bag, two supermarket bags and ten black bin bags. Where had all those bin bags of stuff come from? There was hardly anything in her bedroom when I went to visit Karen's house before Christmas. There wasn't room for them all in the car, and certainly none for her bike. It was a bit disappointing because it felt as though the move was still incomplete with so much of her stuff left behind, but at least it meant there was a very good and pressing reason for John to come down to Oxford soon and so that made the goodbyes easier. We arranged that he would bring the rest of her things down the next week.

Lauren actually didn't seem too fazed by saying goodbye; I suppose she had done it so many times before. Goodbye, old family and old Mum and Dad. Hello, new. John's eyes, though, filled up with tears as she got into my car. He was such a lovely, kind man and I discovered later he had wanted to adopt her himself. I felt as though I was snatching his child.

Karen, who was after all the official foster carer, did not even come to say goodbye. Not that that seemed to bother Lauren. It was clear that any warmth and affection she got in that placement came from John.

I pointed the car back towards Oxford and we sang along to 'Bat Out of Hell'.

When we got home, we put the contents of the overnight bag and the two supermarket carrier bags in her room: some clothes and a few books and toys. We left the black bin bags in the car boot.

Then we had supper – baked potatoes with tuna mayonnaise, one of her favourite meals – and we did something that was recommended to me by a therapist who worked with children who had had very disrupted lives. We placed candles on a cake, one for everyone who had played a significant part in Lauren's ten and a half years. (We didn't debate whether good or bad.) There were candles for her birth parents, four known siblings, her grandparents, seven foster carers, her brothers' adoptive parents, her former would-be adoptive family and key people at each of her three nurseries and four schools. Just as well I'd bought a large cake and three boxes of candles!

As we lit over forty candles, it felt hugely significant and symbolic to me, but I was not sure what impact, if any, it was having on Lauren. She had no time for ritual or symbolism or sentiment. Why would she? She had never experienced any thus far in her life. She was pretty pragmatic, too, about the whole move.

'Can I watch telly?' she asked as soon as she'd blown out the candles.

The next morning I suggested we bring in the rest of the bags from the car, unpack them and then find places for all her things in the house so it could become her home too. She didn't seem very interested, but nevertheless I carried all the bin bags into the kitchen and we started to go through them. The bags I'd managed to fit into the boot contained broken toys and old soiled clothes, virtually none of them Lauren's; most clearly belonged to a boy. Karen had obviously just decided to clear her garage of unwanted junk, the detritus of her life as a foster carer, which I hoped was now at an end.

All this visibly upset Lauren and she stormed off, telling me to just leave it. Eventually I coaxed her down from her room, where she had thrown all her books and toys on the floor. We put most of the junk back into the bin bags, drove to the local tip and unceremoniously threw it into the skips.

'Good riddance to old rubbish!' I shouted.

'And good riddance to old cow Karen,' Lauren gleefully added. 'I hated her.'

Then we went and bought a hamster, Sandy, and a very shiny red cage that cost ten times what he cost. Lauren was very excited and begged me to let her have him in her room, then spent most of the rest of the day happily playing with him.

The next day Lauren was itching terribly, and her arms in particular were covered in bright red blotches and were sore. She said it was eczema, but I wasn't sure. I wondered if she was allergic to the hamster, but it seemed more serious than that. I suggested an introductory visit to our doctor so Lauren could meet her. Reluctantly she agreed, encouraged by the fact that the surgery was on the edge of our local park, so she could try out the playground on the way back and we could take bread to feed the ducks. The doctor was very nice and welcoming. Lauren had scabies and nits.

Lauren spent a lot of time during her first few days in Oxford on the phone to John and other old friends. I realized that one of the people she had phoned was Barbara Spragg, her previous adoptive mother, who had asked for our address as well as our phone number. I found this really upsetting and worrying. This woman was such a bad mother that Lauren was removed from her by order of the high court and yet she still felt she had rights over Lauren. She seemed shameless. I wished Lauren was strong enough to tell her to leave her alone, but the rational adult in me realized it was more complicated than that. One of the things that isn't mentioned when you adopt an older child is how much the former families, and there are usually more than one, will come with them; there is no such thing as a clean break or a fresh start.

Three days later John came down from Stoke, bringing Lauren's bike and another six black bin bags. We didn't say anything to him about the contents of the first lot, or the nits and scabies. He'd tried so hard to care for her; we didn't want to upset or embarrass him. We had a lovely lunch out at the Trout, an old riverside pub just outside Oxford, much featured in *Inspector Morse*. Then we said goodbye again with promises to see each other soon, but somehow I didn't think we would. He needed to let go, and we needed to move on, but it was a shame because he was such a great guy and so fond of Lauren.

'You two should get married,' Lauren said to me as we drove home, 'and then I could have you both.'

We took the six additional bin bags straight to the tip and hurled them into a skip without even looking in them.

At the weekend, my parents, my brother Gerry and my nieces, Hannah and Lottie, who were seventeen and fourteen, came for lunch. When I had first told my parents of my plans to adopt, they had been a bit concerned that doing something like that on my own might be too stressful and potentially heartbreaking, and they were also worried I would have to scale back my career, but they soon came round and were now keen to meet their new granddaughter. Lauren helped me set the table for lunch and wrote out name place cards for everyone, each one saying, 'Enjoy your meal'.

The day went really well, no awkward moments; Lauren was so good at getting on with the new. She had a good chance to laugh at me when we took a walk to the park and while lecturing the girls on how they needed to be careful because the ice on the lake was very thin, I managed to fall through it myself. I was never allowed to forget that one!

The next day was Lauren's first day at All Saints Primary School, the fifth school she'd attended. We were up early, and she looked very smart in her red school jumper, grey shirt and black tights, although it was touch and go as to whether I would get her into the uniform. She had decided to pick a fight over getting dressed.

'I won't be staying here, so what's the point in starting another school?'

I was a bit stunned. 'Why won't you be staying?'

'You don't want me to stay. You love Hannah and Lottie more than you love me.'

'But, but, but what . . . ? I don't. Of course I love them – they are my nieces and I have known them all their lives – but they don't live with me. It's you who I want to become my daughter.'

I made the mistake I would make so many times again of trying to explain, be reasonable, rational, find the words that could change the way she looked at the world, the words that would untangle her very screwed-up view of human relationships . . . I had yet to understand that there had been nothing reasonable or rational in what had happened to Lauren so far, so how could I possibly expect her to think logically?

Some breakfast and getting out the camera lifted the mood and eventually I took a photo of Lauren in the garden in her new uniform and off we went. Choosing a school had been difficult, because although there was a very good primary school just round the corner from home, Oxford still had a three-tier system, so she was too old for the primary and would have to go to a middle school that didn't have a very good reputation. In the end I chose a primary school on the outskirts of the city that went up to eleven but was only three miles from home. It fed into what I felt was the most suitable secondary school for her in Oxford, Hinksey Fields. It was smaller than the others and seemed more structured – it had a uniform, for example – while many of the other Oxford secondary schools were huge and seemed rather wacky and chaotic.

The first day at the new school seemed to go well and she came out holding hands with two girls. But I knew how hard it was to start a new school in a new area halfway through a term: I had done it when we moved from Merseyside to Surrey when I was thirteen, but I'd had my family with me; I wasn't changing families as well.

That night Barbara Spragg phoned to ask Lauren how she had got on at her new school. A terrible scene with Lauren followed during which I suggested that it was not a good thing for her to keep talking to Barbara.

'You can't tell me what to do. You don't own me, and you're not a proper mum.'

'I would like to be your mum, if you'll give me a chance.'

'Just leave me alone!' She stormed off upstairs, throwing a vase on the floor as she went.

I picked up the pieces and left her to it for a bit. She came down after about half an hour as if nothing had happened.

'Can we talk?' I said.

'What d'you mean? There's nothing to talk about. I'm hungry. Can I have something to eat?'

A few days later two separate letters arrived for Lauren. One was from 'Mum (Barbara)', and included a heart-shaped photo of her and Lauren, and the other was from the Spragg seniors, Barbara's parents. They were both full of sentimental and insincere guff. I was sure they were trying to intimidate Lauren. If they really wanted the best for her, they would leave her alone. Lauren wouldn't talk about how they made her feel and shoved the letters in a drawer.

The next day just as Lauren was going to bed after a two-hour battle to get her to have a bath, the phone rang and I answered it.

'Can I speak to Lauren?' said an old man's voice.

'Who is it?'

'Her granddad.'

'No you're not – I know his voice. Who are you?'

'Ernest Spragg. Put her on. I know she wants to hear from me.'

He was Barbara's father. I wanted to tell him to go to hell and how dare he speak to me like that, but Lauren was standing at my elbow, imploring me to give her the phone. Stupidly, I gave in.

That Saturday we were on the M4 on our way to Wales to stay with my brother Michael and his wife, Victoria, for the weekend so Lauren could meet them. This was the route I had travelled so many times trying to decide what to do with my life and promising myself it would change. Now it had.

It was a lovely, sunny early spring day and the Welsh countryside around their hillside home looked glorious. They were very welcoming and, having heard of Lauren's love of horse riding, had arranged for her to be taken out on one of the ponies on the farm next door. We got her into a hard hat and mounted on a very sedate pony and set off down the lane, but she was clearly terrified and we had to turn back quite soon. It was obviously the first time she had ever been on a horse. I had never believed the Silver Shadow story, but I understood the need for her to add such a romantic element to her life and it was clear that she had a young girl's fascination with horses. I knew there would be many more opportunities for her to ride if she wanted them.

The following morning I went into her first-floor bedroom to tell her breakfast was ready. She was sitting on the window seat looking out at the lambs. She was in a strange mood, tetchy and defiant, a bit like the morning of her first day at her new school.

'Fuck off. You're not my real mum and you don't care about me,' she said, out of the blue.

I had never heard her swear before and it sounded shocking coming from such a young mouth. Then she suddenly opened the window and declared she was going to jump out.

I froze for a moment. Oh my God, what? Why? Where did this come from? Trying not to let the panic show in my voice, I started to try and reason with her and joke her out of it.

'Oh, come on, we've got a lovely day planned and we don't want to miss any of it having to get your broken leg fixed.'

When that failed, I took a gamble, which if I was wrong, would have had catastrophic consequences: I walked out of the room.

Michael, Victoria and I were starting breakfast when Lauren came down and joined us. The relief was immense, but I tried not to let it show.

We went out for Sunday lunch and had a windy but invigorating walk to the top of Blorenge and looked down on Abergavenny, and then it was back to Oxford to start Lauren's second week at All Saints Primary School.

By the time Lauren had been with me three weeks, I would have said that it was mostly going well. She seemed happy and positive on the whole, but then in the blink of an eye, for no reason, she could suddenly change and become incredibly aggressive and angry towards me. She challenged almost every request I made and any expectation I had about behaviour and cleanliness. How could social services possibly have assessed her as overly compliant? Dealing with the nits effectively had been a particular challenge: she hated baths and having her hair washed, and particularly loathed having to sit around with the smelly cream on her head. Stupidly but instinctively I'd tried to reason with her, saying, 'I know it must be horrible and uncomfortable to have nits and this treatment really will get rid of them if we do it properly.'

She'd stormed out of the bathroom, her hair dripping wet, and headed downstairs and towards the front door, clearly wanting to go out. I got there first, locked the door and put the key in my pocket. Lauren screamed and shouted at me, ran back up to her bedroom and slammed the door. I left her for a bit, but eventually went up because there was some awful banging going on. She was pounding her head with her fists and slamming it into the bedhead.

'Lauren, whatever's the matter?'

'I've got a worm in my head and it's eating my brain!' she screamed.

'Is it the nits making your head itchy?'

'No, stupid – it's inside my head. I've had it for years.'

I just sat on the bed and stroked her back, and eventually she let me put my arms around her and I held her really tightly for about ten minutes until she calmed down and finally fell asleep.

At other times, when she was trying to pick a fight, Lauren would often say how boring life was with me. Compared with the soap-opera dramas she'd lived through for most of her life up to this point, it must have seemed very dull. Sometimes I felt she started an argument just to raise the tempo a bit . . . Can you be addicted to adrenalin? I was beginning to think she must be; this was more than just the boundary testing I had expected. One morning we were driving to school when she suddenly opened the car door and threatened to jump out. Fortunately there was a bus stop I was able to pull into and no one was hurt and no damage was done. No damage except to my nerves and my belief that all I needed to do to make our relationship work was stay firm and steady and loving.

At the beginning of March, three weeks after Lauren moved in with me, the first of the formal statutory reviews took place at our house. These have to be held every few weeks when a child is in care or placed for adoption. Three social workers came down from Stoke-on-Trent, one to chair the meeting. Liz from NCH was there and Lauren and me. The questions are scripted and set out on a form that is to be completed. Designed primarily for children in a children's home or in temporary foster care, they were slightly irrelevant to our situation, but nevertheless served as an agenda for our meeting.

The questions all seemed defensive or negative: 'Does the young person have any complaints?' Not comments, views or opinions, just complaints. Fortunately the only complaint that Lauren made was that I would no longer allow her to have Sandy the hamster in her room at night because he was so noisy in his wheel he kept her awake.

'Does the young person have a copy of the complaints procedure?' was the next question, and the adults all laughed.

'No, and I don't want it. I was just joking,' said Lauren, hanging upside down off the back of the sofa. 'I'm bored. When's lunch?'

The only question on the pro forma that didn't get answered was the only one that, with hindsight, might have been useful: 'What assistance and aftercare will the child need when she ceases to be looked after by the local authority?'

Part of the arrangement made at the high court when Lauren was removed from the Spraggs in the summer of 2002 was that she should receive some therapeutic support; consequently she had been going to see a play therapist every six weeks for an hour. The social workers were keen this should continue, although Lauren was very unhappy about it and said it was useless. I asked if Lauren could see someone in Oxford and a bit more regularly, but that got kicked into the long grass. So I agreed to take her to see the play therapist, who was based in Sutton Coldfield. I was beginning to understand that some help was definitely needed if Lauren was to process what had happened to her.

I asked about the use of the term 'young person' in social-services-speak these days and was told it had been introduced because it was thought to be more respectful and empowering. When does a child cease to be a child and become a young person? About eleven. Ridiculous! How many parents would describe their eleven-year-old as a 'young person'?

The other bit of social services terminology that bugged me was 'contact'. As in 'having a contact' or 'going on a contact'. So when we met Kirsten the following month at the zoo, it wouldn't be 'two children having a day out together', it would be 'two young persons going on a contact'! I had thought recent changes in childcare parlance had been made to try and reduce the stigma and make it all sound more normal, more like real life. But who the hell talks about 'going on a contact' with their sister in real life? I thought it was cruel to single out children in the care system like this. Was it really that different from the days when they used to have to wear a uniform? I tried never to use those words, but Lauren knew no other way of talking about seeing her sister or other members of her birth family.

Having made an appointment for Lauren to go and see the therapist, I said I would write to her to give her some recent background information. She didn't even know that Lauren had moved to Oxford.

Lauren has been with me now for four and a half weeks and we had three weeks' introduction before that. On the surface, she has coped fantastically well with what must have been the most enormous upheaval and loss for her.

But despite the superficial coping, I must say I think she is a very confused and disturbed child underneath and I am very anxious about how and if she will ever be able to really settle here.

Almost from day one she started being incredibly rude and defiant with me, arguing about anything and everything, and challenging me in a very aggressive manner on anything I said, even passing comments. That behaviour has diminished greatly in the past week or so, maybe because I have got better at managing it. She can still be very difficult and defiant, but I have set certain non-negotiable rules with a set of rewards and penalties for specific things, like bedtimes, cleanliness and health and safety issues, and I try and ignore the other problems.

She finds it very difficult to cope if there are not exciting things happening all the time. She has started doing some very risky things, which she says help her cope with the boredom.

Her mood can switch in a second from happy and cheerful to rude and angry if something frustrates her.

But by far the biggest problem to my mind is that her previous adoptive family are pestering her (my words not hers). Since she has been here they have written six times, sent heart-shaped photos and made several phone calls. Lauren claims to like this, but I think it is hugely unsettling. That whole part of her life is a total no-go area and Lauren is very defensive and angry about what happened. I think she feels it was her fault.

So in summary Lauren needs urgent help in sorting out:

1 What really happened when she was with the Spraggs
   and why she was taken away, and
2 How she can really settle here and feel this is where she
   belongs, what she can do to begin that settling process
   and how I can help her.

As I poured all this out onto the screen, tears started dripping onto the keyboard. I didn't know I felt this bad.

3

The Arrival of Jennifer

Mother's Day was always going to be a difficult and confusing day for Lauren, so I didn't make much mention of it. She gave me a teddy bear that I recognized as one from a box of toys in the attic. I wondered what happened to the money I gave her at her request to buy me a card and a present, but didn't say anything because I didn't want to spoil the moment. We took Meg for a walk, and when we got back, there was a message for Lauren on the house phone from Adrian Spragg, a former adoptive uncle, saying he would phone back. She said she didn't want to speak to him and I deleted the message.

The next day there was another message left for Lauren from him. What a brass neck! They were shameless. They would ring, listen to my voice on the answerphone and then, ignoring the fact that this was my house and my phone, leave a very proprietorial message for a ten-year-old child. I was beginning to think they were trying to intimidate her. Again I deleted it, this time without telling her.

A few days later I let Lauren play with an old mobile phone of mine that she had found, not realizing it still had some credit on it. She spent an hour in her room phoning round the numbers in her address book, including Old Man Spragg, to show off the fact she had a mobile phone. Once again I tried to explain to her why that wasn't a good idea and she became very angry. I dropped the subject, but the next morning she said, 'I need to tell you something.'

'Ernest Spragg' – she used to refer to him as 'Granddad', but no longer did – 'asked me to give him the mobile number and he's put some credit on the phone so I can ring him, except I don't want to. He told me to tell you it was John Harris who put the credit on.'

This time I was really angry with Lauren. I told her it was deceitful and underhand for her to let him do that and that no adult should be telling a child to keep naughty things secret. She was genuinely contrite and said she really didn't want anything more to do with the Spraggs.

I later discovered that Ernest Spragg had also registered the phone as his and put a password on the account, so when I called Virgin to ask if they could issue a new number, they said they couldn't because the phone wasn't registered to me. I had to destroy the old SIM card and buy a new one. Was there nothing that this supposedly poor old man wouldn't stoop to? I wondered why he was so devious.

In early April Lauren went into a frenzied period of bad behaviour, triggered in part by too much Easter activity, chocolate and the fact that John didn't in the end make his long-planned (and much looked-forward-to) visit. We had the most dreadful scene, made much worse, I fear, by me getting very angry and upset. I had no idea how anxious and emotionally exhausted I was feeling!

The immediate cause of the row was my finding out that she had been back in touch with Old Man Spragg even though she had promised to stop contacting him. Unfortunately, just as she seemed to be putting that part of her life behind her, he phoned and asked if she had forgotten him, adding, 'Did you know your mum isn't well?' After that she felt obliged to keep in touch with him. Another of the uncles had been leaving messages for her on the answerphone again, but I intercepted them. When Lauren was in the house, I set the answerphone to automatic answer so the phone didn't ring.

I tried once again to explain to Lauren why I felt a lot of contact with the Spraggs was not a good idea.

'I know they played a big role in your life for those three years, but it wasn't a happy time for you, and you have a new life now if you could just let yourself be part of it,' I told her.

'I can't settle here. The Spraggs say they're going to get me back. They say I belong to them. They say you're no good and don't love me. There are so many of them. They say they'll follow me everywhere.'

'Love, there is no way the Spraggs can get you back. No one would let it happen. They are bad people. This is your home now. I'm your mum, and I love you and want you to be part of life here in Oxford. I really want the adoption to go ahead as soon as possible, as soon as you really feel able to be part of a new family, but to do that, you need to let go of feeling you owe the Spraggs anything.'

'I do want to be adopted, Mum,' Lauren said. 'I do want to be with you, I really do, and then I can tell the Spraggs to leave me alone.'

I realized I too would feel on much firmer ground to deal

with some of Lauren's needs and with the Spraggs when I became her legal parent. I had been warned that there would be several months between Lauren coming to me and the legal formalities being completed but, given that everyone seemed to agree that her placement with me was right for her, I hoped that there would be no unnecessary delays in completing the paperwork and applying for a court hearing.

In the meantime and in view of Lauren's assertion that she definitely wanted to settle with me and for the adoption to go ahead, I decided to be more assertive with her over the Spraggs. I told her that I thought they were bad, sick people and I would not have them invading our lives and was not going to allow the phone to ring while she was in the house. Everything would go straight to answerphone and I would check the messages regularly. If there were any for her from friends or Kirsten or someone OK, I would let her listen to them, but if they were from the Spraggs, I would delete them without telling her.

'Does that mean I won't have to talk to them again?' she asked.

'Yes, but you have to let me protect you from them and stop going behind my back.'

I also wrote to Stoke-on-Trent Social Services to ask if something more forceful could be done to stop the Spraggs trying to get to Lauren. Given that the case went to the high court in the first place, could Stoke consider applying for an injunction? They promised to write to the Spraggs threatening legal action if they didn't leave Lauren alone, but whether they did or not, it had little effect, because throughout the coming months the extended Spragg family hounded us on what must have been an organized basis.

Two letters arrived full of photos. These were masquerading as coming from children in the Spragg family but were very clearly written by an adult trying to look like a child. There were more gushing letters and cards from 'Mum (Barbara)' and her daughter, and dozens of calls to the house phone and my mobile. The caller hung up each time I answered. I put a bar on the landline on all calls from withheld numbers.

Summer had come and a new ice-cream parlour had just opened in town, so Lauren and I went to try it out. We sat side by side on high stools at a table in the window, each facing out into the street. As we were sitting silently watching the world go by, Lauren suddenly said that Ernest Spragg was a dirty old man who did horrible and disgusting things, and she wished he would leave her alone.

I turned to look at her and, trying to keep my voice unemotional, asked, 'Disgusting things to you?'

She turned away and shut up. I went back to looking out of the window and eventually she said, 'Yes.'

'Did you tell anyone?'

'No, but they knew.'

'Who knew?'

'Barbara.'

'Didn't she stop it?'

'No, she used to take me to him and then go out shopping with her mum.'

'And then?'

'He'd say, "Let's go into the cellar and make some raspberry jam and you can have a choc ice." And then he did disgusting things.'

'To you?'

'Yes, and he made me do disgusting things to him.'

'Did he do that to anyone else?'

'Dunno. No, I don't think so. I don't want to talk about it anymore. Don't tell anyone, will you?'

I felt numb and sick. So the old man was a paedophile and it would seem that the whole Spragg family knew what was going on and were accessories to the abuse. No wonder they were trying to control and intimidate her still. That's not the sort of thing you can keep secret, so I said, 'I won't tell anyone if you don't want me to, but I think we should tell Stoke so they can stop it happening to anyone else.'

I told the Stoke social worker, but nothing came of it. Their lack of interest left me speechless but the fact that Lauren had confided in me gave me more confidence that she would let me help to protect her from the dreadful Spraggs.

Despite all the problems with the Spraggs, Lauren seemed to be coping reasonably well with school and to have fitted in quite well. It was a lovely place, with all sorts of activities, and they made Lauren very welcome. She was in the netball team and took part in a brilliant concert. It was such a shame she was in year six and wouldn't have at least another year at primary school. For reasons I didn't quite understand, presumably staff shortages, they taught two years together, so she was in a class with nine-, ten- and eleven-year-olds. She was one of the younger ones in her year anyway, with a mid-July birthday, and I noticed that most of her friends were the younger ones in year five, who had another year to go at primary school. So not only did she have to cope with another change of school in a couple of months, she would also leave most of the friends she had made behind.

I rang Mr Jones, the head teacher, to discuss the situation.

We agreed it would be better for Lauren if she could stay on another year in primary school, which would give her time to really settle in and catch up academically and emotionally with her peers. He offered to talk to the Local Education Authority and sound them out, and if they were amenable, I could then make a formal request.

As Lauren was still technically in the care of Stoke-on-Trent and there was no sign of any progress on the formal legal adoption process, I realized I would have to clear any change to the anticipated move to secondary school with them. I rang Anne Jenkins, one of the social workers, and to my great surprise, she was against it.

'Why?' I asked.

'Because Lauren is in year six and therefore should go on to year seven in September.'

'But she's not ready for it, and another year in a supportive primary school after so many disruptions in her life would give her a much stronger base on which to make the move to secondary school,' I said, but Anne was not convinced.

It was pointless arguing. I had come to realize that with social workers the process was all, and there was little, if any, scope for judgement. Year seven follows year six as night follows day; it is the right and proper order of things. I decided to leave it until we had the approval of the Local Education Authority and then raise it with Anne again.

But we didn't get the approval of the LEA. Mr Jones rang me a couple of weeks later to say they had got back to him and the answer was 'no'. Year seven follows year six; it's just how things are. I could appeal it, but any appeal wouldn't be heard until October, by which time Lauren would already be in secondary school. Also, as Lauren was still 'in care', it would have to be Stoke who appealed it, and they had already indicated that they wouldn't.

Looking back on this, I believe that the fact that Lauren was catapulted into year seven when she wasn't ready for it was disastrous. Most, if not all of the terrible things that happened to her subsequently might have been avoided if she had been more emotionally secure and mature when she entered the bear garden that is secondary school.

A few weeks after Lauren had moved in, she had started wanting me to carry her around like a baby in my arms: just sitting in my lap wasn't enough. Although she wasn't a particularly big child, she was nearly eleven and only a few inches shorter than me, so it was physically quite difficult. It also seemed a bit strange, but as it so clearly met a genuine need in her, I didn't feel I could refuse to allow it. Unfortunately my back was suffering. Then I had a brainwave. The local outdoor swimming pool, which was just down the road, had opened for the summer, so I got us two season tickets. Supported by water, I could carry Lauren around for as long as she wanted. We may have looked rather strange, but it seemed to comfort her so much. Besides, by the end of the summer she had got it out of her system.

One of the many disadvantages children in care have is they are not allowed sleepovers with people who are not Criminal Records Bureau-checked. When your child is invited by a school friend to go to theirs and stay the night, you do what any parent would normally do and make sure you talk to the mum, find out a bit about the family, their address, phone numbers and so on, but what you can't do very easily and without causing offence is ask to see their CRB certificate, which they are very unlikely to have anyway. I realized that sleepovers were all the rage, almost like being invited round to play was when I was a child, and without them Lauren's social life was a bit limited. Even worse, because of the number of times I had to decline sleepover invitations, everyone got to know that she was a child in care waiting for the legal adoption to go through. I tried to make up for that by having lots of sleepovers at our house, and as her bedroom wasn't big enough for more than one bed, the living room became a dormitory.

She had one particularly close friend, Nicola, who sadly she would have to leave behind when she moved on to secondary school. Lauren found special friendships difficult. She handled group situations and initial introductions very well, but more intimate, lasting relationships were a real challenge. I spent a lot of time arbitrating disputes between the girls, but the friendship endured long enough for Nicola to spend many evenings after school at our house and even to come to Wales with us one weekend.

The children who were moving up to secondary school were paired up and given 'moving buddies'. Lauren's was a girl named Jennifer. She was almost a year older than Lauren and a whole head taller, and perhaps as she had older brothers and sisters, she appeared to be much more worldly-wise. Her mum seemed nice and friendly, though, and we chatted at the school gates. It seemed Jennifer, for all her superficial confidence and grown-up appearance, was very anxious about moving on and didn't have many friends, although she had been at the school since she was five.

Jennifer's mum wanted to encourage a friendship between her daughter and Lauren. Given that Lauren would be leaving Nicola behind, I was pleased at the prospect of helping her form another friendship, so Jennifer and Lauren started sharing trips to each other's houses for tea, although sleepovers could only be at our house.

17 July 2003 and 'Lauren is 11', proclaimed the banner my brother Gerry had made to hang up at her party. I had hired the local community centre and arranged a children's disco, and we had invited virtually the whole class, so there were twenty-five ten- and eleven-year-olds charging madly around, plus a few younger brothers and sisters. It was fun, and Lauren was on cloud nine – she had never had a birthday party before, never had the experience of being special and the centre of attention for a day.

Kirsten came down from Stoke for the party, staying in a hotel with two carers. In a discussion I had with Anne, the girls' social worker, we had decided it was best for both sisters that Kirsten didn't stay with us. It meant Lauren could keep part of her new life to herself, and we wouldn't be rubbing Kirsten's nose in how different their lives now were. Kirsten had recently been removed from her foster carer, who could no longer cope with her very challenging behaviour, and was now in a kids' home.

The party seemed to be a great success, although I wasn't sure whether it had been such a good idea to invite Kirsten. The two sisters had a very ambivalent relationship. They loved and loathed each other in equal measure. It was so sad, as they were extremely close in many ways and had been through so much together, more than most sisters would experience in a lifetime, but their relationship had been messed up by a series of uncaring and irresponsible adults. Consequently after the party they had clearly had enough of each other for the time being. Having talked to Lauren, I spoke to the carers and they agreed that they would simply go back to Stoke in the morning rather than us all meeting up for lunch as had been the original plan.

Lauren got some lovely presents from her school friends, but perhaps the star present was a huge water pistol, actually more like a cannon than a pistol, a gift from the head teacher's son. I speculated as to whether choosing presents for his son's classmates gave the head the opportunity for revenge on parents . . . water pistols, maybe trumpets and drum kits!

The day after the party was warm and sunny, so we went into the garden to try out Lauren's new present. She squirted me and I squirted her, and then we got out the garden hose and suddenly we were two shrieking, soaking dervishes charging round the garden throwing water in every direction. What must the neighbours have thought? What would social services say?

A week later and we were heading west, first to Cornwall and then to Devon for our first summer holiday together and Lauren's first ever swim in the sea, first ever mackerel-fishing boat trip, first ever midnight beach barbecue . . . The list was long. Gerry, Hannah and Lottie joined us for the week in Devon in a caravan and the three girls really got to know each other, building fabulous sandcastles, making up daft songs to sing in the back of the car and going on scary rides at the funfair.

It was a great holiday and we had a lot of fun together, and through that we grew much closer. I was thankful for the strengthened relationship as we drove off one sunny day in

August for what was going to be, for both of us in different ways, a very testing day. We were heading up to Staffordshire for the first birth family 'contact' since Lauren had moved in with me. Arranged by Stoke Social Services, Granddad, Nana, half-brother Jayden and birth mother Terri were being driven down from North Wales, the younger brothers, Harry and Jamie, were coming with their adoptive mother, Marjory, and Kirsten was coming with two carers. Thankfully Liz was coming from NCH to support me, and two of the Stoke social workers were coming too.

Early as usual, Lauren and I stopped at the M6 services to get a drink. She was tense and really trying to needle me. First she said I was driving too fast and then too slow. And then . . .

'You don't like Terri, do you?'

'I don't really know her, but I do know that she didn't take very good care of you.'

'Well, you're not a real mum, so how would you know?' The words stung a bit, despite my understanding the confusion that had caused them.

'No, of course I don't really know what happened when you were all together. I am sure she loved you and was very sad she couldn't look after you.'

'Well, she's my real mother, so I have to give her lots of love and attention today and I won't be able to talk to you. I'll be too busy with my real family.'

Lauren insisted she wanted to buy Terri a present and we found a very overpriced trinket box in the shop and a card. She then spent a lot of time redoing her hair. It must have felt awful for her having to re-enter her old world and being so torn as to which mother she owed loyalty. I tried to reassure her that I understood and it was fine for her to spend time with Terri. She told me to shut up and that I didn't understand, which try as I might, I probably didn't. I tried to sound very calm and relaxed about it all, but I didn't really feel it. I was more than a bit hurt by her words, and anxious about how the day would go, but I knew I had to be strong for Lauren.

When we arrived at the play farm, everyone else was already at tables in the courtyard dining area. Terri was sitting down with a can of Coke and a cigarette. She didn't get up when her children came up to her. She just sat there and they more or less queued up to kiss her; it was almost as though she was holding court. Nana and Granddad were very warm and friendly, and did the grandparently thing of exclaiming how much the children had grown. Granddad kept telling Lauren how much she looked like 'her mum'. It must have been so sad for them: not only was their only child a drug-addicted alcoholic who was now living in a homeless hostel, but they had very little contact with their grandchildren, all except Jayden, who lived with them. I knew that they had wanted to foster all five children when they were taken into care, but understandably social services thought that at the age they were, taking one, Jayden, would be enough. They had obviously tried so hard to keep an eye on the children when they were all tiny; in fact, the only happy memories Lauren had from her very early childhood were trips to their house in North Wales.

The social workers and I moved off to a separate table to discuss the next steps in formalizing the adoption, and I tried not to keep looking over at Lauren. She was completely ignoring me. It was fine – I was prepared for this; I understood she couldn't acknowledge both me and Terri at the same time – but it was very uncomfortable, and I suppose deep down I thought Terri really was her mother. Could I ever in Lauren's eyes be more than just another carer?

After a bit the five children went off together to explore and play, and the two tables of adults nodded and smiled at each other, all that is except Terri, who just smoked and stared into space. Liz took me to go and get some lunch.

'You're doing fine, girl. These things are horrible, aren't they?' she said with empathy.

Unlike the Stoke social workers, who didn't seem to get it at all and kept referring to Terri as 'Mum' to the children, Liz, who was herself an adoptive mother, clearly understood how awkward, even painful, these gatherings are for all concerned, including the adoptive parents. She said it simply disrupted a child and delayed them in being able to settle in and bond with new parents.

And then suddenly Lauren came up to me. 'Can we go now? I want to go. I've had enough.' She headed off towards the car park and I had to persuade her to come back and say her good-byes.

Terri, who still didn't get up, half-heartedly hugged her with one arm, the other still holding a cigarette. Lauren squirmed and then legged it back to the car without a backward glance.

In the car, she said, 'I hate Terri. She doesn't care about us. I want to be with you.'

On our way home, we stopped off at Sue's to meet her new baby granddaughter. Lauren sat almost in a trance with the tiny baby on her lap and had such a look of care and tenderness on her face it brought tears to my eyes. Every day I seemed to discover a new facet to this complex and extraordinary child.

4

A Lamb to the Slaughter

The first term of Lauren's move to secondary school was, in the end, mainly uneventful, though she wasn't very happy and seemed quite lost at times. She became increasingly listless and I began to worry she was becoming depressed. Any interest she had had in school and learning had quickly evaporated, but she made it to Christmas and even managed to sing in a small madrigal choir that performed at the school's Christmas concert.

There was, however, a very difficult patch in the second half of the term, when Lauren started telling me that a boy she had known since primary school was becoming quite sexually aggressive towards her. We were driving home from school after what had clearly been a difficult day for her, and she seemed very wound up.

'And that Kyle's a perv too. He keeps touching me up under the desk.'

Kyle may have only been eleven or twelve, but he was already a good head taller than most of the other year sevens and very powerfully built. Apparently he had on several occasions put his hand up her skirt, touched her breasts and bottom, attempted to get her to touch his penis and asked her to have sex with him. A lot of this had happened in the classroom in front of other children. On two occasions teachers witnessed the boy's behaviour and reprimanded him for it. My blood ran cold to hear Lauren tell me this and, despite her protests, I was determined to do something about it.

At first school seemed reluctant to take the matter seriously and I had to write to them and demand that they took concrete action to protect Lauren from assault on school premises. I wanted the boy stopped, but I was also concerned that because Lauren was still technically in care, I would therefore have to let Stoke know what had happened; this might trigger some heavy-handed child protection procedures, which would have been very distressing for her.

Aside from that, a lot of our emotional energy during the autumn of 2003 was consumed by fretting about why the legal process to finalize the adoption was taking so long. There was another statutory review meeting in the autumn, during which a lot of boxes were ticked and Lauren was again advised of her rights and of the complaints procedure. There was talk about progressing the legal formalities but no action plan. I could see that finalizing the paperwork for court was not a priority for anyone. After all, Lauren was placed with me and was no longer seen to be in any need. But the lingering uncertainty gnawed away at both of us. Lauren could still not legally use my surname, she could not go on sleepovers, and I could not take her on holiday without the consent of Stoke-on-Trent Social Services. Over six years after being taken into care, Lauren remained in limbo. She had been placed for adoption before and then been taken away; how could she have any faith that this time would be different?

Lauren sought reassurance from the court-appointed social worker, called a guardian ad litem, who visited us just before Christmas to prepare a report for the court on whether she thought the adoption should go ahead. This was the same woman who had been involved with Lauren and her siblings during previous court proceedings. Lauren said she didn't like her, and it was easy to see why, because she certainly had zero skills in talking to a child.

'The judge will say yes, won't he?' Lauren asked anxiously.

The guardian, Marion Fox, said, 'You see, Lauren, you told us before when you were with Barbara Spragg that you wanted that adoption to go ahead and that wasn't true, was it, so it's difficult for people to know whether to believe you now.'

Sitting on the sofa beside the Christmas tree, Lauren visibly crumpled and she started to cry. I put my arm around her and tried to draw some comfort for her from Marion. I asked if she would be recommending that this adoption should go ahead.

'Oh, I can't comment on that. It's early stages. We'll have to see,' was Marion's stony-faced response.

She saw a child in tears and refused to offer even a crumb of comfort.

On the M4 on Christmas Eve 2003 I still sang carols along to the radio, but this year someone else was singing along with me. Our first Christmas together was in Wales, at Michael and Victoria's, joined by my parents, Gerry, Hannah and Lottie. The presents had been wrapped for days, and in the case of Lauren's opened and then rewrapped. Lauren, who had never really been shown the magic of Christmas and the joy of giving and receiving, had a very pragmatic approach to presents: all that mattered was having the contents. The anticipation and the ritual of wrapping and unwrapping, of giving and receiving meant absolutely nothing. She hunted her presents out as soon as I bought them and demanded to have them there and then. I only managed to keep one gift, a small silver pendant, hidden until Christmas Day. She wore it once and then lost it. This was yet another example of how much of a normal childhood she had missed.

It was a lovely warm, cosy family Christmas, though, marred for me only by a concern that my father did not seem very well. He was more withdrawn than usual and hardly ate.

Lauren entered into everything as though she had been part of McDonnell Christmases for years. We ate too much and played endless games of charades, and she and my nieces performed karaoke songs with the aid of a karaoke machine my brother bought for the occasion. If she was missing previous Christmases or families, she didn't show it. I worked out this was her twelfth Christmas and she was spending it with her sixth family.

The excitement of the festivities over, however, Lauren went into a massive depression once school restarted and refused to go, claiming all manner of vague illnesses and spending day after day either in bed or wrapped in a duvet on the sofa watching television. The formal adoption on which she placed so much significance seemed as far away as ever. Liz took the unusual step of writing to the judge who had been assigned to the case to ask him to resist any approaches by either the guardian or Stoke to further delay the final hearing. But there was still no date on which to focus our minds.

Something fairly big had to happen quickly to help lift Lauren's mood and give her something to be cheerful about. I thought about a short trip to somewhere like Disneyland, but I had taken her there in the autumn and couldn't really afford either the time or the money for another trip so soon. Then I had an idea.

It was a cold, grey Thursday morning and Lauren was lying in bed insisting she had flu. She had been off school all week.

'Why don't you come downstairs and have a change of scene and some lunch?' I suggested.

'No.'

'How are you feeling?'

'Terrible.'

'Too terrible to come out and look at some puppies?'

She was out of bed, dressed and dragging Meg's old puppy crate out of the shed and into the car in ten minutes.

I had researched some Westie puppies online and knew there were some for sale at a kennels about twenty miles from Oxford. I had always planned to get Lauren her own puppy as an adoption present and so decided it could become an 'almost adoption' present. I'd thought about a puppy from a rescue centre but was concerned that it might give an unintended message. A rescue puppy for a rescue child.

Alfie was not the most handsome puppy ever, but Lauren's eyes lit up when he wriggled from under an upturned dog bed in the pen. Probably the runt of the litter, he looked like a little white fox cub with his huge pointed ears, certainly not the breed standard for a Westie. We had been advised to get a male to reduce competition with Meg, and as all the others were female and we couldn't leave empty-handed, he came home with us

– not actually in the puppy crate but snuggled inside Lauren's fleecy jacket as she cooed and cuddled him.

The next day she agreed to go back to school on condition that I would meet her at the school gates with Alfie at half past three. Her friends adored him and suddenly there was a queue of girls wanting to come back after school to play with Alfie.

Lauren was beginning to make some friends at last, but I must say they were a motley crew. Looking back, they represented every aspect of Lauren's fractured sense of self. Some were very young for their age, but many were incredibly sexually developed and streetwise for year seven. Most clearly had fairly troubled home lives. It would have been lovely to see Lauren making friends with more secure and stable children, but I knew that was unrealistic and that she felt more comfortable with those whose own experiences bore some similarity to her own.

Our first anniversary came around on 15 February 2004 and we went out to celebrate at Pizza Express.

'Can I have a glass of wine?' Lauren asked.

'No, you can't.'

'That's stupid. Don't you know I've been drinking for years? And I smoke.'

I was getting better at not rising to the bait and so didn't respond and we had a happy evening.

Not so happy was our trip to a bowling alley in Birmingham the next day for another birth family 'contact'. We had been warned that Terri was pregnant again. The whole event was once more structured as though Terri was holding court and the children were there to pay homage. The Stoke social workers still referred to her as 'Mum' to all the children.

'They're so stupid,' said Lauren. 'They know you're meant to be my mum now.'

This time Terri totally ignored the children; she didn't say a word to any of them. The kids started acting up, particularly Lauren and Kirsten, who got into a fight with some girls in the ladies' toilet.

Why were we there? Who was supposed to be benefiting from this ridiculous charade? Even the grandparents, who were the only ones managing to smile and chat, looked increasingly dismayed at their daughter's refusal to take part in an event set up for her benefit. In the end Granddad took Terri off to a burger bar, where she just sat and drank Coke and ate chips. We again left at Lauren's insistence.

She was angry and upset in equal measure. 'Why did Terri ignore us? Why does she want this baby when she didn't want us? What did we do that was so wrong? Why didn't she love us enough to keep us?'

I knew that my feeble attempts to answer her questions would provide little, if any, comfort, but I tried to console her as best I could.

At least at the end of February we had some good news. A letter arrived giving us a date for the court hearing to finalize the adoption – 16 March 2004. We danced a jig round the kitchen. What a relief!

Anne Jenkins, the Stoke-on-Trent social worker, asked me to provide a written summary of the first year to complete the paperwork for the court. I wrote it feeling resolved and optimistic about the future.

Dear Anne,

We celebrated our first anniversary a couple of weeks
ago with a meal out. In some ways, it seems no time at
all, and in others, it seems as though we have known
each other for ages. Lauren is much more relaxed again
than she was a few weeks ago now there is a date for the
adoption hearing and she is telling everyone about it and
discussing what she will wear!

She seems very settled here now, and she and I have a
really close, happy relationship, except when I am telling
her she has put on too much make-up or can't go out
without a coat, when she can get very angry and defiant,
but it soon passes. She gets on well with my friends and
family, who all think the world of her, and as she is the
youngest in my family and among most of my friends'
children, she gets a lot of fuss and attention, which she
thrives on.

She instantly took to all the pets, especially Meg, and is
lovely with them. Lauren has, of course, helped expand the
menagerie, firstly with Sandy, the hamster she had always
longed for, then with two goldfish and now with her own
puppy, Alfie.

The move to secondary school was too big a move too
soon and with hindsight I wish I had really pushed the
LEA to allow her to do year six again. She was completely
overwhelmed for most of the first term, but being Lauren,
somehow she coped and she is now fairly settled and doing
reasonably well. (I haven't had a progress report for some
time, but there is a parents' evening next month.) She
gets on well with those teachers who bother to take time

to get to know her, but her new-found confidence has led her to be rather naughty and cheeky with those she does not respect, notably the science teacher, and she has had a couple of detentions as a result.

School has an informal support service and Lauren was linked up with them last term when she was finding it so hard to settle. They say she doesn't need it now, but have let her stay on in the weekly sessions because she likes the hot chocolate and marshmallows they serve up!

The problem with the boy that I reported to you has been resolved as far as I can tell. Eventually school seemed to take it seriously and the boy's contact with Lauren is carefully watched. In some ways, some positive came out of that episode, as I think it made school realize how vulnerable she is, despite her cheerful and confident manner.

That and another episode, when a boy she hardly knows persuaded her to give him her brand-new mobile phone, her pride and joy, has made me realize how vulnerable to exploitation by certain boys she is. My biggest task over the next few years is to give her the confidence and skills to deal with the sexual predation she will inevitably encounter and to ensure that the freedom she must increasingly have is nevertheless carefully regulated.

She does have a wide circle of friends at school, and although some of the relationships are very volatile, they have endured. Most of her friends tend to be pretty troubled children themselves, but I have noticed that in the last month or so one or two new friends have appeared on the scene who seem to be much more secure, mature and happy children.

Her health is good. She has grown four inches and three shoe sizes in a year! Illness-wise she has had nothing more than a cold, although she has had a total of twelve days off school since she moved with what I can only describe as stress, firstly during all the trouble with the Spraggs harassing us (which fortunately now seems to have stopped) and more recently when she was so concerned that the adoption would never go ahead. She has lost all her baby teeth and now has an appointment with an orthodontist to be fitted with a brace to straighten her front teeth. To my amazement, she is looking forward to a brace – as long as it's purple.

She says very little about the past, although bit by bit things are emerging. She is wholly negative about the Spraggs and wants no contact or reminders of that part of her life, although when she brings the subject up, I do try to encourage her to talk and to remember the good bits as well as the bad. She is understandably utterly confused about how she feels about her birth family. At the moment she is very angry with Terri (more so after the contact) and feels very let down that Terri couldn't keep them but is now looking forward to another baby. She is even more confused about her birth father, who on the one hand she remembers as a terrifying monster about whom she still has nightmares, but on the other she has written a passionate ode to a caring and protective 'dad' in a notebook. She is very clear she doesn't want to see him, but she desperately wants to have a photo. I don't know if something could be arranged?

Her relationship with her brothers seems quite

straightforward and she really enjoys meeting them. The relationship with Kirsten, although in some ways the closest, is also the most complex, and Lauren is at times rather reluctant to actively maintain it – for example, she absolutely refused to send a Christmas card or present. I think we are going to need to think carefully about how to support the girls to develop a relationship that works for both of them.

In conclusion, I feel terribly lucky to be able to share my life with Lauren. She is a wonderful, warm, generous, funny child who has already coped with more than most people have to in a lifetime and yet has retained her optimism and joyfulness. I think adolescence, however, is going to be a very difficult time for her in a number of ways and she will need a lot of help to understand that there are other ways of attracting and relating to boys/men and dealing with things like drugs and alcohol than she has experienced in her early childhood. She will also need a lot of encouragement to appreciate that she can make choices for herself about how she wants her life to go. Getting the adoption through and being heard, believed and an active party in that final decision will be an important next step for Lauren's confidence and self-esteem.

We travelled up to Birmingham the night before we were due in court. The hearing was scheduled for nine thirty and we didn't want to be late. I knew the hearing was pretty much a formality, but it was important nonetheless, and a big occasion for Lauren. My parents and Gerry, Michael and Victoria all came to court with us. Lauren wasn't just being adopted by me but by the whole family and they were keen to be part of the formal proceedings. We filed into the bright, light, modern courtroom and sat down behind assorted court officials, lawyers and social workers.

'Are they all here for me?' Lauren asked incredulously.

She was only four months from her twelfth birthday, and as I'd said in my letter to Anne Jenkins, I thought she needed to feel that she was an acknowledged party in the decision over the adoption order. Strictly speaking, there is no role or voice for the child, even if they are old enough to fully understand what is going on. There is a fiction that the child is represented by the guardian ad litem and a solicitor appointed by them, but the truth is that as they have virtually no contact with or knowledge of the child, they can represent no one but themselves and the process. To give Lauren some sense that she was involved, I drew up a 'Certificate of Consent to Be Adopted', which the judge was happy to make part of the proceedings. He asked Lauren if she was willing to give her consent to me adopting her, which she solemnly did, and then he signed the certificate alongside her. Lauren beamed with pride at being given such an important role. Then we all went up onto the judge's bench for photos, including one of Lauren wearing his full-bottomed wig. She loved the theatricality of it all.

Outside the court, we smiled and shook hands, and Lauren was given good-luck cards by the social workers. For the first time in seven years she was no longer a child in care and wouldn't have social workers involved in her life. We both felt so relieved.

Of course, being adopted didn't magic away Lauren's problems, and I hadn't expected it would. The excitement of the occasion soon wore off, and back in school, Lauren started to play up – being late for lessons, not doing homework, repeatedly losing her PE kit and making her dislike of certain teachers very plain. She was starting to lie a lot too: no, they didn't have any homework that night; someone had stolen her PE kit. Her year tutor was understanding and not overly concerned. He and I assumed that this was a reaction to everything that had happened and things would settle down eventually.

When they didn't settle down at the beginning of the summer term, I was summoned to see the deputy head, Mrs Coggins, a very dour older woman who belonged in a different era. She was definitely old school, a clone of the schoolteachers who taught me in the 1950s and 1960s. I got such a sense of déjà vu when I was summoned in to see her that I had to remind myself that this time I was the parent, not the badly behaved schoolgirl.

Mrs Coggins said Lauren's behaviour should be 'nipped in the bud'. I started to explain just what had gone on for Lauren over the previous few years, indeed her entire life, when she interrupted me: 'Mrs McDonnell, we don't discriminate in this school. Everyone is treated the same. You would be rightly complaining if Lauren was treated differently because she was black or disabled.'

'I am not suggesting you discriminate,' I said, 'but rather that the school shows some understanding and support for a child who has had such a troubled and disrupted early life. Couldn't we all work together on a plan to support her and help her settle here?'

'But, Mrs McDonnell, I thought I had explained that here at Hinksey Fields School, we treat all our students the same regardless of their background.'

It was futile. She didn't want to understand. She simply re-iterated that Lauren must change her attitude and dismissed us.

Children in care have very little opportunity to develop a bit of age-appropriate independence and so, at nearly twelve, Lauren had never travelled on a bus on her own, run errands to a local shop or walked home from school. Now I was her legal parent, I hoped that by giving her a bit of carefully contained independence, she might start to take some responsibility for herself and enjoy the feeling of being trusted.

Lauren's friendship with Jennifer was also developing. As Jennifer seemed a nice girl with a sensible mother, I was keen to encourage it. They lived very near the school, so Lauren would often walk to Jennifer's at the end of the day and I would pick her up from there a couple of hours later. Jennifer's mother was always warm and welcoming, and seemed to share my approach to appropriate levels of independence for twelve-year-olds. One day I agreed to leave it a bit later. It was June and still light when I went to pick her up at seven. The girls weren't at the house; Jennifer's mother explained that she had let them go to the local park with some friends. They were due back an hour ago, but she couldn't go and find them because she was looking after her granddaughter. She seemed surprisingly relaxed about the whole thing, but I reasoned that she had several older children so was much more experienced and probably knew when to worry and when not to.

I found the two girls in a playground with several slightly older boys; they were smoking. When Lauren saw me, she screamed abuse at me and ran off. I followed, but she ran off again, the obscenities growing in volume and range. I had never seen her like this before and was shocked by her behaviour. I decided that pursuing her round the park with the boys cheering her and egging her on was pointless, and not doing much for my dignity and authority, so I went back to the car and sat waiting and shaking with rage and frustration. Eventually Lauren flounced up to the car, got in and slammed the door. She stank of tobacco and something else . . . Cider?

'Let's go.'

'What the hell were you playing at?'

'We were just having fun.'

'Who are those boys?'

'Just some friends from school. They're in year ten.'

'And you have been smoking and drinking – I can smell it.'

'So?'

'So, you are not yet twelve. You don't smoke and drink at your age.'

'I do.'

'And you broke your promise to me that you would be sensible. I trusted you and you let me down.'

'So? Everyone lets me down.'

'No, they don't – I don't.' I was furious but very disconcerted.

'Fuck off.'

That was when it started – in Botley, Oxford in June 2004 – the downward spiral of risk-taking, defiance and denial. This child, who Stoke Social Services had once defined as overly compliant, started to refuse outright to accept any reasonable rules or boundaries to ensure her well-being and safety.

At a loss, I attended a seminar for adoptive parents a few days later. In a workshop on containing challenging behaviour, I asked how I could successfully tackle lying and defiant behaviour and still show I loved and trusted Lauren. The speaker, an eccentric American expert, chewed me up: 'Don't be ridiculous – of course you don't trust her. Don't let her believe you do or she will think you are really stupid.'

It was very shocking to hear that. It seemed such a betrayal to essentially tell a child you didn't trust them, didn't believe them. It seemed akin to saying you didn't love them. But she was right, and in a way it was liberating to be told that I didn't have to trust Lauren. I was, however, deeply upset to realize that our relationship was not developing into the warm, trusting bond I had imagined. It became clear to me that for parental discipline and boundary setting to work, on some level the child has to be willing to accept your authority. I could not physically impose it, and try as I might, I could find no way of communicating with Lauren in order to enforce it intellectually or emotionally.

So all in all, I was relieved when the summer holiday came around. The park incident had helped me realize that Lauren was always happier and less challenging away from her peers, and dealt with new situations and people well. We went camping in Dorset with friends and spent a lovely relaxed week swimming and fossil hunting, something Lauren really got engrossed in. It was lovely to see her so relaxed and taking an interest in things again, but I noticed how much easier she found interacting with adults than with young people and how she shied away from making friends with any of the kids on the campsite.

We also went up and stayed with Sue, as she was throwing a party for her son's birthday. He didn't turn up, and Lauren's indignation and dismay at him for letting down his mother like that after 'all the trouble' she had gone to, 'making a nice birthday meal for him', came straight from the heart of a very principled and empathetic young person.

And then finally we were off to the South of France, to Michael and Victoria's holiday house, a beautiful old farmhouse set in rolling hills covered in sunflowers. Best of all, at least for Lauren, it had a huge swimming pool. She and her cousins virtually lived in the pool, inventing games such as making videos of sharks attacking film stars lying on lilos complete with sound effects and a musical score. They cooked a Mexican meal one night and dressed up in sombreros with huge moustaches painted on with eyebrow pencil to serve the food. It was nothing terribly unusual by the standards of normal family holidays, but for Lauren, it was a first. She had a wonderful time using little more than her imagination. There were no emotional dramas to overstimulate her, just what came from within. That summer I saw in her a playfulness and artistry that I had never seen before. Sadly that joyfulness and creativity were not to last.

I think I was dreading her return to the dead hand of school as much as she was. Year eight had been described to me as the 'year when the wheels come off' by one of her teachers. He said year seven was usually trouble-free for children, but come year eight, with hormones starting to rage and childhood cuteness on the wane, pupils start to challenge authority and teachers stop making allowances.

Lauren wasted no time in testing authority. Within a week of her return to school she had had a fight in the playground, sworn at a teacher and stormed out of a science lesson. I hadn't been too optimistic about her return to school given the attitude there, but I hadn't expected it to get so bad so quickly. It was becoming difficult at home again too, with Lauren being challenging and defiant a lot of the time. Hardly a day went by without an incident at school, and I now had the phone numbers of her year tutor and the deputy head stored on my mobile phone.

I could get nowhere at all with the deputy head. 'Shape up or ship out' was her attitude. Lauren's year tutor was more understanding, but even he made it clear that there was no capacity in any teacher's day to try and accommodate, let alone take an interest in, a child who was not coping. I was told very firmly that there was no pastoral support available at Hinksey Fields School because they didn't usually have the sort of children who would need it!

By half-term Lauren was having detentions two or three times a week. These became double detentions for not turning up. Of course, she didn't go to these either. Clearly an effective sanction, then! Even when things had reached this stage of lunacy, no one from school was prepared to sit down with us and talk about what we could do to help make things better.

We went off to the Gower peninsula camping at half-term. Lauren was determined to conquer her fear of horse riding, so I had booked her on a four-day riding course, which she thoroughly enjoyed, but we had to divert down to my parents' house in Wiltshire for the last few days of half-term. My mother had rung to say she was really worried about my father. He was refusing to eat and was so thin and pale it was shocking to see. The GP I called out diagnosed depression, although I was certain that was not the whole story. We collected some antidepressants and took him and Mum back to Oxford with us. Lauren was fabulous with him, so gentle and caring. She brought him drinks, and nothing was too much trouble for her when it came to looking after her new-found grandfather.

Even when Dad was dying in hospital a couple of weeks later

of bone cancer – not the depression he had been misdiagnosed with – Lauren would insist she came with me on visits to support me and would sit holding his hand, helping him sip drinks and stroking his hair. It was only when he vomited in his oxygen mask that she became clearly distressed and we decided that it was probably best if she didn't visit him anymore. At first she protested, but I think deep down she was relieved that the decision had been taken out of her hands.

Almost every day for four weeks I would drop Lauren at school in Oxford, drive to Salisbury, spend a few hours with my father and drive back in time to collect Lauren from school or Jennifer's. Several of these journeys were interrupted by phone conversations with the deputy head about Lauren's further deteriorating behaviour in school. I would have to pull into a lay-by to listen to the latest catalogue of misdemeanours before continuing my journey.

On one of these visits, my father lapsed into unconsciousness and we were told it would probably only be another day or so. My brothers and I arranged between us that one of us should be at the hospital with my mother and father round the clock. School had just broken up for Christmas and I asked Lauren if she would be prepared to go to Jennifer's house and stay the night. I spoke to Jennifer's mother, Lynne, who was more than happy to have Lauren, so the next morning I dropped her off. This would be the first time in nearly two years that we would spend a night apart. Jennifer, her mother and Lauren all promised there would be no repeat of the previous escapade. I really had no option but to trust them.

My father died that evening, 22 December 2004. I had rung Lauren a couple of hours earlier and she seemed well and happy at Jennifer's, so I decided to leave it at that for the night. It wasn't the sort of news I wanted to give her over the phone.

I brought my mother back to Oxford with me, arriving in the early hours of 23 December. I left it until half past nine to ring Jennifer's house and Lynne answered.

'I'm really sorry but I don't know where the girls are. They went out last night, promising to only be an hour, but they didn't come back.'

My heart stopped. 'Oh my God, do you know where they could be? Have you called the police?'

'No. I didn't want to bother the police. Jennifer texted me to say they were OK. She said they were with friends.'

'What friends? Where? They are twelve and thirteen years old. Anything could have happened.'

'I'm sure they'll be OK. Jennifer has done this before. Teenagers, eh!'

I was staggered at how laid-back she was about it all. Lauren wasn't even a teenager, and Jennifer only just. They were still children and I had trusted her.

I rang and texted Lauren's phone in a blind panic. She didn't respond; her battery was either flat or the phone switched off. I tried to make light of Lauren's continued absence to my mother, who was in no state to cope with this on top of everything else.

Eventually Lauren called me from a withheld number. She was in Wood Farm, a housing estate on the other side of Oxford from where Jennifer lived.

'Who are you with?' I asked, trying to hide my extreme anxiety.

'Jennifer's boyfriend.'

'Jennifer doesn't have a boyfriend.'

'Yes she does, but her mother doesn't know.'

'Give me the address and I will come and pick you up.'

'He says he doesn't know his address. I'll meet you at the laundrette in the parade of shops.' She hung up before I could say anything else.

I waited ages outside the laundrette – for so long I was about to give up, thinking this was a wild goose chase, when Lauren and Jennifer appeared across the road. They were ambling along, laughing.

'Can we give Jennifer a lift home?' Lauren asked non-chalantly, when she opened the car door.

'Get in the car. I've a good mind to make you both walk home.'

'How's Grandpa?'

'Dead.'

There was a gasp, followed by barely audible sobbing from the back of the car.

I was so exhausted and angry I had wanted to shock her, to get through to her, and I obviously had.

That afternoon I iced the Christmas cake while on the phone to the undertaker arranging my father's funeral. My mother was keen that for the sake of the grandchildren, we should salvage some sort of Christmas, so everyone came up to Oxford. It was very last minute and chaotic, but warm and supportive, and caught up in all that, I didn't have much time to reflect on what might have happened to Lauren and Jennifer in Wood Farm.

5

The Wheels Start to Come Off

Lauren and I spent New Year 2005 in Folkestone with a large group of my friends. It was jolly, cosy and supportive, and felt a world away from death, illness and crazy pubescent behaviour. Except for when we had a party on New Year's Eve, Lauren was the only child there. As always, she was so much more relaxed surrounded by sensible, caring adults. I spent most of the three-day break trying to organize the details of the funeral service – readings, drafting the eulogy and booking flowers. The others were very helpful and kept taking Lauren out to give me some space. I must admit some of the time I just went to bed. I felt as though I hadn't slept for months.

Dad's funeral was in Wiltshire on 5 January 2005. It went as well as these things can. Lauren was wonderful: kind, caring, empathetic and helpful. She stood up and read a poem in the service, and helped to hand round the trays of food at the wake, coping with a lot of elderly friends and relatives, most of whom she had never met before. I never failed to be amazed at how she could rise to the occasion even in the midst of her most defiant and out-of-control behaviour. It felt at times as though I had two very different daughters.

Back at school, however, Lauren began getting into trouble on a daily rather than a weekly basis. She was excluded twice in February and thrown out of school before I could get there to collect her. On the second occasion she disappeared, I searched everywhere for her but couldn't find her.

She eventually came home at 10 p.m. in a terrible state, clearly having taken something. She was wild, giggling one minute and moaning the next, then throwing herself from one piece of furniture to the next. God knows where she had been – she said with friends.

'Have you taken something?'

She giggled stupidly in my face without answering.

Who did she know who would have access to drugs and give them to a twelve-year-old? I had reported her missing to the police, but they hadn't found her; she'd just suddenly turned up at the front door.

I took her into school the next morning: we had been summoned to see the deputy head. Lauren didn't want to go and I was beginning to understand how she felt. The staff had clearly made up their minds to reject her. Their model of the pupil was middle of the road, unchallenging, compliant. They were not interested in the children as individuals. Mrs Coggins was sitting behind her desk when Lauren and I were called in, and she produced a ledger-like book full of ticks and crosses and red marks, ran her finger up and down the figures counting and announced Lauren was almost the worst-behaved child in the school, based on the number of reported incidents of bad behaviour. She was second only to a fifteen-year-old boy who was about to be permanently excluded. Lauren feigned pride at this achievement.

I tried to suggest that if there was more understanding and more accommodation of Lauren's situation, her behaviour might improve, but Mrs Coggins simply kept repeating, 'Mrs McDonnell, here at Hinksey Fields School we don't discriminate. All children are treated the same, regardless of their gender, ethnic origin or background.'

'But surely you can make adjustments for different abilities and needs and the very different issues some children have to cope with?'

'Mrs McDonnell, I am sure you would be the first to complain if we singled Lauren out for different treatment just because she was adopted. No, what Lauren needs to do is to buck up her ideas.'

I felt like we were having an exact repeat of every conversation we had ever had. It was like talking to a brick wall.

Following the exclusions, Lauren was placed on a restricted day in school and told she could only be on the premises on certain days between nine and twelve, during which time she would be allowed no contact with any of her friends. She was going to be sent to 'B12'. It sounded sinister, like something out of Big Brother (Orwell, not Channel 4), and it was the school sin bin. It was, however, run by a very experienced and wise teacher, John Morgan, who showed considerable interest in and empathy towards Lauren. He took the time to ask me about her background and what I felt were the key issues for her. He spoke to Lauren about her hopes and fears, and what she found so difficult about school life. Unfortunately, the overarching school regime clearly restricted him greatly in what he could do to help.

Although I tried to collect Lauren from school each day, that was not always possible. She would also sometimes be sent home from school much earlier than I was expecting because of bad behaviour and would take herself off and hang around Oxford city centre, where she was becoming involved in the street scene. There was a notorious and very grotty bit called Bonn Square, which, despite being in the main shopping area, was at all times of day and night full of street drinkers and drug users and other groups of disaffected people, including a gang of young Albanian men. I had warned her many times not to hang around there, but banned from normal school life and from association during the school day with her friends, this was where twelve-year-old Lauren would head, to cadge fags and look for companionship.

As usual, it was a very different Lauren who came down to Wales with me at the weekend after her second week in B12. Michael, Victoria, Lauren and I took all four dogs down to the beach. The tide was right out and there were miles of sand. The dogs ran and ran, and so did Lauren, in ecstasy, with the wind bowling her along the water's edge. She almost took off. She shrieked out, 'I want to live like this forever! I feel like I'm flying.'

Returning home that night, just as we got to the outskirts of Oxford, her phone rang, and at the next traffic lights, without any warning, she jumped out of the car. By the time I had safely pulled up, parked and run back, she had disappeared. It was dark and teeming with rain.

My heart pounding, I rang the police as soon as I got home, and at 3 a.m. they brought her back. I was going up the wall with worry. She'd been seen on CCTV in the city centre in the company of two much older men. She said she couldn't remember where she had been, and as she was clearly in such a stupor, this was probably true. Drink? Drugs? Exhaustion? Probably all three. I got her into bed and she became very distressed, so I sat with her, stroking her hair. She started to make gurgling, bubbly baby noises, and as I stroked her hair, she sighed and sucked more energetically on her thumb. She stank of tobacco, cheap perfume and something else. Where had she been? Why had she just jumped out of the car like that? Who had phoned her? She wouldn't answer any of my questions.

One of the places Lauren told me she went to was a busy evangelical church, St Aldate's, which is right in the centre of Oxford, opposite Christ Church College.

'See, you think I'm going off with dodgy people when I'm actually going to church!' she said whenever I asked her where she'd gone.

She told me they had a service on a Sunday evening that anyone could go to, followed by the serving of refreshments. Despite the location, I was worried, because it sounded as though this service might be something for homeless people. I rang them many times and eventually wrote to 'whoever is responsible for child protection' saying I was concerned about my twelve-year-old daughter who often went missing and who said one of the places she went to was their church. I gave them my address and phone numbers. No one ever got back to me.

By this time, my paid work consisted of twelve hours a week running a small charity working with severely disabled children, and some freelance work in the housing and mental health fields. I tried to limit any work I did away from home to three mornings a week, in the hope that Lauren would be at school or, failing that, in bed sleeping off the excesses of her last escapade. Providing that I left out a couple of cigarettes, she would usually be at home when I got back about 1 p.m. I wasn't particularly happy with this arrangement, but I hoped it was a good way of keeping her safe for a few weeks.

But by early February we were in the midst of the most incredibly chaotic behaviour. She wouldn't get up or go to bed at a reasonable time, wouldn't wash or change her clothes and often refused to eat the food I cooked for her. At the slightest challenge to her behaviour, she would go into violent rages that could last for hours. Door panels would get kicked in, vases thrown and smashed, and – a new development – she would attack me with whatever came to hand. It was like living in a war zone.

Somehow the shock of it all and the need to find a way for us both to survive this tumultuous time deadened my emotions. I didn't let myself feel anything too much, neither the physical pain nor the sadness and worry. Only survive, I would say to myself as her eyes started to flash in response to my refusal to give in to some outrageous demand. Don't plead, I would tell myself as she picked up one of my most valued ornaments and smashed it onto the floor with a crazy grin on her face. Don't let her see you're in pain, I would remind myself through clenched teeth as she twisted and bent my fingers round in circles, and above all try not to cry.

I was starting to walk around like a jailer, with bunches of keys round my neck. I had locks put on all the windows as well as extra ones on the doors. I put a lock on my office door so I could keep money and my phone safe, as she had started stealing from me, and I stopped putting credit on her phone in the hope that it would stop her contacting whoever these so-called friends were.

By mutual agreement, early in 2004, we had given up

making the six-weekly treks to Sutton Coldfield to see the play therapist. The round journey from Oxford was expensive and time-consuming, and by then it didn't seem to be helping Lauren, who refused to enter into the process. However, as things continued to deteriorate, I had found a local therapist, Peter, who I thought might be able to help Lauren. He came highly recommended as someone with great skill in working with the most damaged, disruptive children. Lauren was very resistant to the idea.

'I don't need a fucking shrink. I'm not mad.'

'No, of course you're not mad, but you are angry and unhappy, and I think it might help to be able to talk to someone who understands how you're feeling.'

'No one can understand how I'm feeling because I'm not feeling anything.'

When I offered to make it worth her while financially (she would get an extra £3 pocket money every time she went), she reluctantly agreed to give it a go. It wasn't cheap, but I would have paid any price, gone anywhere to find someone who could help her process all the stuff that had happened to her and which was clearly making her so furious and unhappy. Often she would come out from sessions with Peter angry and upset, but after some visits she would come out looking relieved, as though a huge burden had been lifted from her. She said to me once, 'I tell Peter things I've never told anyone.' I was so relieved; maybe we had finally found someone who could help her.

Generally, though, she was becoming angry and distressed on an almost daily basis. More disturbingly, she had started to talk again about the worm in her head that was eating her brain. One morning, during half-term in February, while Lauren was still in bed, I rang Peter and he agreed to see me urgently, ahead of Lauren's appointment that afternoon, to give me some feedback on what he thought was going on for her and some advice on dealing with her outbursts. Our cleaner was in the house, so I jumped in the car and drove out to see him.

When I got there, Peter told me, 'Elizabeth, I have to tell you Lauren is an extremely troubled girl and I feel that unless she urgently gets some very intensive therapeutic help, her acting-out behaviour is likely to get a lot worse.'

He continued, 'The situation you are trying to deal with is on the edge of being uncontainable by one person. What Lauren really needs is intensive residential therapeutic treatment.'

Hearing that, I was almost relieved: it wasn't just that I was hopeless; Lauren really did have huge emotional difficulties. We discussed the realities of being able to find something appropriate, and Peter said it would be difficult, partly because Lauren was now almost too old for the sorts of places he had in mind and partly because without the support of school or some statutory authority, there would be no mechanism for funding or referral.

However, he did give me a few tips, such as minimizing any emotional demands on her and keeping life at home very simple and straightforward, with limited treats and privileges in return for clear behavioural expectations. He suggested I encourage Lauren to reflect on how she felt about herself in order to deflect her anger away from me.

When I got back home from my meeting with Peter, there was a note from Lauren pinned to the front door saying she had gone to the cinema with Jo, a friend from school. Are cinemas open in the morning? I wondered. Maybe, as it's half-term. But then Jo phoned asking to speak to Lauren. If Lauren wasn't with Jo, then who was she with?

When she got back during the afternoon, I asked her where she had been, saying I knew she hadn't been with Jo. She went berserk and there followed two hours of being screamed at and called a fucking cow, a hopeless mother and a loser who was not up to the job. I eventually got her into the car, still ranting, to take her to her appointment with Peter. Taking his advice, I said, 'Look, you don't have to like me – I understand that's hard – but you should try and like yourself a bit more.'

This shifted the rant up a gear. 'What the hell do you mean? Don't you dare say that, you fucking cow. Are you trying to wind me up? What have I ever done to make you think I don't like you?'

'Well, constantly calling me a "fucking cow", for example.'

'Are you having a laugh? Calling you a "fucking cow" doesn't mean I don't like you.'

She gradually calmed down, though. I stopped at a pet shop and ran in to get some dog food. When I got back to the car, it was covered inside with dozens of Post-it notes saying, 'Sorry'. Lauren was sitting in the passenger seat playing with the radio. 'Don't say anything,' she said. She didn't want to talk to Peter either and walked out of the session after just a few minutes.

The next day was very quiet. Lauren was exhausted and stayed in her pyjamas on the sofa watching TV. I let her because she clearly needed to rest. She seemed like a small child and said she felt safe when she was at home with me.

'Can I ask why, if you feel safe at home, you keep going out and getting into very unsafe situations? I don't understand it. It must be horrible to feel unsafe so much of the time.'

She shrugged. 'That's just how life is for me. I don't deserve to feel safe.'

I started to say, 'Of course you deserve to feel safe – everyone does, and you are a wonderful young girl and deserve the very best in life,' but I could tell it was making her uncomfortable and angry again, so I stopped.

During the evening she wanted to watch a programme on out-of-control preschool children and kept asking me if they were worse than her. I was uncertain how to play this, but it seemed like an opportunity to get some points across, so I decided not to completely fudge it. I said her situation was different and she was a lot older, but her behaviour at times, at school and to me, was really shocking and very worrying, and I wondered what was making her feel so bad that she had to behave like that and what I could do to help.

She said, 'Nothing. Fuck off!' and stormed off to bed.

About an hour later, when I was in bed, she came in saying she was having bad dreams and asked if she could sleep in my bed.

I didn't have to work the next day and I devoted almost all of it to Lauren's pleasure. I bought her new jodhpurs, took her to a riding lesson and put streaks in her hair, which took hours. Then Lauren accused me of having stolen her savings because I wouldn't let her have access to the £51 she had carefully saved over the last few years to fritter away. The abuse and aggression started to escalate, and mindful of Peter's advice, I walked quietly off to my office to make some phone calls. Lauren followed shouting, which made phone conversation impossible, so I turned on the computer and pretended to work, managing to more or less ignore her. After about twenty minutes she started to calm down, but still went to bed shouting and spitting. A couple of hours later she climbed into my bed saying she was too scared to sleep in hers and that I made her feel safe.

'I do love you, Mum. Don't take any notice of me when I say I don't.'

How did she manage to change so suddenly? It was exhausting and very confusing trying to keep up with her. I couldn't change as quickly as Lauren, so my emotional responses were always lagging behind her. She would suddenly be all bright and loving when I was still feeling angry and despondent about the last outburst, possibly only an hour earlier. And then I would force myself to cheer up and be jolly and positive again only to be told I was an insensitive cow to be so happy when she was having such a terrible time.

To finish off half-term, we had arranged to meet up with Kirsten at Dudley Zoo. Kirsten came with a carer from the children's home. Lauren was in a tense, tetchy mood and being very rude and defiant towards me.

'You should show Elizabeth more respect, you,' Kirsten exploded. 'She's meant to be your mum. You shouldn't disrespect your mother.'

Lauren pushed the table, threw over her chair and stormed out of the cafe where we were having lunch. I left it a couple of minutes and then went after her and found her in tears by the giraffes, cursing Kirsten. We all patched things up and had a reasonably harmonious afternoon looking at the animals, but then over tea Lauren stormed off again, having had another argument with Kirsten. We decided it was time to go and the girls managed to hug each other before getting into the cars and being driven off in opposite directions.

From the zoo we headed to nearby Stourbridge to spend the night with Sue. As Lauren was usually more relaxed and happy away from Oxford, I took as many opportunities to get her away for a night or two as possible. On the way there, Lauren's anger was building.

'It's not fair – Kirsten's been talking to Terri on the phone and the cow hasn't phoned me.'

'Well, Kirsten is in a very different situation to you. She hasn't been adopted and she's planning to go back and live with Terri in a few years when she leaves care.'

'You stupid bitch, that doesn't make any difference. Terri should still ring me.'

'It does make a difference: Terri knows you are adopted now.' I took a deep breath. 'In fact, I don't want Terri to ring you. It doesn't help you.'

I had to grip the steering wheel tightly as even fouler abuse rained down. Apparently I was the worst mother in the world; I stole someone else's child because I couldn't have a child myself.

What Lauren didn't know at this point was that a social worker had recently told me that Terri had been hospitalized following a heroin overdose and was now a registered heroin addict. Kirsten believed that Terri had been in hospital suffering from fits, but of course this was far from the truth. I hadn't told Lauren what I knew, because she was in enough of a state without that, but now I decided the time had come to tell her about Terri's heroin use. Big mistake on my part, in hindsight. I had to stop the car; she went completely crazy and tried to pull the steering wheel. I was every piece of lowlife imaginable, including a fucking whore, and I was lying about Terri. Lauren had never been quite so awful in terms of personal abuse and it was impossible to drive for about fifteen minutes, but as the rage seemed so clearly related to the contact with Kirsten and revelations about Terri and all the pain and confusion of that, I managed not to feel it was personal.

Then Lauren said, 'I have a secret to tell you. I'm actually a serious smoker and often smoke weed.'

Trying to sound calm and matter-of-fact, I replied, 'That isn't very sensible, is it? What a waste of money.'

'It's really strong weed too,' she needled. 'Not that you can stop me – I'm an addict now.'

I tried not to react, and just repeated that it wasn't a sensible thing to do, I didn't approve, and smoking weed was illegal.

'You fucking cow, you don't care that I'm smoking weed and am virtually a drug addict and will probably die. You don't care about me at all, do you? If you did, you'd be very angry and try and stop me. Not that you could, though. I like it. It makes me feel good.'

Back at home, it wasn't just me on the receiving end of her rages but her beloved puppy, Alfie, who was regularly subjected to torrents of abuse and the occasional kick. He was ugly, pathetic, the runt of the litter, she only took him because no one else would want him, and she was going to send him back and then he would be on his own forever because he was so horrible. I was very concerned that she might actually hurt the little chap, who would rush and sit at my feet looking at her with his head on one side in bewilderment as she railed at him. It was distressing to hear the amount of pain behind what she was saying, but the projection of her feelings and worries about her security with me were so blatant that it actually helped me to see a lot of what was going on in her head more clearly.

But it was beyond me to find ways to use that insight that could help her. I tried but was just told to 'fuck off' each time I attempted to reach her. Peter the therapist wasn't making enough of a difference; we needed more specialized professional help, so I made an appointment to see our GP. She was very sympathetic but explained that the only thing she could do as a health practitioner would be to refer Lauren to the Child and Adolescent Mental Health Service. Experience told her they would try and reject such a referral because Lauren's symptoms didn't fit any of the traditional mental illness classifications. She was at times psychotic, manic, she was certainly very depressed and a massive risk to herself and others, but she didn't have the right set of symptoms to fit their acceptance criteria. The doctor felt that continuing with Peter was probably the only option, but Peter had already told me that he, too, was at a loss to know how to reach her. He felt that Lauren needed medical psychiatric input rather than simply a talking treatment that she was too disintegrated emotionally to be able to engage with.

I had also approached Oxfordshire Social Services three times for help, and the police had informed them of their concern when Lauren was missing, but Oxford said that because Lauren had been adopted from Stoke-on-Trent, it was them who must take responsibility for us. The fact that the Stoke social workers were over a hundred miles away and had no knowledge of services in Oxford and no contacts there cut no ice. Nor did the fact that I had lived in Oxfordshire for sixteen years and Lauren was my legal daughter. Even more galling was the fact that they freely admitted that if we had *both* just moved into the area, they would have had to help.

After much persistence, Lauren and I finally got an appointment with the duty social worker at Oxfordshire County Council's offices in Cowley Road to discuss my request that Lauren should go on the Child Protection Register in order to try and get her on the radar as a vulnerable child. The social worker we saw was very thorough and understanding, and said she would talk to our adoption support worker and Lauren's therapist and promised to get back to me the next day. I heard nothing more.

I was getting desperate. Lauren was a very young, very vulnerable, very frightened twelve-year-old who had endured and survived so much in her life; I could not accept that there was no one who would help us. Walking the dogs one morning, I bumped into a neighbour who was the recently appointed head of the Oxford University Department of Child Psychiatry and I told him some of the story. He recommended a child psychologist who worked part-time for the NHS Trust and part-time in private practice. I rang our GP, who agreed to write an immediate letter of referral.

The following week Lauren was missing three nights in five days. On one occasion, after she received a phone call from one of her friends and said she had to go out, I rushed to the front door to try and drag her back. She tried to push me off and we ended up on the floor. I had one arm round her ankle and one round the banister and she kicked me in the head with her free foot. We were both sobbing.

'Mum, you have to let me go,' she screamed. 'You don't understand – I have to go out.'

I let go. I wish I had known what she meant.

She came back at three o'clock in the morning with her usual boozy, smoky scent. She sat on my knee and sucked her thumb as we waited for the police to come and 'sight her', a procedure that happens every time a missing person turns up. They asked her where she had been and she said with friends; they advised her to choose nicer friends and left.

After a couple of days of calmer behaviour, I agreed to let Lauren come home from school when she left at noon on the bus on her own. This would give me an extra hour at work before I needed to leave to be at home when Lauren got back. I was still trying to focus on any glimmer of positive behaviour and to support and model what I felt was age-appropriate freedom in order to reward her when she was behaving sensibly. She rang me from the bus and all seemed well. She then rang me again to say she had just got home. I said I was two minutes away. When I got home, she wasn't in, and clearly never had been. I rang her mobile again, but she had turned it off. Despite what I had learned from the seminar with the American psychotherapist, I still wanted to trust her. It was hard to maintain a positive, loving relationship without at least some degree of trust: I had to keep trying. Despite the locks on the doors, I couldn't become her jailer. I was her mother.

One night, I was whiling away the hours sitting up late waiting for Lauren to come home or the police to visit by trying to work out what, if money were no object, I would do to keep Lauren safe and help her work through whatever was going on in her head. I decided if I were Richard Branson, or at least had his money, I would hire a round-the-clock personal protection team to be with her at all times. We would have live-in tutors and therapists and probably have to move to a remote island or a castle with a moat and drawbridge!

I was shaken out of my reverie at midnight by the phone. It was Lauren. I had reported her missing that afternoon.

'Mum, I'm at the JR!' The JR was the John Radcliffe Hospital.

'Oh God, what's happened? Are you all right?'

'Yes, I'm OK. I'll tell you all about it.'

'I'll come and get you.'

'No. I don't want you to. Don't you dare come.' She was suddenly hostile and furious.

Just at that moment the police arrived. I put the PC on the phone to Lauren and he calmed her down, went to the hospital and collected her. I was grateful to him for going, but saddened by the fact that she didn't want me there.

She was still angry and hostile when she got home, and by the look in her eyes had clearly been taking something. She told us that she had been with her friends at 227 Iffley Road. The PC visibly winced at the mention of the address and asked her who her friends were. She was very vague, but said one of them, John, had had a fit, and as no one else knew what to do, Lauren had dialled 999 and gone with him in the ambulance.

Why neither the ambulance people nor those in A & E had the wit to question what a twelve-year-old was doing with a strange man at midnight, heaven knows!

A few days later I made what was possibly an illegal and what many might regard as a stupid decision. I was going to buy a twelve-year-old cigarettes. I knew that one of the main reasons she went to Bonn Square and all these other dodgy places was to cadge fags. I reasoned to myself that if I kept a packet in the house and allowed her, say, three a day, it might just keep her at home.

Lauren was very excited and said it would. 'It's only the fags I go out for, Mum.'

I took the dogs out for a quick walk, and when I came back twenty minutes later, Lauren and what I had thought was a carefully hidden packet of cigarettes, kept in an old vase right at the back of the top larder shelf, were both missing. It was 2 p.m.

While I was out looking around the local area, I bumped into two friends and burst into tears. The sense of worry, betrayal and utter bafflement was overwhelming at times. Just when I thought there was some kind of understanding and agreement between us, Lauren would break it and take the defiance and challenging behaviour to a new level.

One of my friends, Joanne, offered to help me search properly after seeing my distress. We went first to Bonn Square. It was unusually empty. Perhaps the police had just done one of their regular clear-ups. Next we talked to a couple running a kebab van. I showed them a photo. They knew Lauren, although they hadn't seen her for a couple of days. They agreed to keep my phone number and ring me if they spotted her.

As we were trawling around town, I suddenly remembered the address Lauren had mentioned – 227 Iffley Road. Joanne and I got in the car and drove over.

God, what a dump. A large, detached, late-Victorian house, it must have been quite something in its day. It now looked more or less derelict. There were torn curtains hanging in broken windows, and the garden was full of rubbish, including some hypodermic needles by the front door. As Joanne and I walked up the path, a crazed, unkempt young man burst out of the front door, shouting, twitching and talking to his voices. After walking just a few steps, he turned on his heel and stormed back into the house. Joanne went pale and was clearly terrified. I felt sick . . . Were these Lauren's friends? Looking up at the front of the house, I thought I could identify the room where she might be. Lauren had said the man, John, had had his fit on a balcony. There were two attic rooms with balconies. One had a light on, and the window was open.

I knew I had to go in to look for her. If she was inside, I had to get her out of this hellhole. Not knowing what she had let herself in for when she agreed to come with me, Joanne clearly didn't want to go in the house. In any case, it seemed sensible that one of us stay outside to raise the alarm if something happened. I told her to call the police if I was not out in five minutes.

As I went up to the front door, two young men answered it, completely stoned. I asked them if they knew John or a girl called Lauren. They obviously wouldn't give information to someone like me, but they mumbled and pointed to a door just ahead of me off the hallway. I knocked and opened it, but there was just a large middle-aged man in his underpants asleep on the bed. I'd been set up.

I pushed past the two stoned men and walked up two flights of stairs. There were all sorts of people hanging around, including young mums with babies and a couple of men who were clearly mentally very unwell. One man was lying on the stairs and told me he was Jesus Christ. I finally reached a door on the top floor with a light shining underneath. Listening outside, I could hear a TV on in the background. I knocked and a voice said, 'Come in,' quickly followed by another gruffly asking, 'Who is it?'

'Is Lauren there?' I asked, and the door opened. Lauren was sitting on a bed with six men and women. Most of them were out of their heads. The room was full of cigarette smoke, dirty takeaway boxes and beer cans, and *EastEnders* was on the television. The minute she saw me, Lauren screamed in horror, jumped up and stormed out, brushing past me. She ran down the stairs, out of the front door and down the path past Joanne, who ran after her and tried to reason with her. I stayed and talked to the people in the room, who stared blankly at me. I wasn't cross with them and didn't want them to get into trouble, but asked them if they realized she was only twelve. I said they must not let her come into their rooms and for their own sakes should have nothing to do with her. I doubt they heard me.

Back in the street, I found Lauren hiding round the corner pacing wildly up and down, and tearing at her arms with her nails. When she saw me, she ran off, swearing and shouting at me. Then she started running in and out of the moving cars on the busy road in the Friday-evening rush. Desperate, I called 999, but it took the police nearly an hour to come. All the while Joanne and I stood outside the house while Lauren played cat and mouse with us. She kept appearing, and then the moment we said anything to her, she would run off again. When the police did eventually come, Lauren fled once more and was very aggressive towards them, so she was restrained, handcuffed and arrested. I had never seen anything as shocking as my daughter attacking police officers, being brought down and handcuffed.

They took her to the police station, where, because she was refusing to come home, she was made the subject of a police protection order. She was returned home three hours later because social services said they could not take responsibility for her.

The next day I took the morning off work and wrote a letter, which I sent by recorded delivery, to several important people in various authorities. I outlined the attempts I had made with each local service to get help for Lauren. I said that although several people had advised a multi-agency conference might be beneficial, no service was prepared to act as the lead agency and convene such a meeting. I went on, 'The purpose of this letter therefore is to convene such a meeting. As the parent, I suppose I am in a good position to act as lead agency.' I set out a proposed agenda, offered our house as a venue and suggested three possible dates.

I had worked in the public and voluntary sector all my adult life, I had run two complex national charities, I was a non-executive director of the Oxfordshire Mental Health Trust, and I was on the board of several local agencies. I knew the director of social services professionally. I knew how the system should work. Surely the multi-agency meeting would be the breakthrough we needed.

Most of the people I wrote to came to the meeting; school even provided a room for us to meet in. I chaired the meeting as lead agency, summarized the current position as I saw it and then invited each agency to comment on how they saw the situation and what they could do to help. We went round the table and each person agreed the situation was pretty desperate, that Lauren was in great need, and then each person gave a carefully drafted reason why their agency could not help and passed the parcel to their left. Eventually, of course, it ended up back in my lap. A lot of time and effort and hand-wringing seemed to have achieved almost nothing.

But after the meeting and behind the scenes, the social services departments of Stoke-on-Trent and Oxfordshire became embroiled in a battle to establish who didn't have to help us. I wasn't party to all the gory details, but it was hard fought, with lawyers brought in on both sides. Ironically, the excuse for this battle was some new legislation that was meant to help adoptive children and their new families by conferring a right to post-adoption support for a period of three years after a child moved to a new family. Oxfordshire were determined that no matter what, this meant that they didn't have to do anything to help an adopted child in their area if that child had not previously been in their 'care'.

Eventually, Stoke capitulated and agreed to take lead responsibility for trying to coordinate support for us, but at such a distance, with no local knowledge and with the continued opposition to any local help for us from a senior member of the Oxfordshire Social Services team, it was difficult for them. They did, however, appoint a senior and very experienced social worker, Dave Marshall, to take the lead on the case and liaise with me. For the first time in two and a half years, I had an informed and empathetic person to whom I could talk. And someone with the willingness to attempt to get something done for us.

After commissioning an initial assessment of the situation and our needs, he started talking to his opposite numbers in Oxfordshire to see what they might be prepared to do to help if Stoke were willing to pay for it. He also arranged for me to be paid a weekly adoption allowance to help make up for my dramatic reduction in income: I had kept having to reduce my working hours in order to be with Lauren, who, by spring 2005, was only allowed in school about nine hours a week. This took one worry off my plate. I had already remortgaged the house to give us some cash to live off, but at least now there was an additional regular monthly income.

One other tangible outcome from the meeting was the offer of a home visit by someone from the Child and Adolescent Mental Health team to talk to Lauren and see if they might be able to do an initial assessment. I hoped this might be the breakthrough we needed. Only the previous evening things had become really violent and Lauren had picked up a knife and threatened to kill me, making me feel truly frightened for my own safety for the first time. She said, when she'd finally calmed down, 'I really need help. I need to see a doctor. I think I'm going mad.' The home visit could not, I thought, have come at a better time.

On the day of the visit, I explained to Lauren that someone was coming to see us at 2 p.m. and with some difficulty managed to keep her in. By half past two no one had arrived and Lauren was going up the wall. I rang the office but got no answer. Ten minutes later two women – not one, as I'd told Lauren it would be – arrived, forty minutes late. Lauren was furious and tried to leave the house, but I managed to persuade her to stay.

'It's just a twenty-minute chat and then we can go out and do something nice,' I promised.

However, when we finally got talking, the women were very patronizing and uninformed, despite all the information I had provided. They kept asking Lauren to tell them about her 'real family'.

'Which one's that?' Lauren said.

'Your real family. You know, your proper family, your natural family.'

Lauren pulled her pink hoody right over her head, turned

to me and rolled her eyes, then refused to say another word. I didn't blame her – they were utterly clueless.

The two 'experts' left a few minutes later, offering to come back next week to talk to Lauren about school. Arriving late, then blundering straight into the two most painful issues, they certainly knew how *not* to engage with a child like Lauren. Oh God, I had been pinning a lot of hope on the Child and Adolescent Mental Health Service. Was there no one out there who would help us?

6

Hot Potato

'Is that Elizabeth? This is Enfield Hospital.'

'Enfield? What, in North London?' It was 4 a.m. and I felt groggy, pulled out of a fitful sleep by the phone ringing.

'That's right. We've had two girls come in by ambulance. One of them, Jennifer, is very unwell, I'm afraid. The other girl said she was called Lauren and she gave us your name and phone number.'

My heart sank. It was not the first time I'd received such a call. Jennifer was now bunking off school regularly, and with Lauren partially excluded and in B12, they would frequently disappear together, often overnight. They would usually meet up during the daytime for some ostensibly innocent activity – swimming or a visit to the library or popping round to one another's homes – and then not return. I was increasingly concerned about Jennifer's influence on Lauren, but she needed the company of friends her own age. I knew where Jennifer lived and knew her mother, so she seemed like a better option than some of these other so-called friends I never saw, who were not given names but who would ring Lauren's phone and entice her out.

Jennifer and Lauren would be happily in Lauren's room, playing music and reading magazines one minute and gone the next. Our house was over four floors, with the kitchen in the basement. There were two front doors, one in the kitchen and one on the floor above. Consequently, if I was in the kitchen, I couldn't see who was going in or out of the upper door. They had slipped out that way a couple of times, and on one occasion let in some dodgy-looking young man, another of Jennifer's seemingly never-ending entourage of boyfriends. I had started keeping the upper front door locked and had added that key to the bunch I had clipped to my belt, becoming more and more like a jailer. But with every window now locked and double locks on each door, I worried about how we would get out of the house in the event of a fire.

While it was difficult, but not usually impossible, to keep an eye on the girls when they were in our house, I couldn't do this when they were at Jennifer's and so it was usually from there they would disappear. Jennifer's mother didn't even seem to notice whether they were at home or not. Sometimes they would emerge from some dubious house somewhere in Oxford demanding a lift home in the early hours of the morning, but increasingly it would be later and further afield.

Over a twelve-month period Jennifer and Lauren disappeared together over thirty times. On one occasion they were gone for four days. Luckily, and this is going to sound like a very strange use of the word, but luckily Jennifer was an insulin-dependent diabetic. After two or three days without her medication, she became very unwell, often losing consciousness. Lauren would then call an ambulance and I would get a phone call from a nurse in an A & E department somewhere in the Greater London area. I collected the girls from hospitals in Harrow, Waterloo, Battersea, Brentwood, Southall and Dagenham. And now Enfield.

On this occasion Lauren had been missing for two days. Gasping with relief when I realized where she was, I briefly explained the situation to the nurse and said I would contact Jennifer's mother and we would come up. I rang Jennifer's house, but there was no answer, so I got in the car and drove to Enfield. It was a typical general hospital – sprawling Victorian buildings interspersed by car parks and Portakabins. Eventually I found the children's emergency department, explained who I was and was pointed towards a curtained cubicle. I pulled back the curtain and looked at the pale, dirty, skinny child on the bed. It was Lauren.

'Hello.'

'You keep coming for me, don't you?'

'Yes, and I always will, so you better get used to it.'

Jennifer wasn't well enough to be discharged, so we went home, leaving her behind. I felt a bit uncomfortable doing that, especially as Jennifer's mother didn't drive, but Lauren was enough for me to deal with.

I had no idea how Jennifer and Lauren got to all the places they did. All Lauren would say was that they went to visit friends of Jennifer's.

During this terrible time I was surviving on a heady mix of strong black coffee and adrenalin. I found it impossible to sleep while Lauren was missing. I would doze off for a bit and then wake with a start, thinking the phone was ringing. It might be Lauren, the police or an A & E nurse, but often it was nobody. I had started to hallucinate a ringing phone. Occasionally I would come to feeling confused and wonder if I had made it all up. I didn't have a daughter; I had never adopted; it had all been a dream. Then I would go into her room and see the clothes, toys, posters, all the clutter of a young girl, but no girl, no Lauren. I would sit on her bed and cry, then fall asleep.

After she had been missing for more than a couple of nights, I would steel myself for what the eventual outcome might be. What might happen to a twelve-year-old girl miles away from home in the company of God knows who? Time after time I psyched myself up for the knock on the door in the middle of the night, the journey with a couple of kindly police officers, the walk into a cold white room, the small form under a sheet. 'Yes, that's her. That's Lauren.'

In the midst of all the crazy behaviour, I still tried to keep a semblance of ordinary life going. I tried to make sure normal meals were produced at normal times. Supper would always be available at seven even if she wasn't there to eat it. I would try and get her up by 7.30 a.m. even if she hadn't been home until 1 a.m. There were rules about appropriate clothing, personal hygiene, earning and losing pocket money, and so on. I tried to negotiate written agreements with her about how long she could stay out and how many cigarettes I would buy her to try and stop her going out on the streets to beg for them. She would enter into such agreements quite enthusiastically to begin with, providing I picked the right time for the discussion, almost as though she wanted these boundaries, but would usually break them within twenty-four hours.

I knew all about the importance of boundaries, discipline

and consequences for children, and tried to ensure that they were there at all times, but I came to realize that even in the most ordered of families, these are not unilaterally imposed. Lauren would have had to have been literally tied up and gagged to keep her in when she wanted to go out. She would even take on police officers at times if challenged by them, and such was the power of her rage and fury that it could take three police officers and a pair of handcuffs to restrain her and still she would be shouting and cursing. Consequences were pretty meaningless to her too. If, as a result of some breach of our agreement about behaviour, I were to cancel a planned treat, she would go out anyway; if I stopped pocket money, she would just steal it; if I withdrew the cigarette allowance, she would simply go on the streets and beg for them. She was determined not to allow me to have any power or control. Although I tried not to let her know that I knew it and tried to carry on behaving like a parent, she actually had all the power. She would set the terms on which she would have a relationship with me, when she was prepared to let me be her mother and when she would simply ignore my existence.

She would demand to sit on my knee and suck her thumb one minute, and then, after a phone call from Jennifer or one of the mystery friends, she'd be out on the streets the next. It was a relationship of two extremes, both problematic and hard to handle. And neither was what I had imagined my relationship with my almost thirteen-year-old daughter would be. I had either a very clingy two-year-old or an angry, violent and rejecting stranger to deal with. There were fewer and fewer glimpses of the warm, funny, empathetic, caring person I knew, who was in there somewhere but who rarely surfaced, and certainly not when we were in Oxford.

On the advice of a very insightful police officer responsible for liaison with schools about truanting children, I tried to reframe how I thought about and dealt with some of her most difficult behaviour, in particular the outbursts at home, which would trigger Lauren to storm out of the house if I challenged her about her conduct. The police officer suggested that I make an agreement with Lauren that if she was starting to feel angry and worked up about something, instead of me trying to stop her storming off, I should agree that she could go out for a bit to calm down but only under certain conditions, such as not after dark, only for forty-five minutes and that she must take her phone, keep it on and answer if I rang her. It sounded a bit bizarre and counterintuitive – I was trying to set firm boundaries, not relax them – but I tried it and it worked for about a week. After that Lauren's need to deny any authority, especially mine, meant that the forty-five minutes rapidly drifted to hours and she would turn her phone off the first time I tried to contact her.

Courtesy of the internet and with the help of friends, I was becoming an expert in theories on post-traumatic stress disorder, conduct disorder, oppositional defiant disorder, attachment disorder, ADHD, early onset bipolar disorder and many others. I was also discovering that there were specialist services designed for children with the sort of complex needs Lauren had – services, usually residential, designed to get alongside the most 'damaged', disturbed and disruptive children, work out how they were hurting and why, and then try to find ways to heal their shattered souls. But how to get Lauren referred? I started ringing round. Time and time again experts in these services told me Lauren was exactly the sort of child they set out to help. They also warned me that they were expensive and treatment would take a long time, but the key was to get all the services who were currently working to help and support Lauren to agree to share the cost through joint funding. But in our case there *were* no services currently providing anything for Lauren, and there wasn't a cat in hell's chance of anyone agreeing to something called tripartite funding, whereby education, health and social care all shared the cost. As someone in social services said, Lauren was a 'hot potato'. All anyone wanted was not to be left holding it when the music stopped.

I had thought Jennifer was bad, but then Lauren suddenly started associating with Kasey, who was about a year older. According to a guy called Chris who ran a youth club and who had been trying to keep an eye on Lauren for me, even the police were wary of Kasey. He said she was bad news, always trying to set up fights and situations that got other children into trouble. She was very violent and banned from almost every youth club in Oxford.

One day Lauren had been missing for several hours. I rang Chris, explained the situation and asked if he had seen them. He hadn't but said he had heard that Kasey was now associating with a group of much older Asian boys and men on Cowley Road who had a bad reputation. I sent Lauren a text saying I knew all about Kasey and that she was bad news and hung around with very undesirable people. Lauren rang me back and was extremely abusive and then put Kasey on, who called me a 'fucking cunt' for disrespecting her. She demanded to know why I had been checking up on her on the internet. I told her she wasn't that famous and she said she was going to come round and glass me. I detected that even Lauren thought that Kasey had gone a bit far because she was rather more conciliatory when she came back on the phone but still refused to return home or let me come and get her.

Her battery must have died because she then started calling reverse charge from a phone box, trying to negotiate with me, promising to come home if I would buy her fags. I kept trying to appeal to her sensible side but stonewalled on the cigarettes. And then at midnight I got a panic reverse-charge call from Lauren. The girls had been chased by a gang of Asian men and her 'friends' had run off and left her and she was scared. I went to collect her from outside the Firtree pub on Cowley Road. She was silent and subdued when she got in the car. She said, 'I hate men. They only want one thing,' and then clammed up when I said, 'Men? Not boys?'

She was, however, very intrigued as to who I had been talking to about Kasey. I said I had a very high-up contact in the police who knew pretty much everything about Oxford lowlife. If only.

Although Stoke had stepped in to try to sort out some support on the social care side, there was nothing they could do about the lack of appropriate schooling for Lauren. Apart from the few hours a week that she was allowed to spend in B12, but frequently didn't, there was no education available for her. She was slipping further and further behind, and becoming more and more isolated from her peers. I rang and wrote to Oxfordshire County Council's Education Psychology Service, and after several attempts to have a proper conversation with someone who didn't just promise and fail to ring me back, I found someone who confirmed that they did deal with Hinksey Fields School and expressed surprise that Lauren hadn't already been referred to them by the school itself. She agreed to follow it up with the school, and after a lot of huffing and puffing on all sides, it was agreed that she would see Lauren in school on a particular date to do an initial assessment. It turned out to be a day when Lauren bunked off school and after that they washed their hands of her.

What was becoming shockingly apparent in all my dealings with Oxfordshire's education, social services and mental health agencies was firstly how administratively flaky they were: letters never answered, phone calls not returned. Secondly they were not in the least robust in their professional practices. Despite all being there to help children in need who were often very troubled, they had no ability to deal with a setback like a child not being in school on a particular day. They took any opportunity to find an excuse not to help.

This approach was exemplified by the team in the Education Department who dealt with applications for statements of special educational needs. Statements are awarded to children who need more than just ordinary mainstream schooling, and if awarded, a statement unlocks additional money to provide extra resources or support. I was therefore expecting some resistance when I first applied for a statement for Lauren. I knew our case would be rigorously tested. What I hadn't expected was the sheer breathtaking incompetence of the system. In June I started to chase the application I had made in April. At first I was told they had never received it, but eventually they rang me back.

'We have found your application; it had got onto the wrong desk. Unfortunately it is now out of date, so we can't process it.'

'What do you mean, out of date?'

'Well, the procedures state that all applications for statements of special educational needs must be dealt with within six weeks, but because yours was put on the wrong desk, those six weeks have elapsed, so we can't process it.'

Almost speechless with disbelief, I responded, 'I will hand-deliver a fresh application to your offices this afternoon.'

'Oh no, that wouldn't work, because we can only process applications during term time and there isn't enough of this term left to process a fresh application. If you sent it in now, it would expire again during the summer holidays and you would have to start all over again in the autumn term.'

I was to make five separate applications over a two-and-a-half-year period before it was finally accepted in autumn 2007 that Lauren, by then fifteen, did indeed have special educational needs and therefore was entitled to have additional support and resources allocated to help her with an education.

Another extraordinary example, which I can laugh at now but which at the time reduced me to tears, was the fate of the referral our GP had made to the child psychologist who had been recommended to me. I was a non-executive director of the Oxfordshire NHS Mental Health Trust but had resisted trying to use my position to gain help for Lauren because I felt it was wrong to do so. That changed, however, in May, when the board meeting coincided with Lauren having gone missing for the third night that week. Exhausted and frustrated, I decided to talk to the chairman and chief executive. About three words in, I started to sob. I felt so embarrassed and unprofessional.

Anyway, they got the drift and leaped into action to try and find out what had happened to the GP's referral and why there had been no follow-up to the visit we had had at home from the two rather inept women.

That night the chief executive phoned me. She was very apologetic. The GP had indeed written to the child psychologist recommended by my neighbour. Unfortunately that person had now retired. To make matters worse, the admin office in the Department of Child Psychiatry had failed to remove the doctor's name from her pigeonhole, so any correspondence addressed to her personally was still being put in there, despite the fact that she hadn't worked for the trust for nearly two months. The pigeonhole was very full – so full, in fact, that an additional tray had been created to hold all this mail. We speculated as to how long it might have taken for the admin office to spot that one of their doctors wasn't collecting their mail and had indeed retired if it hadn't been for this intervention.

Around this time, at the suggestion of a friend, I went to see a solicitor to see what legal pressure I might be able to exert to get some comprehensive help for Lauren. After several discussions and the reading of the already vast amount of correspondence I had accumulated, he informed me I had a very strong case to apply for a judicial review, a court order to compel a local authority to do its duty. Unfortunately this would not happen overnight and would be expensive to pursue. Sadly I didn't have the luxury of the time or the money to follow it up.

One sunny afternoon in early June Lauren, who was in a fairly calm and happy phase, was sitting in the garden with one of her slightly older and relatively stable, well-behaved friends and the friend's eleven-year-old sister. They were listening to music and eating ice lollies. I needed to pop into town for half an hour and asked them if they wanted to come too. No, they were happy just 'chilling'. They seemed to be having a really nice time. I would be back inside the hour. What could possibly go wrong?

As I walked down the hill from town fifty minutes later, I could see a commotion. A figure was running about in the middle of the road, in and out of the cars and buses, which had all come to a stop. The figure ran back towards the pavement and fell in the gutter and lay there. It was Lauren. I started to run towards her. I managed to get hold of her and lift her out of the gutter and onto the pavement, but she broke loose and, kicking and swearing, ran up the hill towards the city centre. She was drunk but also seized by something that always seemed to go with alcohol for Lauren, a crazed, maniacal frenzy and superhuman strength.

I pursued her up the hill as far as the police station, but gave up, went into the police station, reported the incident and went home to wait. I got a phone call a couple of hours later. She had been arrested for being drunk and disorderly. In town she had clearly got access to more alcohol and had been brandishing an empty wine bottle and threatening people with it.

'Can I come and take her home?'

'No. We'll be charging her, but we can't do that until she has sobered up, so she will have to stay here until she does.' The custody sergeant added, 'She's making a nuisance of herself, throwing herself around the cell, smashing herself into the walls and screaming.'

I could hear her shrieking and wailing in the background.

'You can't let her do that – she will really hurt herself. She is not yet thirteen and very disturbed. This isn't just drunkenness; she is unwell. Please can't you either let her come home or get her transferred to a secure medical setting?' I was begging now. 'Please – she may kill herself.'

'I will try and get a police doctor in to see her, but I can't release her and there is no secure medical place in Oxford other than our cells here. We are the local designated place of safety for disturbed and vulnerable people.'

I rang off and spent the next two hours ringing round the duty social services and mental health services numbers trying to find somewhere more appropriate than a police cell for a child in meltdown. No one could offer anything.

About 11 p.m. the police rang again. Lauren had stopped throwing herself around the cell, and although she wasn't in any fit state to be interviewed and charged, they were going to bail her into my care overnight on condition that she return the next day. They had not been able to find a doctor who could come and see her.

Jean, our next-door neighbour, who had been keeping me company as I rang round the various services, walked up to the police station with me. Lauren, almost unrecognizable with a swollen face and covered in dirt, was more or less dragged out of the cells by two Group 4 security guards. It soon became clear she couldn't walk and so they each took an arm and dragged her down two flights of stairs. On the pavement, they just let her slip down and walked off.

'We need to get her to hospital. I'll call an ambulance,' I said, scarcely able to believe what had just happened.

'No, I'll run home and get my car. It will be quicker.' Jean headed towards home, while I tried to support Lauren and keep her off the wet pavement.

At the John Radcliffe Hospital, she was rushed into the resuscitation room, barely conscious, and a specialist in paediatric trauma was called in. She examined Lauren carefully and discovered that although there were no broken bones, she had had some concussion and extensive deep bruising all over her head and upper body, a result of repeatedly throwing herself at the cell walls.

'But,' she said, 'there is something else going on inside, isn't there, and it isn't just the alcohol.' I gave her a potted history of Lauren's life and told her how no one would help us.

Lauren spent five days on a children's ward in the John Radcliffe Hospital. Physically she was well enough to have returned home after three days, but at the suggestion of a second, very concerned and empathetic paediatric consultant, they kept her in longer to try and get a psychiatric assessment carried out. Perhaps this awful incident would enable us to get the help Lauren so desperately needed. Eventually a stand-in locum child psychiatrist was found. With bad grace and a very patronizing tone, he spoke first to me, referring to me as 'Mother' throughout, presumably because he couldn't be bothered to remember my name. He then said he would go and talk to Lauren. He spent less than three minutes with her – I timed it – and on the back of that eventually, two months later, produced a report saying she did not have any identifiable mental health needs. Lauren was discharged later that day. All that terrible, awful stuff that had just happened and yet again everyone just washed their hands of her. This was all apparently just normal twelve-year-old behaviour – drunken violence, being excluded from school, massive self-harming, going missing day after day . . .

Don't bother your head about it, Mother; we certainly won't.

One hot day in late June I got back from work just before one to find Lauren gone. A concerned neighbour came round to say she had seen Lauren leave the house at about midday and get in a car with blacked-out windows that had pulled up outside our house. My heart sank. If she had left in a car, she must have gone with someone much older, and the blacked-out windows worried me. I rang the police immediately.

The next morning the police called to say that they had found Lauren and Jennifer in McDonald's in the city centre. The girls claimed to have been in a house in Cowley Road with some men who had given them a lot of drink and drugs. Because the girls seemed the worse for wear, the police had taken them to A & E at the John Radcliffe Hospital as a precaution, but they were fine. Would I go up there and collect her?

I went on the bus, partly to avoid feeling obliged to have to chauffeur Jennifer and her mother around, and partly not to make it too comfortable and easy for Lauren. If I had known what a state she would be in when I found her, I would have taken the car. She was filthy and wearing a hideous and very revealing pink boob tube I hadn't seen before. She was also sullen and defiant. The doctor who was treating her flat out refused to talk to me. The nurse explained to me that as they suspected sexual activity had taken place, they couldn't discuss anything with me even as the parent. It was purely a matter between the medical staff and the patient. This rule applied to any child over ten, and Lauren was twelve. This was lunacy. At this point in time there was a fairly vociferous national debate in the media fuelled by statements by the likes of Tony Blair, then prime minister, about how parents should be made to take more responsibility for their children; meanwhile, here was one arm of the state, the National Health Service, actively working to ensure that parents couldn't take responsibility for something as important as their child's sexual health and well-being.

'Don't worry,' said the nurse, 'we have given Lauren all the information she needs about pregnancy tests, contraception and treatment for sexually transmitted diseases.'

'There's no way Lauren will have taken any of that in,' I said wearily, and as if to prove a point, Lauren very ostentatiously threw all the leaflets she had been given in the bin in front of the nurse as we left.

Lauren was furious when I marched her to the bus stop rather than the car park, and even more so when I refused to stop at the shop to buy her some food. Back home, I made her a sandwich, got her to have a bath, and she went to bed. I wasn't going to be able to get to work that day, so instead I arranged for my colleague Anna to come to the house that evening. We sat in the garden, while Lauren, I thought, watched television in the living room upstairs. It was a beautiful summer's day, the longest day of the year.

I saw Anna off at about 9 p.m. and decided to put the bins out before going upstairs to Lauren. As I was carrying the last bin up the basement steps, I saw Anna walking back up the road with Lauren, who was sobbing, her face streaming with blood. She had got a phone call from two friends asking her to meet them on the corner of our road, where the ghastly Kasey had jumped on her, headbutted her, knocked her to the ground and kicked her face. She had clearly been set up for this attack, but why? I didn't like Kasey and had of course been told she was bad news, but she was supposed to be Lauren's friend. Why had she done that to her?

We were back in A & E less than twelve hours after leaving it that morning. Lauren had a broken nose, a split lip and a black eye. Kasey, we were told, received a police caution for the attack but couldn't be prosecuted for lack of independent evidence. We never knew why Kasey had done it, or why the two other friends who had lured her out of the house had done so. Lauren just said, 'It's the sort of thing that happens to me.'

The next morning, her face swollen and throbbing, Lauren was a very different girl, clinging to me and seeking reassurance that she was safe. I persuaded her to come to work with me. It was a lovely place, a restored barn with a beautiful sensory garden, which I suggested she could sit in. I was the only person due in that day, so she need not worry that anyone was going to see her face.

I had discovered that car journeys where there was no need for eye contact were often good opportunities to have difficult conversations with Lauren. Driving round the Oxford ring road, I asked her if anything had happened to her in that house on Cowley Road. She said nothing had happened; some men they had met had just given them a lot of vodka and weed. I could sense there was a 'but' hanging in the air.

'But . . . ?'

'But, Mum, I have been raped. Not that night, though.'

We were on the elevated section of the ring road by the Cowley motor works; I gripped the steering wheel tight and tried hard to concentrate on the road. As soon as I could, I pulled over. Lauren clearly wanted to talk now. We sat in the car both looking straight ahead out of the windscreen. I knew she would clam up if I looked at her.

'Do you remember last week when Jennifer and I said we were going to her house and you dropped us at the bus stop in town? We didn't go to her house. We stayed in town and met Jennifer's new boyfriend and some friends of his and went back to their house. They gave us a lot of vodka, and when Jennifer went into the bedroom to have sex with her new boyfriend, one of the other men raped me.'

For some reason, telling me this seemed to enable her to start talking more about some of the other sexual assaults that had happened to her. She told me more about what Dirty Old Man Spragg used to get up to in his basement, and then if all that wasn't enough, she started describing how, when she was three and four years old, her birth father used to bring men back from the pub to sexually assault his small daughter for money. She told me she used to try and make herself invisible under a blanket and would lie there trying not to breathe but would gradually be overwhelmed by the stench of booze, fags and body odour before the blanket was pulled away and some drunken pervert was leering down at her.

As this torrent of depravity washed over me, I went numb, literally physically numb. I couldn't move my arms. I couldn't speak.

'Mum, you're not cross with me, are you, for telling you?'

'Oh God, of course I'm not cross with you. You can always tell me things. You know I just want to be able to help you and protect you.'

I turned to her and tried to put my arms around her, but she pulled away from me.

We didn't continue our journey to work. She didn't sit in the sun in the sensory garden and smell the flowers and listen to the birds. Instead we went home, and with her agreement, I rang the police.

Lauren spent the rest of the day being interviewed by various police officers. And the next day she spent several hours doing a video interview in a special house set up to examine and interview victims of sexual assault and rape. Over the next few years we would become quite familiar with the various 'rape houses' run by Thames Valley Police, with their incongruous mix of the forensic and medical, TV studio and cosy domestic touches like boxes of chocolate biscuits, fluffy towels and shower gel.

Lauren refused to be medically examined but gave a detailed description of the house where she was attacked and the men involved, and later that day the police raided the house and arrested its occupants.

For some reason, a particular detail of the information Lauren gave stuck in my mind and brought tears to my eyes. She was asked to describe the living room where she and Jennifer were sitting with the men before the attack. She described a sofa and two chairs, and said two men were sitting on the sofa, another on a chair and Jennifer on the second chair.

'And where were you sitting?'

'I was sitting on Jennifer's knee.'

She was just a babe.

The men were Albanian asylum seekers who operated as a gang and the police seemed to have some concerns for our safety and advised us to leave Oxford for a bit. I found a cottage near Hay-on-Wye and we packed up the dogs, asked a neighbour to look after the cats and went. We had just got to the cottage when the police rang and said Lauren would have to go back to Oxford to do a video-linked identity parade the next day, where she picked out the man who attacked her and became very distressed. Apart from that we stayed away for ten days, during which time one of the gang was charged with rape and remanded in custody.

While we were in the cottage, we had one of the worst scenes we had ever had. A woman from a post-adoption support charity who had been asked by Stoke-on-Trent to carry out an assessment of our needs rang my mobile. I briefly explained the situation and she asked to speak to Lauren. I put her on, although Lauren was indicating that she didn't want to speak to her, and she became very abusive, telling the woman to 'fuck off' and then throwing the phone on the floor.

On the back of that, I tried to initiate a conversation. 'Look, Lauren, if you are not even prepared to cooperate with those people who are trying to help us, I don't know what more I or anyone else can do to keep you alive. The way you are going, meeting the awful people you do, taking drugs and drinking alcohol, you will probably be dead by September – murdered or killed by a drugs overdose.'

She feigned scorn and contempt for me and the rest of adult society. 'You don't understand anything, do you? You're all just a bunch of wankers. I can take care of myself.'

I threatened to leave her in the cottage and call Stoke-on-Trent to come and get her and put her somewhere secure. 'I simply don't know any other way to keep you alive if you won't cooperate.'

I started to pack up my things; I was, I think, prepared to go through with it. Lauren must have thought I was, because she took the car keys and went off and locked herself in the car. After about thirty minutes she came back to the cottage, taunting me.

'Oh, so I see you haven't gone. You didn't dare to, did you, because it would show what a bad mother you are for even thinking of abandoning your child.'

I explained it would have been a last act of desperation to keep her alive. She sat down at the table and said, 'Let's have a conversation.' She didn't really have anything she wanted to say, but I talked and tried to get through to her about the risks she was taking. Eventually she agreed to another deal, never to be out for more than four hours, to always have a mobile switched on and be back by half past nine. I wasn't convinced she had any intention of keeping to it, but at least she had calmed down and I had managed to get a few points across.

The next day she said she would like to go back to school for the last two weeks of term. For one reason or another, she hadn't been at school for over a month. I rang John Morgan, the man who ran the B12 unit at the school. He was surprised but agreed. He asked if I had heard anything from the Education Department about their plans for Lauren from September, as she was soon to be permanently excluded and would not be allowed to return to Hinksey Fields School. I said I had still heard nothing and told him about the farce over my application for a statement of special educational needs. He offered to have another go himself.

We returned to Oxford and Lauren did go back to school for half a day, but knowing that she was going to be permanently excluded in two weeks anyway, and forbidden from associating with her friends, there was no incentive for her to keep going.

A month later I got a letter from the Crown Prosecution Service, telling me they were going to drop the case against the man who raped her. The woman who wrote it offered a telephone conversation to explain why. I rang her and she was apologetic. Lauren's evidence was quite clear and convincing, and she was sure a jury would have believed her, but Jennifer's statement was full of inconsistencies and what were very clearly lies. They wouldn't take the case to court purely on the evidence of Lauren, even though she was the victim, and no jury would believe Jennifer. I couldn't understand why Jennifer was messing about like that. Did she not understand how serious what had happened to Lauren was? Didn't she care? Was it all just a lark to her? That was the day Jennifer became Bloody Jennifer. I could never again think of her without the adjective.

The gang of young Albanian men continued to roam the streets of Oxford city centre. I used to see them regularly when I was out looking for Lauren. They often had very young girls with them, possibly as young as ten or eleven. On two occasions I intervened, once with another adult who was concerned about what was going on. The girls ran off while the young men hung around laughing and mocking me in Albanian. I waited until the police arrived and then left. The police said afterwards there was nothing they could do because they never caught them with the girls. But they were there in broad daylight right in the centre of Oxford, a group of up to six men with two or three very young girls in tow. If we could see them, why couldn't the police?

7

The Care System That Didn't

Two days after our return from Hay-on-Wye and despite the shock of the rape, the time we had spent away and all her promises, Lauren and Jennifer disappeared again.

Lauren had been happily amusing herself at home looking at water from our pond under a microscope when Jennifer rang and asked if she could come round. I hesitated for a moment but said yes, adding that providing they both behaved, Jennifer could stay for supper and I would run her home. Supper was going to be lasagne, Lauren's favourite, and given that and her quieter behaviour during the day, I didn't feel too concerned about letting Lauren walk up the road to meet Jennifer off the bus. After about half an hour, during which time I had started to get a bit twitchy, Lauren came back incensed. Jennifer had got off the bus and then said she needed to go and meet a man to get money to buy drugs. Lauren said that meant she was going to 'give head' to men who waited at the back of the college of further education. She said Jennifer was disgusting. It was so revolting, even for Jennifer, that I was shocked.

At about 6 p.m. Jennifer rang Lauren again. Lauren said

Jennifer was now walking to our house from the college, had got lost and wanted Lauren to go and meet her.

'I don't believe it – Jennifer knows how to get here; she's done that walk dozens of times,' I protested.

'Well, I don't care what you think. I'm going out to rescue a lost friend. You can't stop me.'

I tried to stand between her and the door, but she pushed past me so violently that I lost balance, slipped and hit my elbow hard on the corner of a radiator. I yelled with pain and Lauren looked back at me and hesitated for a minute, but then stormed out of the front door. After about half an hour I phoned her. It rang twice and then she switched it off. I knew I wouldn't be seeing her again anytime soon. Once again I was left feeling angry and upset, utterly bemused at how fast things could change from a happy evening together to defiance, violence and Lauren disappearing.

Jennifer's diabetes once more came to the rescue and thirty-six hours later I got a phone call from an A & E department in Ealing, West London. Again Jennifer had started to feel unwell, so Lauren had called an ambulance and gone with her. The difference this time was that not only did Lauren not want me to collect her, she didn't want to come home. I was devastated when the hospital told me this. She had never said that before; she had always been so pleased to see me when she had decided to surface again. I was upset, but I was also very angry that she was messing about again after everything that had happened and after all her promises. Life was becoming impossible. My elbow had swollen to the size and colour of a beetroot, and I had had two sleepless nights.

A police officer then came on the phone and I gave her the brief details of the situation. She said if Lauren was refusing to come home, she would have to phone Oxfordshire Social Services and they would have to come and collect her and take her into care.

Four hours later I had a phone call from a social worker in Oxford. 'We've got Lauren here in the office and have arranged to send her to a placement down in Kent. Can you bring a bag for her?'

'What sort of placement? Why does she have to go so far away? How long is she going for?'

How could it be that one minute they were saying they could not do the tiniest thing to help us and now they were whisking her over a hundred miles away from home?

'There's no time to go into details, but it's an organization that works with very disruptive children. We don't have anything like that in Oxfordshire. She will be there for a six-week assessment.'

I packed an overnight bag and put in a little toy rabbit I had given her and some tubes of sweets. I met the social worker in Tesco's car park in Cowley Road to hand over the bag. I couldn't bear to go into the offices knowing Lauren was there and refusing to see me. I was absolutely devastated.

Was this it? Was this the end? Just there and then, almost in the blink of an eye. Less than thirty-six hours had elapsed between us being together at home in the kitchen, me making lasagne as Lauren looked at pond life under the microscope, and now me standing in the car park of Tesco handing over her bag to a social worker who was about to send her miles away to an unknown place for God knows how long, perhaps forever. Had I failed so badly that this was a better option than trying to help me cope at home? Would I ever see her again?

The social worker said she would ring to let me know that Lauren had arrived safely and that I would have to go into their offices the next day to sign papers saying I was voluntarily entrusting her into their care. I went home and a friend came round and we put away a bottle of wine and tried to make sense of everything. Maybe it had all been a terrible mistake. Maybe I was just wrong for Lauren.

The next day, feeling emotionally and physically exhausted, I went to Oxfordshire Social Services offices in Cowley Road. The social worker was there with her manager. I signed the forms and we talked about the situation.

'Children like Lauren should never be adopted,' the manager said. 'They are better off in care. You should prepare yourself for her not coming back to live with you.'

That restored my fighting spirit. I was not going to give in and let that happen. 'As far as I'm concerned, adoption is for life. I didn't take Lauren on approval. My commitment is to give her a home and a family forever, to be there for the rest of my life for her and for the children she will eventually have.'

I had worked with young people leaving the care system and knew it would just spit her out again at sixteen or seventeen. Then where would she be? Even more angry, distressed and unhappy, and with no one to help and support her. It didn't bear thinking about. I knew how desperate life was for so many of these kids. That was not going to happen to Lauren. With this in mind, I added an amendment to the consent form saying that I agreed to the placement for just one week as a place of safety and that I would only consent to extend it if there were clear plans to facilitate contact between Lauren and me, and provide therapeutic support for Lauren.

I added that there should be a written care plan, with the goal of the permanent return of Lauren to me within one month. I then said that there should be appropriate ongoing support for us both thereafter, and that it was in Lauren's best interests for her to live with me until adulthood rather than in the care system.

I signed the papers and went home. I did finally have an address and a phone number for Lauren. She had been placed in a private house near Maidstone with a woman employed by a private organization that carried out educational and psychological assessments of children with multiple needs. I rang the organization to find out more. There was no one who knew anything about Lauren, and they said they wouldn't be able to tell me anything until they had received the paperwork from Oxfordshire, which could take two or three weeks. But that was nearly half the time that the whole assessment was supposed to take!

Feeling frustrated, I rang the house. The woman who answered said she was a foster carer. She was cold and disinterested almost to the point of hostility. I tried to tell her a bit about Lauren as she said none of the paperwork had come through.

'I really don't need to know any background. That's a matter for the office.'

'Can I tell you a bit about her likes and dislikes? She is very young for her age in many ways and needs a lot of reassurance and comfort.'

'I am sure if Lauren wants anything, she will ask me herself.'

'Do you know it's her thirteenth birthday at the weekend? Will anything be done to mark that?'

'If the office confirm it's her birthday, I will be given a budget for a card and a cake.'

'I would like to ring each day and especially on her birthday. Is that OK?'

'If the office confirm that you are allowed to ring, you can try, but I'm often in the garden and don't hear the phone.'

'Can I speak to her now?'

'I don't know if she wants to speak to you.'

Lauren did come on the phone.

'Hi, love. How are you?'

'OK.'

'Are you getting everything you need?'

'I am sure if I want something, I can ask.'

'Are you excited about your birthday? Have you told them?'

'No. They wouldn't want to know about that sort of thing.'

'Can I ring you again tomorrow?'

'I don't think the office will allow you.'

'Well, I'll try anyway.'

'We probably won't hear you – we're usually in the garden.'

I told her I loved her and she rang off.

She had just parroted everything the foster carer had said to me, even using her tone of voice. I had been told that was what she used to do with Barbara Spragg when she was scared and uncertain.

I sat down and wrote Lauren a letter explaining that as she was refusing to come home, she had to be taken into care, but I loved her very much and wanted us to be together again.

The next day I sent Lauren a photo of the dogs and a note with a paw print from Alfie. A couple of days later I sent another note full of inconsequential chat, but still heard nothing. This was awful; it seemed I was deliberately being blocked.

I began to worry that I had made a mistake in signing the papers. I thought about how lovely Lauren could be when she was with me. After all, she was a vulnerable child who had only recently been raped; no wonder her behaviour was odd and difficult at times. We didn't need another assessment; her needs were plain for anyone who could be bothered to see. Maybe being at home around family and friends was best for Lauren after all.

I was particularly concerned that we would miss an appointment that had been made by Stoke-on-Trent for us to see the Attach Team. The Attach Team was a group of clinical psychologists and senior social workers with experience in the field of attachment theory and the impact of abuse and neglect on children who had been taken away from their birth families and were either in care or adopted. They sounded like just what we needed. Although they were part of Oxfordshire Social Services, Oxfordshire wouldn't refer us, but thankfully Stoke agreed to, and also to pay for the service if it was felt we could benefit.

I rang the lawyer who had advised me earlier on the possibility of going for a judicial review and he told me that as I had full parental rights, I could simply retract my permission to put Lauren into care.

The following day I rang Lauren and told her I was coming down to bring her home in time for her birthday. I rang social services and told them that the placement in Kent was not appropriate for Lauren's needs, was too far away and that I was going to bring her home and continue my search for local support that would enable us to stay together.

The long motorway journey was hot and tedious, which made my mixture of anger and apprehension harder to bear. When I got to the house near Maidstone, I was fully prepared for a very hostile reception from the foster carer, but a woman in her fifties with a dark tan and a sundress opened the door and smiled. She apologized for her attitude on the phone and said that as she hadn't been given any information about the situation, she had assumed that I was an abusive parent and that Lauren had been taken away from me for her own safety. This was almost understandable, but then she handed Lauren the bundle of cards and letters I had sent, which she had kept from her, assuming she wouldn't want to read them. Could she not have asked or checked?

Lauren threw her arms around me, and we fled to the car and submitted ourselves to the M25 in the Friday-evening rush hour. It took over four hours to get home. Lauren said the woman had been OK, but she kept trying to discourage her from thinking or talking about home. She also encouraged her to smoke and smoked with her, which even Lauren thought was a bit inappropriate, given the woman was an official foster carer and Lauren was a twelve-year-old child. And this set-up were supposed to be experts in helping very troubled children!

Lauren's thirteenth birthday the following day was a fairly subdued affair. There had been no time to organize much, and now that she was cut off from school, she really only had one friend, Bloody Jennifer. We had balloons and presents over breakfast and then set off for Wales. Down there, in the middle of nowhere, without dodgy friends or other Oxford low-life to distract her, Lauren once again reverted to fairly normal thirteen-year-old behaviour. She went horse riding, played games with the dogs and, as the only child, basked in the un-divided attention of safe, boring adults.

We then went camping in Dorset with a friend of mine and her fourteen-year-old son. Again she was calm and happy, thoroughly enjoying days on the beach swimming and fossil hunting and attempting to fly kites.

However, we hadn't been back ten minutes when she announced she was going to go out and see Jennifer that night. They were gone for twenty-four hours, emerging from an in-salubrious part of town very much the worse for wear.

The girls then started to behave even more oddly, spending hours out looking for the rapist, who had by then been released. He had been told he could not return to the house where he had raped Lauren because it was only about half a mile away from where we lived. Instead he was now holed up somewhere near Cowley Road, and the girls were determined to find him to 'talk to him'.

'But why on earth would you want to do that?' I protested. 'You know how dangerous he is.'

Lauren said, 'I want to find out why he did it.'

Jennifer said, 'I want to find out where he's living.'

I warned them that whether they wanted to reconnect with him socially, which I think was Jennifer's motive, or try and exact revenge, which may have been what Lauren fantasized about, they were playing with fire. What had caused both young girls to lose any natural instincts for self-preservation and sur-vival, and to actively seek out danger and harm? I couldn't get my head round it all. They really couldn't distinguish between abuse and affection when it came to men.

I did, however, think there were a couple of possible glimmers of light on the horizon at last. The Education Department promised to give Lauren a four-week placement in a school reintegration unit to get her back into education, assess her potential and decide which school it would be best to place her in. When I told Lauren about the plan, I was expecting a 'Well, they know where they can stick that' response, but she was excited.

'I really would like to go back to school again, Mum. I miss it, and I miss having friends. I need to catch up. I just want to be normal again and have friends. I'm so lonely.'

But the weeks went on with nothing confirmed. She said nothing more about missing school; she was either sleeping, weeping, raging or out on the streets, and had started stealing from me in a much more concerted and aggressive way than she had ever done before: money, bank cards and my mobile phone – I couldn't put anything down, even for a moment. I really didn't know how much longer I could go on trying to hold things together and keep her alive without help from someone.

And then in September I got a phone call from the Education Department saying there would not, after all, be a place for Lauren at the school reintegration unit because of some administrative error. She hadn't been put on the list and all the places were now allocated to other children. I had to calm myself down first and then try to pick a reasonably good moment to break the news to Lauren. She screamed, she wept, she tore at her face, smashed a mirror, and with a broken shard she first threatened me and then tried to hack at her arms. I got the shard off her and she ran screaming down the street. It was heartbreaking to see her distress. All she wanted was to be normal.

She was gone for four days, surfacing in London. I had prepared myself for this; there was no other way. I rang the police, and I rang social services. I told them where she was and that this time they would have to sort it out. She could not return home until/unless there was some support for us in Oxford.

Social services retaliated by sending her miles away, this time to King's Lynn, a six-hour return journey from Oxford. It was a small children's home run by KidzKare, a commercial company. This time there was meant to be a twelve-week assessment. It felt like Oxfordshire chose to place children as far away as possible to punish both the child and the parents by making it almost impossible to stay in touch. Or perhaps it was to ensure the county's troublesome children were as far away as possible from the dreaming spires, leafy suburbs and country cottages. Out of sight, out of mind? But then again, even when they were in sight and right under their noses, they still seemed to be out of mind.

The journey from Oxford to King's Lynn took forever. Although only 140 miles, it was across country with no motorways, and the route seemed to consist of just roundabouts, one after the other, mile after mile. On Saturday morning, five days after Lauren had gone there, I set off to see her, unsure of the reception I would get. The staff on the phone had been friendly and encouraging, which was reassuring after the hostility I had encountered in Kent.

When I first saw Lauren down a long, dark hallway, and smiled and said hello, she turned away. The home's manager must have seen my face because she said, 'Lauren, why don't you take your mum upstairs and show her your room?' Up there, she softened a bit when I gave her the things I had brought her and we sat on her bed and played one of the games like a pair of strangers.

When I left, I felt a certain sense of relief because the staff seemed to know what they were doing. If the home did provide what it said it would in terms of an assessment and some education, it would offer fairly good respite for us both and give me the time not only to catch up on a bit of sleep, but also focus on trying to pull together the Oxford-based services, this time backed up by a proper assessment of Lauren's needs. I drove home after that first visit feeling reasonably optimistic.

While it was hard to get any joined-up support from the statutory services in Oxfordshire, I was much luckier with the voluntary support I had. Not only did family, friends and neighbours all do whatever they could to support and help, I now had a huge network of concerned advisers from all sorts of third-sector agencies. NCH (now called Action for Children) were very supportive, convening meetings and writing letters on my behalf. Our old adoption social worker, Liz, was a rock, providing sympathetic, wise counsel over the phone and accompanying me to many of the meetings. Through Adoption UK, the charity that supports adoptive parents, I got a lot of useful assistance and access to some very informed legal advice and to some of the country's leading experts on caring for children with the most complex problems.

Peter, the child psychologist I had engaged privately, wrote a very detailed and helpful analysis of Lauren's problems resulting from all the abuse and neglect she had suffered in early childhood and setting out the sort of support and treatment she needed.

All these agencies and experts supported my analysis that Lauren needed an integrated package of therapeutic support and education, and the longer she was denied this, the worse the problems would get. Above all, everyone agreed that it was vital to nurture the tentative bond she had formed with me and that the distances involved in the only support we were currently being offered was a real threat to maintaining that bond.

I was determined to do what I could to keep that bond going, so I made the journey to King's Lynn every five or six days and rang Lauren every night. Gradually a warmth returned to her tone of voice. The staff remained kind and welcoming to me, but it was becoming clear that almost nothing was being done in terms of education or in assessing her underlying needs. She was simply being 'warehoused'. More worryingly, she and the only other resident in the house, another girl of a similar age, called Sheri, had inevitably formed a rather complex relationship, either giving staff the slip and running off to meet young men in the local park to cadge cigarettes or arguing with each other.

The staff at King's Lynn didn't have the training to deal with these episodes, or to contain the behaviour of either girl. Lauren's behaviour rapidly deteriorated and she started to self-harm, cutting her arms. The home took her to hospital twice but never thought to inform me about these incidents. One or two members of staff started to bait her, something they freely admitted when I challenged them, making comments like 'Get a life' when she was upset or kicking off.

Then one day I got a phone call from a police sergeant in

King's Lynn telling me they had arrested Lauren for fighting in the home. He was thoroughly unpleasant and officious, saying she was going to be cautioned for battery. Shockingly, he refused to allow me to get a solicitor for her or to go up and be with her, so she was entirely on her own in the police station. Staff from the home hadn't been allowed to accompany her, as they were the complainants.

Lauren pretended not to care about what had happened, but I made a complaint both to the police and to the home, and eventually I was successful in getting the caution removed from her record, but it took months. It was now clear that this placement was not going to be able to achieve anything for Lauren. It was, in fact, doing more harm than good.

8

Meadowside

Sue persuaded me I needed a break away from everything. I was very tired and stressed and finding it hard to sleep. I agreed to go away for two nights on a city break to Lisbon. It was so good to escape all the cares and worries at home and to catch a bit of late-summer warmth.

At first I was worried about being so far from home, but after a few hours I found myself beginning to relax and enjoy a city I had never visited before. We walked for miles, exploring old Roman sites, cathedrals, museums and, of course, a few shops and cafes. Then, while sitting in a restaurant on the second night, the home called my mobile to say that the girls had had another fight and had caused a great deal of damage in the house. The police had been called and Lauren had been evicted and sent to another home run by the company all the way down in Devon. The home had hired an escort service to drive her down. They assumed she had arrived, but they hadn't heard, and no one from the home had travelled with her. They gave me a phone number for the new place, but it just rang and rang.

I felt terrible for going away, although it had only been for two days, and given that the home had only told me after the event what had happened, I couldn't have done much if I'd been in Oxford anyway. Nevertheless I felt I had failed Lauren.

I kept ringing the Devon number and eventually the phone was answered. I explained who I was and asked if Lauren was there. They refused to answer my questions because they hadn't been told whether I was allowed to know anything or not. They did say they had received a child in the early hours of yesterday morning. The person on the phone didn't know her name. This child was, they said, still asleep, and when she was awake, they would find out more. I heard nothing else that day from anyone and just had to assume the child was in fact Lauren.

I rang the Devon number again the next day, and after four unanswered messages I spoke to someone, who confirmed that Lauren had arrived. They still hadn't received any files on her and didn't know if she would want to speak to me. I asked them to ask her, which they did reluctantly, and she came on the phone. She sounded completely traumatized and disorientated. She described the fight with Sheri.

'And, Mum, the staff just laughed at us, and then when we really started to kick off, the fucking cows just locked themselves in the office and called the police. The pigs arrested me, put handcuffs on and threw me in the police van. I got another caution.'

The home had sent a message to her in the police cells saying she wouldn't be allowed to go back and after six hours a prison escort service had come and taken her off. She was locked in the back of the car and they refused to tell her where she was going. They also refused to allow her to have anything to eat or drink and only once agreed to stop for a loo break on the six-hour, 300-mile journey. When she told me this, I wondered how much could be right – she must be making at least some of it up. Surely no one would treat a vulnerable thirteen-year-old like this? Later, when I got the full story from one of the company's directors, I discovered that it was unfortunately only too true. 'It's policy,' he said.

Lauren said she was in a house called Meadowside, which was set in the middle of a field. There was normally another girl staying there, but she was away for a few days, so Lauren was on her own. The girl, who was a year older, was due back the following day.

As Meadowside had no information on Lauren, I wrote a letter briefly setting out Lauren's background with details of the recent problems, including those at King's Lynn. I also said that if there were any behavioural problems that they couldn't handle, under no circumstances were they to remove her yet again. I asked that they instead ring me and I would go and fetch her. They had already told me that they only answered the phone for a period of a couple of hours each day and that their answerphone was broken, meaning they couldn't retrieve messages, so in my letter I said that in view of their telephone difficulties, I would send Lauren a mobile phone, which I would keep topped up.

I also asked if they could organize an HIV blood test. This had been due to happen while she was in King's Lynn, but the staff never organized it despite several reminders from me. All sorts of tests had needed to be done as a result of the rape, but the doctors advised us that an HIV test had to be left about ten to twelve weeks after the attack. Any earlier and it would not be conclusive.

When I rang Meadowside the next day, Lauren said the other

girl, whose name was Carley, was back and she was OK because she had smuggled some cigarettes back in. She and Carley were having fun hanging out of their bedroom windows smoking. Two hours later the phone went. The caller display showed it was the same number, but it wasn't Lauren.

'Hello. My name is Joyce. I work at Meadowside. I am afraid I have to tell you that Lauren and Carley have run off. They managed to give us the slip by climbing out through a toilet window with a broken lock. We chased them across the fields, but they were too fast. We think they will have made their way to Plymouth.'

'Have you rung the police and reported the girls missing?'

'Not yet, but we will. We'll let you know if we get any news or if she comes back. How late can we ring?'

'Anytime at all! Just call me if you hear anything.' I knew I wouldn't be sleeping much that night. Where could they have gone to? Lauren wouldn't have a clue where she was.

The next morning the home rang again. They had still heard nothing from the girls or the police. They sounded completely out of their depth and I ended up advising *them* on what actions they should be taking!

That night I got a call from Lauren from a withheld number.

'Hi, Mum. Just to let you know I'm fine. I'm with Carley. We're in London staying in a really posh hotel. It's fun. Love you. Bye.'

Before I could say anything she hung up. She didn't sound fine – she sounded as high as a kite – but at least she was alive. I rang the home and told them. Two more days went by as I anxiously waited with no news, and then on Saturday afternoon I got a reverse-charge call from Lauren, who was in a phone box. She was at Paddington Station. She and Carley had tried to jump a train to Oxford because she wanted to come and see me, but they had been spotted and stopped. I said I would go to Oxford Station and, using something the train companies called 'silver service', pay for tickets for them, which they could then collect from the ticket office at Paddington. I was so relieved to hear from Lauren and so anxious to see her that I didn't argue about paying for Carley too. I didn't want to give her any reason to fly off the handle and not come home.

I rang Meadowside and left a message for them, telling them what I was doing, and went to Oxford Station to wait for the girls. They walked through the barriers laughing and giggling as though they had just been out for an afternoon's shopping together rather than missing in London for four days. Carley was obviously a couple of years older than Lauren, although not as tall. She had bleached-blonde hair and even more make-up than Lauren. I decided to keep things fairly light and uncensorious rather than start asking too many questions and risk them running off again. On the way home, we chatted about the dogs, what they would like to eat and what might be on TV that night. About anything other than the important stuff.

Back in the house, Carley rang her mother and I persuaded them both to have baths. I found clean pyjamas and dressing gowns for them, and they came and snuggled on the sofa in our big, cosy kitchen while I cooked them spaghetti bolognese.

Lauren looked around her and said, 'Why do I keep running off? I love it here.'

It was lovely to hear that, but it just deepened my bewilderment. Why *did* she keep running off?

Over supper they showed me some photos on Carley's phone. There was a photo of a bed in a hotel room with money all over it. Not just coins but £5, £10 and £20 notes, and lots of them. There must have been £200 or £300 in total. I was horrified. There couldn't be any good explanation as to how two young runaways staying in a West End hotel might have come by such an amount of money. Still I knew I must try and keep the tone light and casual, and they wouldn't tell me the truth anyway, so it was better to try and engage them in chat and see what I could glean that way.

'Wow, that's a lot of money!'

'Yes, it's Carley's. She took it out of her savings. We had loads of fun. We ate in a very posh restaurant near Oxford Circus.'

'Oh, which one?'

'Garfunkel's.'

'And the hotel, was that near Oxford Circus too?'

'Yes, just round the corner.'

'Oh, which one? I wonder if it's one of the ones I used to stay in when I was working late and missed the last train home.'

'Can't remember its name.' She wasn't going to fall for that.

The next morning the girls went out to buy cigarettes with some of Carley's vast wealth. As soon as they were out of the door, I went up to Lauren's bedroom to look through the bags they had brought back from London. In Carley's bag was the return portion of an open adult return train ticket from Newton Abbot to London Paddington, priced £78. Presumably Lauren had a similar ticket. Where had two children got £156 from, plus all the cash on the hotel bed? They were not going to tell me, but I was determined to try and find out, and I was pretty sure I knew what the answer would be, sadly.

I eventually managed to get the girls in a car back to Meadowside; two members of staff had driven up to Oxford to pick them up. Lauren was in floods of tears and turned and stared imploringly at me out of the back window of the car as they disappeared from sight. I felt that I had utterly let her down, but I didn't know what else I could have done. I wanted nothing more than to have her at home, and most of the time that was what she wanted, but without the support of local services, I knew the set-up would break down again.

Lauren rang me from Meadowside to say they had arrived safely but that she didn't want to stay there. Sure enough, she didn't stay long. The next day at about lunchtime the staff rang to say the girls had disappeared through the WC window with the broken lock – again! The staff offered to come up and stay in Oxford. I said, emphatically, 'No, thanks.' I have no idea what they thought they were achieving by offering to come up. Although it wasn't saying much, I felt I was a lot more knowledgeable and skilled in the matter of troubled children than they were.

Three days of absolute silence. Nothing from Lauren, nothing from the police, nothing from social services. Meanwhile a friend and neighbour asked if I could help out a young friend of theirs for a few days. Roman was a nineteen-year-old Canadian who was taking a gap year to travel across Europe. He had planned to spend two weeks in Oxford, but halfway through his accommodation had come to an end. Could I give him a room for a week? I decided to let him use Lauren's room. At least it would stop me from going in there and crying, and it would be nice to have another young person in the house.

At about midnight the next night I got a phone call from Lauren. Whether she was putting it on or not I couldn't tell, but she did sound quite distressed. She said they were in London again and now owed money to someone who was demanding it back. I asked who this was and where they were. She refused to say. I begged her to go to the police, but she said, 'We'll just be in trouble then.'

'Where are you?' I asked. 'I'll drive up and get you.'

She said that no, they would be all right for the night. We arranged that I would meet them at Paddington Station first thing in the morning. I rang Meadowside to let them know she had been in touch, but there was no answer. I left a message, although I knew that it was unlikely they had got their machine fixed.

The next morning I was waiting on the main concourse of Paddington Station scanning the tail end of the morning rush-hour crowds. Eventually a girl advanced towards me shouting, 'Mum.' I didn't recognize her at first. She had hair the colour of tomato ketchup and an orange face, skintight mock-leather jeans and stilettos. It was Lauren. I was so shocked I didn't know what to say, just that I mustn't show any reaction for fear they would run off.

'Hi, love. You OK?' I tried to sound as nonchalant as possible.

Carley was with her too, and together, right there at the station, they made a rather half-hearted attempt to get me to give them £120, which they said they owed someone.

'Who?'

'Just someone.'

Um, yes, and I could imagine just what sort of someone. Pimp? Drug dealer? Both?

I took them to a cafe. They were starving, and over bacon rolls and hot chocolate I tried to persuade them to go back to Meadowside. They told me they had return tickets again. Another £156 had bought two more adult train tickets from Newton Abbot. I thought they owed money.

'Why are you buying adult tickets when you could get cheaper child fares?' I asked.

'Because they don't look so hard at adult tickets,' Lauren said. 'They don't question you about how old you are.'

I was certain they hadn't worked that out for themselves. Someone must have bought the tickets for them, or at least told them to buy adult tickets.

They refused point blank to return to Meadowside, so eventually I persuaded them to come back to Oxford again. I promised Carley she could use our phone to call her mum and her social worker to try and explain why she wouldn't go back to Meadowside. It was clear that Lauren wouldn't leave Carley behind, and I definitely didn't want any excuse for her to go off again.

Back in Oxford, I made up a bed for Roman in my office and the girls settled into Lauren's room. I rang Meadowside and managed to speak to a member of staff and told him the girls were safe and well with me. Carley phoned her mum, who was happy for her to spend the night with us again, and her social worker, who was not. I spoke to her social worker, who said she couldn't stay.

'That's fine,' I said. 'Come and get her, then.'

I had thought it was better for her to be at home with us than still on the streets of London, but if they felt otherwise, they knew where she now was.

'Well, this is highly irregular. I will have to talk to my manager.'

Blinkered by their training and hobbled by the procedures, most of the social workers we encountered operated purely like robots running on tracks. Meanwhile, fleet of foot and totally chaotic, their charges ran rings round them. Social services' inability to understand real life, make informed judgements about situations and exercise discretion was to dog us for years.

Three staff from Meadowside arrived in the evening to take the girls back to Devon. They both refused point blank to go. I said I wasn't getting involved with the situation with Carley, as I had merely intervened to get her once more off the streets. I wasn't very happy about Lauren going back to Meadowside because it just did not seem like a very safe place. I wanted time to think it over and talk to Lauren's social worker, who I couldn't get hold of. The three Meadowside staff returned to Devon empty-handed.

Although forbidden by procedures, Carley did stay the night with us in our unregulated and unapproved home, but first thing in the morning there were not one but two Buckinghamshire social workers on the doorstep. Two middle-aged women, one clutching a clipboard and the other a file with papers spilling out, stepped into the house.

'Oh good,' I said. 'You've come to collect Carley?'

'Oh no, we've come to assess you as a temporary foster carer. Carley can't stay here unless you are vetted,' said the one with the clipboard.

'But I don't want Carley to stay here. I have my hands full with my own child. I thought I was doing the right thing in getting Carley out of London. I would now like you to assume responsibility.'

She ignored me. 'What's your date of birth? Are you CRB-checked?' She pulled yet more papers from her bag.

'I repeat, I am not going to be a foster carer for Carley. I merely did what any responsible adult would do and removed her from a potentially dangerous situation. It is now your responsibility to sort something out for her longer term.'

'Well, we will have to phone our manager to get instructions,' said the other one, as the papers in the file cascaded onto the kitchen floor.

'That's fine. You're welcome to stay here while things are sorted out. Would you like a coffee?'

Their manager said she would need to consult further and the social workers were to remain in our house and await instructions.

I woke up Carley and she came down into the kitchen and told the pair to 'fuck off'. 'Fuck off' was pretty much a universal greeting given by Lauren and her associates to any adult in a position of responsibility or control. The social workers accepted it as a greeting and nodded back at Carley. She stated categorically that she would not under any circumstances go back to Meadowside, which she described as a dump run by morons.

Lauren then came into the kitchen, asked who the 'cows' sitting on the sofa were and demanded to know what was going on. 'So what's happening to Carley, then?'

'We are still consulting. No decisions have been made,' said the first social worker, holding the clipboard in front of her a bit like a shield.

'Well, fuck off out of our house, then,' Lauren said, picking up a mug and throwing it in their direction.

It smashed on the tiled floor with a crash and the social

workers snatched up their bags and file, and fled out of the front door, up the basement steps and down the street.

Although I was furious with Lauren for reacting the way she had, especially as these were not her social workers – they were Carley's, so it didn't really concern her – it was a relief to have this ridiculous pair out of the house. Unfortunately it left me still holding the baby, so to speak. The flight of the social workers also spoke volumes about the lack of robustness of their profession. Lauren's tantrum hadn't posed any real threat to their safety, and running like that just made them look weak and silly, not only to me but more importantly to the girl they were supposed to be in charge of.

I managed to get the girls to calm down and eat some food, which put them in a better frame of mind. We talked about what should happen, and after a bit of reflection they both agreed they would give Meadowside another go. I said I would drive them back there, but we would first need to let everyone know what was happening. However, when I spoke to Carley's social workers' manager on the phone, she had a go at me for undermining their plans to transfer her to foster care! That was the first I knew what their plans were.

Bloody cheek! They had just left me lumbered. I thought they would be pleased that Carley had agreed to go back.

'Can you please just make a decision, communicate it to Carley and put it into action?' I said, adding that it was immaterial to me what their decision was, but I required them to take responsibility for getting Carley out of my house so I was free to try and sort things out with Lauren. What both girls needed now was clarity and action from the adults who were supposed to be in charge.

The girls, realizing that everything was up in the air again, flew into identical rages and stormed out of the house. As they were stomping up the outside steps, the phone rang. It was the two social workers. They were lost. In their blind panic to escape Lauren and the flying mug, they had failed to notice which way they had gone and now could not find their way back to our house or their car, which was parked in the street outside. I worked out where they were and talked them back. Eventually, after waiting a few hours with no sign of the girls, they decided to call it a day and go home.

The girls didn't come back, of course, and when I rang, their phones were off.

For the next two days I heard nothing from anyone, despite making dozens of phone calls myself to services in Oxford, Devon and London. As usual, all the authorities squabbled among themselves as to who had responsibility for the girls. One police inspector in Devon who I eventually managed to get hold of told me children from across the country were just dumped in Meadowside, which was a 'honeypot' for drug dealers and pimps, and that there had been other incidents involving children from there that the owners had done nothing about. His force would not, he said emphatically, take responsibility for trying to sort out this latest incident.

Finally, a woman I had spoken to in a Metropolitan Police call centre rang me. She had been sympathetic and concerned, and had promised to make enquiries and get back to me. 'Do you think your daughter could be in Camden Town?' she asked.

'Possibly. The first time they were in the West End, but Camden Town isn't far from there, is it? But why are you asking?'

'We had a 999 call last night to say that a girl had been thrown in the canal in Camden Town and we haven't been able to trace who she was, so it was thought she might be a runaway.'

My heart stopped. I went so numb I dropped the phone. My hand was shaking when I picked it up again. 'Did you not find anything? Did you speak to the witnesses?'

'No, but officers did attend and concluded that she must have got out. There was another 999 call, this time from a girl in a call box in Camden Town, claiming she had been set upon by a gang; we think the two incidents are connected.'

'Oh my God. So what happens now?'

'Local officers are keeping an eye out. I will let you know if we hear anything more.'

I knew Camden Town pretty well; I had lived in and around that part of north-west London for nearly fifteen years. If no one else was going to actively search for a missing thirteen-year-old, I would go and look for Lauren myself. I went and told our next-door neighbour Jean what I was going to do and asked if she could feed the dogs and cats for me.

'You're not going on your own – I'll come too. Give me ten minutes.'

I hugged her. It would be so good to have company and support. I made a flask of coffee and ran off twenty copies of a poster I had made a couple of years earlier which I'd periodically updated with Lauren's latest photo and description and my phone number, and put everything in a basket. We met in the street by my car; Jean had brought her harmonica with the intention of going undercover as a busker at Camden Town Tube station.

Camden Town is used to many an unconventional sight, but looking back, we must have made a strange and incongruous pair. Two middle-aged women, one dressed in black playing a harmonica and the other in a very mumsy coat (I had just snatched the first thing that came to hand) with a large basket handing out pictures.

With Jean's support and in a place I knew, I felt reasonably optimistic we might find Lauren. At least we were doing something and not just sitting at home waiting for the phone to ring. We started at the Sainsbury's supermarket at the back of the Tube station. There can't be many other supermarkets anywhere in the country with that degree of security. There were steel shutters, barbed wire and security guards everywhere, a stark reminder that this was not an area for a thirteen-year-old child to be hanging out in for long. I approached a young security guard and told him we were looking for my daughter who was missing and possibly in Camden Town. I showed him the photo and said she was thirteen.

'How long has she been missing?' he asked.

'Three days,' I replied.

'Well, she's dead meat, then,' he said in a chillingly matter-of-fact voice.

A cold shiver ran through me and I had to struggle hard not to start crying.

He told us where some of the brothels were and that there were regular drugs drops outside the Tube station and it might be worth putting up some of the pictures there. 'But,' he called after us as we walked away, 'I wouldn't hold out much hope, though.'

We decided not to put up posters in case it made Lauren even more of a target. I wasn't sure how much use they would be anyway, as she was unlikely to bear much resemblance to the photo of a fresh-faced child on a summer picnic, the most recent picture I had of her.

We found the canal and climbed down and walked along a bit. I kept staring into the water. It was dark and I don't know what I expected to see, but I had become a bit fixated by the police report of a girl being thrown into the canal. It was, I suppose, just the sort of end I feared Lauren might meet one day. Had she met her end in those cold, dark waters in Camden Town?

It was pointless just standing there getting maudlin, so we tore ourselves away and headed back to the Tube station. It was about 9 p.m. when the dealers were due to make a drugs drop. It was quite extraordinary; from almost every side road, alleyway and doorway people, clearly addicts, were converging on a lay-by at the side of the Tube station and then, clear as anything for all to see, a large, dark four-by-four with blacked-out windows pulled up, a rear window was wound down, and the dealing started. I stood back and watched and hoped Lauren and her dodgy friends might appear. They didn't. I did approach a couple of the more with-it looking punters with her photo, but they just shrugged and walked away.

I went into several local shops with her photo, but everyone just shook their heads. I remembered that Carley and Lauren, when recounting their adventures on the first trip to London, had talked about something called the Chicken Hut or Chicken House or similar. I couldn't exactly remember the context, but just round the corner from the Tube station was a fast-food cafe called Chicken Palace. Could it be the same place? I went in with a photo.

'Um, I wonder if you can help me. I'm looking for my daughter, who is missing. Have you seen this young girl around here? She is only thirteen. I'm so worried about her.'

The men behind the counter looked at the photo, looked at each other, passed it around, shook their heads and handed it back. A fairly animated conversation, which wasn't in English, broke out as I left the shop, but it could have just been about the price of cooking oil.

Having come so far and being, we assumed, right where Lauren had last been heard of less than two days ago, it was hard to tear ourselves away. We kept saying, 'Just another quarter of an hour. She might walk round that corner any minute,' but in the end we had to go and we drove back to Oxford in the early hours feeling very despondent. I resolved I would go back the following night and perhaps stay over.

The next day I had a phone call from PC Jane Crump, who ran the police's Missing Persons Unit in Oxford. They had had a discussion and decided that as neither Devon Police nor the Met would assume the lead role in coordinating the hunt for Lauren, Thames Valley Police would. Bless them, it was good of them, as out of the three forces they probably had the least responsibility. Jane said if Lauren wasn't found by the morning, she would go up to London with me and we would look together.

Lauren had now been missing on and off for most of two weeks, most recently for five days. During all that time I had no contact from Oxfordshire Social Services, from whose care she had disappeared. They were supposed to be able to keep her safe; they were supposed to be the experts and were paying a small fortune for Lauren's place in Meadowside. They hardly seemed to know or care that she wasn't there.

Jane was due to pick me up from our house at 10 a.m. the next day. At ten to ten I was in the bathroom cleaning my teeth when Roman came and knocked on the bathroom door.

'There's someone here for you, Elizabeth,' he called.

'I know. It will be the police – just tell them I'll be down in a minute.'

'No, it isn't the police. There is an Oompa-Loompa here to see you.'

Couldn't I even clean my teeth in peace? I threw open the door in annoyance and there, standing on the stairs, staring at me through the banister, was Lauren – this time with purple hair but still the orange make-up. An Oompa-Loompa indeed. I just looked at her, blinking. I couldn't take it in at first: I had been certain that she was dead.

'Hello, Mum. I thought I'd come and see you.'

I didn't know whether to laugh or cry or scream. I probably did all three. She refused food or a bath, so I made her a hot, sweet tea and she deftly hand-rolled a cigarette herself, something I hadn't seen her do before.

'I've got to go back to London – I'm doing some work for friends – but I wanted to come and see you. I miss you, Mum.' With that she burst into tears. She was shaking and exhausted, so I persuaded her to go to bed for a bit.

'Can I sleep in your bed, please, and will you stay with me till I fall asleep?'

She was too tired to bully into pyjamas or anything, so I just let her take off her filthy sweatshirt and torn jeans and fall into bed. Underneath she was wearing a black and red lace corset. It was grotesque and shocking, particularly on a skinny child's body. (I learned later that the black and red lacy corset and

Lauren's purple hair dye had been bought for her by staff from Meadowside while on a supervised shopping trip 'because she wanted them'!) Lauren got under the duvet and I sat on the bed beside her.

She said, 'Let's sing songs.' We sang nursery rhymes until she fell asleep. The whole scene was so incongruous I couldn't get my head round it. I was sitting with someone dressed as a hooker singing songs for babies. Where was my thirteen-year-old daughter in all this? She seemed to have completely disappeared.

It was easier to relate to the baby than the hooker, so I stroked her hair and made soothing sounds and wondered what the hell was going to happen next.

I knew that Lauren had had many sexual encounters, some apparently consensual, but most clearly not, but looking at her lying there in the hideous corset and thinking about the three recent escapades to London, I suddenly knew for certain that she was being trafficked as a child prostitute. I was to raise this many times with both social services and the police but they did not see it as something that was being done to Lauren, rather it was a conscious, if poor, choice on her part.

Later, I found out that Oxfordshire County Council had somehow managed to get word to Lauren via Carley that if Lauren didn't voluntarily return, she'd be locked up in a secure unit. It beggared belief that Oxfordshire, who had consistently refused to provide any services locally for her, should send threats via a third party, and another child at that, to a vulnerable missing girl. I checked this threat with another solicitor from the adoption charity which had been advising me. She was confident that because of Oxfordshire County Council's refusal to provide any local, home-based services for Lauren, any judge would throw out an application to 'secure' her because that should always be used a last resort. She felt as I did that I should resist vigorously any attempt to send Lauren to a secure unit as the company and regime in such a place was likely to inflict a lot of damage on a child as emotionally battered as Lauren.

I had worked in and around social care services all my life; I had friends and colleagues who were social workers. I had always instinctively taken the side of social workers in debates in the media on failings in child abuse cases. I simply couldn't believe the downright heartless incompetence with which Lauren was being treated by Oxford social workers. That day, hearing about the threats to lock up Lauren, knowing how hard they were still fighting not to have to provide her with any support or help at home, any last vestige of trust or respect I had had for social services died.

The cause of most of our problems was a well-intentioned but misguided, or at least misdrafted and misinterpreted, piece of recent legislation. The Adoption and Children Act 2002, which came into force in 2003, shortly after Lauren moved in with me, had awarded local authorities some ring-fenced money to provide therapeutic support to adopted children with psychological and behavioural problems. There was also some funding to coordinate the provision of services from different agencies. But the legislation hadn't anticipated the situation where a child on adoption might move to another part of the country and make the provision of services almost impossible by the placing authority. It also relied on the appointment of specially recruited and trained adoption support services advisers in each local authority. At the time our needs started to manifest themselves, neither Stoke nor Oxfordshire had appointed such a person.

I first wrote to our local MP, Andrew Smith, about our predicament and the problems caused to us by this piece of legislation in early October 2005. He was immensely sympathetic and took the matter up not only with Oxfordshire County Council but also on the floor of the House of Commons. He got a response from Maria Eagle, the minister with relevant responsibility, fairly quickly, although it did nothing but reiterate the intentions of the recent legislation. She would not be drawn on the fact that the legislation was not working in practice and had in our case the completely opposite effect of that intended, in that it was being used as an excuse to deny us any support at all.

Oxfordshire County Council took weeks to respond to Andrew Smith, and when it did, the response bore no relation to the situation we were in.

Despite all the trouble with Meadowside, Oxfordshire Social Services were still trying to insist that Lauren go back a fourth time. I argued that it was not a safe place for a child like Lauren given the lack of basic security. I asked again if they would provide us with local services back in Oxford. They said they couldn't do that until KidzKare completed the supposed assessment. But the assessment wasn't being done. Originally KidzKare said it would take six weeks, then twelve, but after Lauren had spent nearly eight weeks in the two KidzKare places, it hadn't even started. That seemed not to matter to the social workers. The theory was that Lauren was with KidzKare for an assessment of her needs, and the theory was all that mattered. It was shocking how lightly they wasted what must have been a very large amount of money, possibly as much as £2,000 a week. The council tax payers of Oxfordshire were paying for something that wasn't happening. If they had been prepared to spend a quarter of that on local support services, Lauren could have remained at home.

In eight weeks at KidzKare thirteen-year-old Lauren had acquired two criminal convictions, been evicted at 2 a.m. and driven 300 miles across the country by total strangers, and spent a total of eleven days missing. She had gone into complete emotional meltdown, received no education and no psychological assessment, all her clothes had been lost, and the HIV blood test that had been urgent two months ago had still not been done.

But Oxfordshire Social Services remained insistent there would be nothing provided for Lauren at home; they were adamant on that. Whatever the risks or dangers down there, Lauren must return to Meadowside, which our social worker told us was the best of a bad job. I still had legal parental authority for Lauren, so it was theoretically my decision to place her in care, but there was always the threat hanging over me that if I didn't go along with what was offered, they would simply take away my parental rights. Two solicitors I consulted were of the opinion that I should refuse to allow her return to Meadowside and let Oxfordshire Social Services try and take away my parental rights, but I didn't want to run the risk. I think it would have absolutely finished Lauren to lose another parent.

With a very heavy heart I agreed that Lauren could go back to Meadowside for a fourth time. I was told they really would take better care of her, that the broken window lock would be repaired, that they now had more staff down there and would start her assessment right away.

Lauren, of course, did not want to go back to Devon, and when the time came for us to leave Oxford and drive the 180 miles down to Meadowside, she became very tearful. She went next door to say goodbye to Jean, but rather than coming back home, ran up the street. She had recently been on the phone talking to Jennifer, so I guessed they might be heading for the station. Jean and I drove there.

A London train was just pulling in to the platform as Jean and I ran onto the concourse. I shouted to the ticket collector that we were after two runaways and pushed past other passengers just in time to see Lauren and Jennifer getting into a carriage. The girls squealed when they saw us, and I shouted to them to get off. Lauren turned towards me and I put my foot in the closing automatic door, grabbed her arm and pulled her off the train. Back on the platform, she wriggled free and ran down the platform and onto the track right in front of the train. I waved frantically at the driver and pointed to the track, while Jean pulled her off. We manhandled her onto the side of the platform, where Jean, as a teacher having been trained in restraint, brought her down to the ground and held her, securing her flailing legs and arms with her own. How I wished I had had that training. I had never been able to hold on to her for more than a few seconds.

Looking back on the episode, it all seems very dramatic, but I knew that if Lauren went back onto the streets of London again, she might not survive a fourth time. We sat at the side of platform 1 on Oxford Station for nearly an hour. A full-scale emergency procedure was invoked by staff, which meant that the train couldn't leave for fifteen minutes while various safety checks were made. I turned my head away from the angry stares from the delayed passengers.

After about sixty minutes of screaming and trying to break free, Lauren eventually calmed down and agreed to go back to Meadowside. We went straight from the station. I didn't want to risk going home, not even for a couple of minutes. I drove out of Oxford a bit like a bat out of hell, praying that there wouldn't be any red lights or people on pedestrian crossings who I would have to stop for, giving Lauren the opportunity to change her mind and jump out of the car. Fortunately there were none. By the time we reached Swindon heading down to the M4, along which so much of our life together had been played out, Lauren started to relax and turned on the radio looking for a music channel.

'Oh, it's our song,' she said suddenly. 'I always think of you when I hear it. It makes me cry, but it makes me happy at the same time. It's called "You Raise Me Up".'

I listened. I hadn't heard it before.

It was all about lifting someone up and making them strong and helping them through troubles.

'That's what you do for me, Mum – you raise me up.'

Blimey . . . I had no idea she even for a moment felt that I did anything positive for her. I knew she was fond of me, but no more. It was cheesy, but just then I needed a bit of cheese. I put my hand on her arm, the tears streaming down both our faces. So I wasn't the cause of all her problems as far as she was concerned. If she felt even a tenth of what the lyrics implied, why was she setting out to destroy everything we had together? Did she really have no comprehension of the risks she was taking, either of being murdered by a pimp, punter or drug dealer or being locked up in a secure unit by Oxfordshire County Council?

It was agreed that Lauren should remain at Meadowside on a part-time basis for another ten weeks, coming back to Oxford for three or four days each week. During this time I was promised that local services would be identified to enable Lauren to return to the Oxford area; in particular they said they would try to find a therapeutic residential care placement for her.

The staff at Meadowside were pleasant and friendly to me on my weekly visits, but the regime they worked under was ill equipped to provide for the needs of a child like Lauren. She was simply warehoused there with little real education or purpose to her day. For most of the time she was the only child there and she was lonely and bored. To try and entertain her, she was taken out to the amusement arcades of Torbay, where she would spend hours dancing on her own on dance machines, or to the zoo and Dartmoor Prison visitors' centre!

She was stuck in an aimless, ineffectual, procedure-driven regime that was the 'looked after child/young person' system. One of the procedures was the statutory review meeting, bringing in an independent 'expert' periodically to review how things were going for a child in care. Later on, in a different setting, we would benefit from the great wisdom and knowledge of a reviewing officer, but here in Devon we had Roger.

Roger arrived forty minutes late for the scheduled statutory review meeting in Meadowside. He had great difficulties with maps. As it was a day out in the Devon countryside, he had brought his wife along. She needed the loo and a coffee and to be shown the garden. The meeting was now over an hour late starting.

No papers were ready. The home's manager was sitting at the computer frantically pounding the keys. He then had to run off eight copies of the paperwork and was absent from the first hour of the meeting. No conclusions could be made on any of the items discussed because the manager was not in the room. 'Well, we will just have to wait for Keith to join us on that one.'

After about half an hour the reviewing officer asked, 'Now, why is Lauren here?'

'Because there is no local help for us,' I said.

'To carry out an assessment of her needs,' the Oxfordshire social worker said.

'We're not quite sure, because we haven't been formally told by Oxfordshire,' the care worker from the home said.

Lauren said with total clarity, 'Because you're all wankers.'

Roger cleared his throat. 'Let's talk about dental checks, then. Have they been done?'

Lauren seized the opportunity to say she wanted coloured braces. 'Good heavens, whatever next? Coloured braces indeed!' chortled Roger. 'Tell me, what colours can you get nowadays?'

At this point, less than halfway through the agenda and without any key decisions having been made, the social worker had to leave to catch a train back to Oxford.

'Safe journey,' beamed Roger, overlooking the fact that now no decisions could be made, as the only person with any authority had just left.

Roger then decided to pad out the time until lunch by asking Lauren if she had any complaints. The floodgates opened. One of her complaints was that she did not have enough time on the dance machines in the amusement arcade.

'Now, what is a dance machine? Good heavens, whatever next?'

Knowing absolutely nothing about the child, her background, the issues and dangers there were for her and now in full benign uncle mode, Roger started agreeing to all sorts of demands that Lauren was making.

'Of course you should have unsupervised time with your sister' – who in absconding terms makes you look like a rank amateur – 'and of course it will be fine for you to go with your sister to visit your' – sexually abusive – 'birth father' – about whom you still have nightmares and from whose care you were removed by court order. 'Anything else you would like?'

At this point I threatened to remove Lauren from Meadowside there and then if any of that was allowed to happen.

'Oh dear,' said Roger. 'I didn't realize there were difficulties with the birth family.'

On my next visit, I was dismayed to find Lauren slumped on a sofa watching two women screaming at each other on *The Jeremy Kyle Show*. She seemed very down and was dressed virtually in rags. She was pale and grubby-looking. She was wearing black plastic stiletto boots that were so small she could hardly walk in them, a filthy, ripped and stained zipper top, and trousers that were so small they didn't cover her bottom and wouldn't zip up at the front.

'Why are you wearing those awful clothes?' I asked. 'Where did they come from? Where are yours?'

'Mine have all been lost, and anyway, I like these – they suit me.'

She looked like the most neglected waif, the sort of girl that stares out of advertisements when homeless charities appeal for funds to help young people living on the streets.

I hit the roof. The deputy manager said they had allowed her to dress like that because she wanted to.

'Lauren is a young person making choices about how she dresses and whether she wants to wash or not,' she said in a lecturing tone.

'She is not a young person,' I snapped. 'She is a thirteen-year-old child, and emotionally a very young thirteen-year-old, and if she were capable of making sensible choices for herself, she wouldn't be here. You are supposed to be looking after her as a parent would, and no responsible, caring parent would allow their child to dress like that.'

I took a complete new wardrobe down for her a couple of days later and wrote a letter to the home manager setting out how I felt she should dress, saying that clothes should be the correct size for comfort and decency, and ripped and stained clothes should be mended, washed or discarded. I told them her shoe size and asked them not to buy her any more stiletto heels, as they were bad for growing feet. I concluded, 'When Lauren moved in with me, she came with scabies, nits and bin bags of dirty clothes and broken toys. I have struggled for nearly three years to get her to feel she is worth more than that, and it is heartbreaking to see how much she has slipped back since she has been in care again.'

*

The first week in December I did the Oxford–Plymouth round trip three times, clocking up over a thousand miles. As the date set by Oxfordshire for the end of her placement in Devon came and went and there was still no sign of a completed assessment or any possibility of a place in a care home nearer to Oxford, I decided that the only option was to plan for her to return home to me and start again the struggle for appropriate local services. This began gradually, with Lauren returning to Oxford each weekend. The staff at Meadowside were good and used to drive her halfway and we'd rendezvous at services on the M4. This saved me some of the driving, but it still meant Lauren was sitting in a car for hours on end each week.

I now know Lauren was trafficked and sold for sex by an organized paedophile gang while living at Meadowside and in the care of Oxfordshire County Council. A white man called Mark who lived in Plymouth dressed the girls in sexy underwear, photographed them, emailed the pictures to associates in London, bought the girls train tickets at Newton Abbot, gave them hundreds of pounds in cash and put them on the train to London on two separate occasions. They were met in London by other men, who then sold them for sex in various hotels in the West End. To my knowledge, neither Mark nor his London associates have ever been caught or even looked for.

9

Now What?

Most people on the beach at Gorran Haven in Cornwall on New Year's Day 2006 were wearing woolly hats, anoraks and wellies. It was bright and sunny, so the vivid blues, oranges and yellows of the Rajasthani dance troupe's clothes made for a particularly eye-catching sight. But no January day in Britain really has the right weather for sandals and cotton skirts and light trousers, and the troupe's noses and toes were starting to turn purple as they posed for photos taken by locals and holidaymakers who were blowing away the cobwebs of New Year's Eve with a brisk walk on the beach.

Lauren and I spent two weeks together over Christmas, including a few days in Cornwall staying with our friends Caroline and Kate at their house on the cliffs above the little fishing village. The Rajasthani troupe was performing at the nearby Eden Project, and Caroline, who was involved with the project, was hosting a New Year's Day lunch party for them.

It was almost impossible to believe that the girl who was now very graciously helping to show them round, hang up their jackets, find towels for their sodden feet and serve them lunch was the same child who less than two months before had been on the streets of Camden Town with dyed-purple hair and a black and red lace corset, or as recently as a month ago had sat in the children's home dressed in rags watching *Jeremy Kyle* and uttering four-letter words and threats to anyone who came too close. But here, away from Camden Town, Oxford and Meadowside, she was a relaxed and seemingly happy thirteen-year-old in big pink fluffy jumpers and teddy-bear slippers, her face without a trace of make-up. During our stay we had been ice skating, and on New Year's Eve had played several games of Boggle before walking down to the beach at midnight to listen to the foghorns on the ships in the distance sounding in the new year.

With a family Christmas in Wales as well, we'd had a lovely break together. My heart started to sink, though, as the time approached for us to leave and head back to God knows what.

On the bright side, at least Oxfordshire Education Department were saying they would at last look into Lauren's needs and had accepted they would have to provide some proper education for her in the new year. There was to be a meeting in Oxford on 13 January to decide how to proceed. Although not officially due to leave Meadowside until the first week of February, Lauren was now spending more time back with me in Oxford than she was in Devon.

The one really positive service that was available to us in Oxford was the support of the Attach Team, which Stoke was paying for. Both Lauren and I met with them early in January to discuss how they could help us tackle the issues that would arise when Lauren was back in Oxford for good. Lauren was initially very reluctant to say anything, but with their expert probing, she started to open up. She talked about how angry and confused she felt about the past, and how she missed and worried about her birth family, even her parents, despite knowing how neglectful and abusive they had been.

'Don't get me wrong – I hate them for what they did to us, but I feel worried about them too. I sometimes wish they would just die so I didn't have to worry about them.

'I want to know why social services took us away and sent us to so many shit holes full of paedos.'

She agreed that her anger was at times so extreme that she put herself and others in danger. She said that she hated being like that but didn't know what to do about it.

'I just feel angry all the time now and at everyone, even if it isn't their fault. I hate being like this, but I don't know how to stop. That's why I do drugs: they take away the bad feelings for a bit.'

She said she had found it was easier to block out the bad feelings than work through them.

'And, Mum, you make me so angry when you don't get mad when I hit you or break your stuff. It's so weird and wrong. You should get mad and hit me back. People always used to, and when you don't, it makes me even worse.'

Although it took a bit of mental gymnastics to get my head round her contorted logic, these comments gave me a real insight into why her outbursts would often just escalate and escalate. Essentially, she wanted me to get angry and violent to bring the 'outside temperature' up to what she was feeling inside.

She also said she often felt she couldn't talk to me about the bad feelings and the awful things that had happened in case I got upset or felt I ought to tell social workers or the police about what had been done to her.

At last 13 January came and there was the meeting to discuss how to re-engage Lauren with education in Oxford. It was agreed that the formal assessment of her special educational needs, which I had requested in writing four times, should be done urgently. I was surprised and delighted that the case for such an assessment was supported by a very succinct, empathetic and insightful analysis from the Oxford social worker who was involved with us. It was the first time I had felt any understanding or concern from social services. She wrote, 'Lauren is an extremely troubled little girl . . . The most significant positive in her life is that Elizabeth remains committed to her care and the provision of a stable base.' It was a nice surprise to see that, but why, then, didn't they give me more help to make it work?

Maybe we could work in partnership after all. Perhaps their agenda was not simply to dump her back into care. Apparently at last accepting they should try and support us, Oxfordshire Social Services said they would try and find Lauren a few hours a week of respite care to give me a break and at least enable me to keep some work going.

The meeting was full of good intentions, including the possibility of some education eventually. I left feeling more optimistic than I had in months. Lauren was back home, and it was accepted that she should have some specialist help and support in Oxford to allow her to remain there and catch up on missed education. Not only that, there seemed now to be people who actually wanted to help us to stay together.

Lauren had been invited to the meeting but had refused to come. She had been out with Jennifer the afternoon before and had not returned at 7 p.m., when she should have done. I had reported her missing to the police at 10 p.m. I was now used to the process of reporting a child missing and had already memorized the 0845 number of the call centre. The woman who took my call was sympathetic and went through the standard list of questions: Name? Age? Height? Appearance? Last seen? Did I believe her to be the victim of a crime? I never knew how to answer that and usually said, 'Yes, probably. I think she is being used by various men for sex.'

She then went through a suicide assessment, gave me a reference number and said I would get a visit from some police officers as soon as they could be spared.

Before the police officers arrived, I got a very distressed reverse-charge call from Lauren, who was in a call box. Jennifer had taken her to see some friends who lived on Cowley Road. There were some rough men there and Lauren felt frightened and had run out. One of them tried to follow her and she had hidden in an alleyway. I suspected some of the distress was being put on in an attempt to deflect my anger, but I drove to Cowley Road and picked her up outside Tesco. She had clearly been drinking and had possibly taken drugs, but I wasn't sure what.

I always found it quite difficult to tell whether Lauren actually was on drugs because I was a bit naive when it came to illicit substances. Despite being a child of the Sixties, I had only twice tried cannabis, never anything harder. The first time, I was in my twenties and it made me feel very sick. The second time was many years later at an Oxford dinner party where spliffs got passed round with the coffee and mints. I took two drags and got very giggly. If she would admit to taking anything, Lauren would always say it was weed or skunk, but it certainly didn't make her giggly and silly, or even just sick. Whatever it was that she was being given made her wild, angry, paranoid and sometimes even psychotic.

This time she said the man who had pursued her out of the flat was going to kill her. She seemed genuinely frightened, hiding on the floor of the car as we drove down Cowley Road. Once over Magdalen Bridge and heading home, she sat up in the front seat and started berating me when I told her there would probably be police officers on the doorstep at home.

'You fucking cow, what did you call the fucking pigs for?'

I regretted retorting, 'What fun to live in a farmyard,' as soon as the words were out of my mouth, and her punch slammed into the side of my face.

Needless to say, Lauren was not in the mood a few hours later to come to the education meeting with me. I asked if there was anything she would like me to say on her behalf at the meeting and of course got the response, 'Yes. Tell them they're all wankers and should fuck off and leave me alone.'

Her mood was no better when I got back. Although she had been saying she wanted to return to education, she was not pleased to hear that there was a possibility of a place somewhere for her fairly soon. As I was feeling really encouraged and excited for her, I tried sharing my enthusiasm.

'But won't it be good to start learning again, discovering new things, reading new books, maybe doing plays and singing? You like singing, and you have a lovely voice.'

'Stop trying to make me posh. I don't need to know those things. I'm not clever, and I'm never going to be posh like you.'

Lauren's definition of 'posh' seemed to be anyone who went to school or worked and didn't take drugs or hang around the streets. I certainly didn't see myself as posh in the usual sense of the word.

'Stop trying to make me like you,' she said angrily.

'I'm not trying to make you like me. I'm trying to encourage you to find out who you really are. The life you are living is no life for a thirteen-year-old. You are worth so much more.' Again I tried to find words to reach her, to unlock within her some desire or ambition to change.

'I'm fine like I am. This is just how it's always going to be for me. I'm just different. Leave me alone.'

'But that's nonsense, and deep down you know it. Your life could be very different, but only if you're prepared to let it be.'

If only there had been education on offer at this point, it might have been possible to re-engage her, but of course there wasn't, and that simply told Lauren that the services didn't care and that she didn't matter, that she really was different and everyone but me knew it.

Lauren disappeared again that night, and for much of the next month. She didn't seem to always be with Jennifer either. Although she was careful not to let me near her mobile phone when it rang, I could hear the deeper tones of a man's voice, though never distinctly enough to make out words.

I no longer tried to stop her leaving. I knew I couldn't. When I tried, it always ended in a brawl, with one of us, usually me, getting hurt and things in the house smashed. And in fact the police had advised me not to try to prevent her leaving physically. So when she put down her phone and said, 'I've got to go out,' I would feebly say that I didn't want her to, that she was putting herself in danger and that if she wasn't back by 9 p.m., I would call the police and report her missing.

'Whatever!' And the door would slam.

Sometimes I would follow her down the street for a bit. She would disappear round the corner and then there might be the sound of a car engine, the door slamming and then driving off. Had she got in that car, or was it just coincidence? I was aware of a green Vauxhall that seemed to drive around our streets quite a bit, but could never see who was driving and only got half the registration number. A couple of times I followed her as she walked on foot over the river and into the city centre, but I always lost her in the crowds. Mostly I sat at home fuming at my own inability to stop her and utterly at a loss to understand what she was doing and why. If she wasn't home by ten and I had heard nothing from her, I would report her missing. If she had been in touch and I therefore knew she was OK, I would leave it a bit longer.

The night of the education meeting when she wasn't back by 10 p.m., I rang the police and then, armed with my home-made posters of her, set off into town. I started with my old friends in the kebab vans. They hadn't seen her that night. Next I went down the rows of those wrapping themselves up in cardboard in shop doorways for the night. I avoided the most obviously ill, but recognized several I had spoken to before who had always promised to keep an eye out for her.

That night I met a young woman sitting on the narrow pavement wrapped in a blanket, begging outside the Oxford Union. Thin and pale with that ghostly pallor of hunger and drug addiction, she told me her name was Charley. She was pretty and articulate and probably about eighteen. We chatted for ages.

'Yes, I know Lauren. She often comes and sees me when she's

in town. I didn't know she was thirteen; she said she was sixteen. I always tell her to go home. The streets are no place for a kid like her. I'll send word round that she's missing again and see if I can find out anything. You can usually find me here or near Sainsbury's or the bottom of St Giles'.'

I wouldn't give her money, as it would probably go on more drugs, but I bought her a sandwich and a drink, and we talked about life on the streets, about Oxford and the senior academics she swore her friends supplied with drugs.

As I left to go home, she called after me, 'Keep looking. Don't give up. I wish someone had come looking for me when I was thirteen and running away all the time.'

Lauren returned that night at 3 a.m. very distressed and covered in love bites. All she would tell me was that she had been with friends. I made my usual comment that real friends wouldn't let her get into that state.

'These *are* my real friends! Things are different for me and that's just how it is.'

As ever, the only service that was really involved with us was the police.

'Where have you been, Lauren?' they asked when they came to sight her.

'With friends.'

'Well, I should choose nicer friends if I were you.'

I was always a bit surprised that they were not more curious and pushy with her, but I think they lost sympathy with her and saw her as just a bit of a nuisance. I was beginning to realize that there was a lot of Oxford that lived beyond the reach of the law and the norms of mainstream life, and neither the police nor social services had the slightest understanding of it, or any expectation of being able to do anything about it.

I had lived in Oxford for seventeen years before Lauren's behaviour started to introduce me to its other side, to the shadows in dark streets, the cars that hovered just down the road, the muffled voices on the phone, the people who could spirit away a child virtually from under your nose. I hadn't been naive enough to see Oxford as the place of croquet on college lawns, punts and dreaming spires, the Oxford of TV and the movies, but having lived and worked there on and off for much of my adult life, having run services for homeless people, ex-offenders, young care leavers and having served on the boards of various Oxford-based public services and charities, I thought I knew it warts and all. How wrong I was. I knew nothing of the Oxford that Lauren lived in.

By now I was getting calls from Lauren from all over the country. She would take every opportunity to disappear.

The nights when Lauren was missing were torture, either spent in futile searches or in agonized phone calls to sympathetic but baffled friends. On my own, I often resorted to tears, not something I had ever really done as an adult before. There were tears of frustration, of anger, of bewilderment, of exhaustion and often of pure grief for the loss of the child I had never really had.

I could cope with the days much better. I would throw myself into fevered activity, catching up with work, spring cleaning, walking the dogs for miles and writing letters to anyone who might just possibly be able to do something.

'Dear Prime Minister,' I wrote to Tony Blair in February

2006, 'you are probably my last hope . . . I have been begging and battling with local services for over a year.' I outlined at some length everything that had happened to Lauren and the pitiful, begrudging response of the services, and went on:

> What she needs is active, engaging care and therapy to
> rebuild her shattered soul, perhaps the sort of thing that
> is offered to victims of torture, which in effect she is.
> After everything this child has been through, it would
> be a criminal failing of society if it will not give her the
> support she needs to be able to embrace the new life we so
> desperately want to provide a wonderful, bright, kind child
> with so much to contribute. Is there anything you can do
> to help us?

A month later I received the inevitable, perfectly polite reply saying my letter had been passed to the Department for Education and Skills.

One day in early March I got a reverse-charge call from Birmingham. 'Mum, I came to Birmingham with friends, but they've abandoned me,' Lauren sobbed.

I went to Oxford Station and paid for a ticket to be phoned through to Birmingham New Street for her. I didn't go back to meet her when she got to Oxford, though. I told her she could walk home from the station. Probably risky, but I was beginning to ask myself if by always bailing her out and taxiing her home, I was making these escapades too easy.

My approach didn't work: two days later she rang in distress from Barking in Essex. This time I went to collect her on the train.

It was after the episodes in Essex and Birmingham that the police first mentioned to me the possibility of them taking out an order to get Lauren locked up in a secure unit for her own protection. To date I had reported her missing thirty-seven times. The situation was escalating and the police felt they were at the end of the line.

I had always opposed the idea of a secure unit for Lauren, especially as it had been proposed almost as an alternative to trying to do anything less draconian locally for us. Just as the threat of sending Lauren to a secure unit reared its ugly head again, the Howard League for Penal Reform published the report of an inquiry into the treatment of children in secure units chaired by Lord Carlile. Raising concerns about violence, restraint, strip searches and solitary confinement, it did nothing to reassure me that such places actually helped the children in their charge. Fortunately, I think the media coverage the report received caused many of those involved with Lauren to think again. Certainly the police backed off and suggested instead that Lauren should enter into an acceptable behaviour contract with them. This set a curfew of 10 p.m. and prohibited acts of public disorder. It threatened that an application would be made to the magistrates' court for an antisocial behaviour order (ASBO), and beyond that she might be imprisoned or fined or both if she breached the contract. I wasn't enthusiastic or optimistic about it, but if it put off the threat of locking her up for a bit, I was prepared to go along with it.

As a teenager, I had read *Erewhon* by Samuel Butler, a satire on Victorian society and the hypocrisy of its values. It had made a great impression on me, especially the topsy-turvy approach to morality whereby the sick were punished and sent to prison and ostracized, while criminals were pampered and treated with enormous sympathy and care. And now a child whose only 'crime' was being born into a family who abused and neglected her, and being dumped by officials in several more abusive situations, was being threatened with prosecution and incarceration rather than being given any effective support or help. Meanwhile the gang of Albanian rapists and the men who, I later found out, were sending her up to Barking and Birmingham were free to saunter through the streets and do as they pleased. It felt as though Samuel Butler's satire had become reality in twenty-first-century Oxford.

That is not to say that I didn't recognize that Lauren's behaviour at times was now bordering on the criminal. She was, for example, found in a house during a drugs raid where class-A drugs were discovered and claimed that she was being used as a runner – she seemed to think that was quite clever. She was arrested and held in the custody suite in St Aldate's Police Station for hours, making a thorough nuisance of herself, then bailed but never charged with anything. There was no evidence she had handled any of the drugs and the police decided she wasn't a runner. She was just a reckless and impulsive child playing with fire.

Her risk-taking and impulsive, self-destructive behaviour were now at such a level that the Attach Team and our GP joined forces with me in April to again try to get her a psychiatric assessment. Dr Anne Stewart, a child and adolescent psychiatrist from the Park Hospital, agreed to take this on and saw us both. Her conclusion was that although Lauren was not suffering from any conventional mental illness, she still needed intensive monitoring and support. Dr Stewart offered to convene regular multi-agency meetings under something called the Care Programme Approach, a procedure set down by government to ensure that those with severe mental and emotional health problems received appropriate help.

It was such a relief to have an Oxford agency willing to stand up and take some responsibility for pulling things together to support Lauren. It took a huge burden off me and was much more likely to be successful than I was. Being Lauren's mother was hard enough, but also having to act as care coordinator, support worker and so on was becoming too much. I was permanently exhausted, and I knew at times that my judgement was probably marred by the stress and the conflicting roles I was trying to play. I was particularly glad to be shedding those roles as Dr Stewart warned me that as Lauren became more secure in her relationship with me, something she was certain that was happening, the likelihood was that her challenging behaviour would, at least in the short term, become worse. It was reassuring that Dr Stewart thought Lauren was becoming more secure in her relationship with me, but it was hard to get my head round the fact that the more secure she felt, the worse her behaviour was likely to become!

In fact, I had been told something similar by both the Attach Team and by Peter. Strange though it seemed at first hearing, the more secure and attached Lauren became, the more the traumatic memories and anger about the past would surface. As she lacked the emotional maturity to be able to process these feelings constructively, it was likely that her behaviour would become more disturbed. In a wretched vicious circle that such problems create, the more she experienced her emotions and behaviour as damaging and out of control, the more she would see herself as unworthy and unlovable. And in a final cruel twist, the fact that I was showing Lauren that she was in fact worthy of love would just be too disconcerting for her to handle. She couldn't live with the conflict between what she believed about herself and what I was telling her about herself and therefore tried to make me despise her so that her self-hate was validated.

Daunting and worrying though the prophecy of even more difficulties to come was, the fact that I now had sensible professional explanations and support in what might still be to come made all the difference. With the backing and help of the Attach Team and the Child and Adolescent Mental Health Service, I finally felt prepared for more or less anything.

True to her word, Dr Stewart called a multi-agency case review the following week. The police, our GP, social services, education, mental health and the Attach Team were there. All agreed to provide more support, and as a group we also decided that while recognizing the risks, there would be no move to get Lauren sent to a secure unit for the time being. Everyone concurred that the plan for now would be to provide support to enable Lauren to stay at home. The minutes recorded that as far as delaying any action to get Lauren secured went, all agencies, including me, 'would hold the risk together'. It was so different from our previous multi-agency meetings; I couldn't have asked for more.

I was full of hope that we would now get some concerted integrated help from the various agencies.

Another small positive was that a draft statement of special educational needs was finally issued. It recognized the complex set of needs – educational, social and emotional – that Lauren had, but couldn't identify how they might be met. In the short term four days a week there would be a couple of hours a day of activities from outreach workers at PRUIS, a support unit for children excluded from school. Hopefully, when resources allowed, Lauren would also get a few hours a week in Tier 4, a therapeutic unit, but there was nothing full-time or long-term available. PRUIS also said that they couldn't provide Lauren with any formal education; their input would be largely activity-based.

Although Lauren did not attend the case review – indeed, she made some very disparaging, mainly four-letter-word comments about the whole process – the positivity at this time must have rubbed off on her somehow because things calmed down for a bit. Maybe it helped that I was more relaxed and confident. Despite running off now and then, she was enjoying the outings with the PRUIS staff and the support worker provided by social services on the day there was no educational input.

There was an evening when she disappeared with Jennifer, but by 10 p.m. she was back pounding on the door. I let her in and she rushed into the living room and peered out at the street from behind the curtains. There, in the street outside, was a nondescript dark car with blacked-out windows. Lauren said there were two men in the car and Jennifer. Apparently Jennifer had had sex with one of them for weed, but the man said afterwards that he didn't have enough money to get it for her. Lauren said she felt frightened and wanted to come home, so she had suggested that she go home and get some money to buy some if they would take her. They fell for it and here she was.

'I'm not going back out. They're horrible men, and Jennifer's a slag. Don't go out there, Mum, and don't answer the door.'

'But what about Jennifer? Is she safe with them?'

'One of the men, Ziggy, is Jennifer's boyfriend. Her mum knows him.'

Jennifer did come and knock on the door but returned to the car fairly quickly when we didn't answer and it drove off.

I wondered if I should have called the police or gone out to the car to find out what was going on, but my main priority was to keep Lauren calm and in the house, so I didn't. I reasoned with myself that if Jennifer's mother wasn't concerned by all the boyfriends her daughter had, then why should I be? I knew that Jennifer, like Lauren, was putting herself at great risk, but I felt I could still do something to help Lauren, whereas there was now little, if anything, I could do for Jennifer, although I did mention my concern for her in my all-too-frequent conversations with the police.

Lauren crept into my bed that night, saying, 'Thanks for protecting me, Mum.'

Lauren also produced a boyfriend about this time and asked if she could bring him round for supper one evening. This was a first. I knew she had male friends, if that is the right word for them, but she had never wanted me to meet any of those – quite the contrary. Anthony, who she said was fourteen, came round on his bike. He had been invited for supper but wouldn't eat it and went and sat in the living room while the rest of us ate. If he was fourteen, he hadn't worn very well, as he looked much older, but here he was plain for all to see, not someone lurking down the road, and he seemed quite polite and presentable and didn't even smoke.

They went up to her room to listen to music, but I noticed with relief and surprise that she kept the door open and every twenty minutes or so came down to me. 'Just checking you're OK, Mum.'

After a couple of hours she came down looking slightly upset.

'Mum,' she whispered, 'he's going through my underwear drawer. I don't like it, but I don't know what to say.'

She allowed me to play the fussy mother, and I went up to her bedroom to say it was time for him to go, especially as he was cycling and it was getting late.

'After all, you're only fourteen. I'm sure your mother will be worrying.'

I think I saw him blush.

It was strange – this would have been a troubling event to many parents of a thirteen-year-old girl . . . A daughter brings home a boy clearly several years older than her who proceeds to ransack her knicker drawer. But it was for me a light-hearted moment of near normality. Here was Lauren experimenting with an almost normal relationship with an almost normal young man. Anthony was vaguely on the scene for several months as a sort-of boyfriend, but things eventually fizzled out.

That year Lauren made me a beautiful Mother's Day card. It felt like the first time she had really wanted to do that. And although our relationship was still a long way from the sort idealized by Mother's Day, it was, I felt, improving and strengthening quite a lot now, three years down the line.

10

Finding Lara

Things with Lauren were definitely more stable and settled, but one sunny afternoon in June a police officer cycling along the bottom of our road glanced up and saw Lauren and a friend sitting on a wall in our front garden smoking. There being no matters of crime or disorder in Oxford for him to bother himself with, he turned round and came up to our house, into our garden, snatched the cigarettes from Lauren and her friend, leaned over our garden wall and threw them in our neighbour's bin. I heard Lauren shouting for me and went out. He was standing looking rather like Spiderman, with Lycra-clad legs planted far apart, arms akimbo, wraparound sunglasses and a cycle helmet. It was clear from his pose he was trying to intimidate or provoke. He was, he informed me, enforcing a new act of Parliament that made it a criminal offence for anyone under sixteen to smoke.

'The prime minister has personally asked all police officers to be vigilant. He feels strongly about smoking.'

Fortunately I was fairly clued up on the piece of legislation to which he was referring. 'It's an offence for anyone under sixteen to smoke . . . in public,' I corrected. 'You are on private property, and so is Lauren. I may not like her smoking, but she is doing no one but herself any harm here, and at least she is not in Bonn Square cadging cigarettes off drug addicts. If you're in touch with Mr Blair, perhaps you could tell him that . . .'

But he had already jumped on his bike and was pedalling off to right more wrongs.

Lauren said, 'He's horrible. He's always looking for me to have a go at me.'

I was pleased I had been there to back her up this time.

Two days later the long arm of the law overreached itself again. Lauren and two girlfriends had, with permission, got the train to Reading to go shopping. It was, I knew, not without risk, but I was anxious to allow and encourage some freedoms and independence to show that normal life for a teenage girl didn't mean being tied to apron strings. But, perhaps inevitably, it did not go to plan. One of the girls had friends in Reading, the friends had lager, and they all went off to a park to drink it, arriving back at Reading Station at 9 p.m., not 4 p.m. as agreed. Three slightly inebriated young girls drew the attention of some police at the station, who questioned them and ran their names through the computer. Lauren rang me, very distressed, saying the police officer was insisting she had an ASBO and was in breach of it. The officer came on the phone and I tried to explain that she didn't have an ASBO, rather an approved behavioural contract, which was a voluntary agreement. The officer refused to listen and arrested and handcuffed Lauren. By the time the mistake was realized and the girls were released, the last train to Oxford had gone. The three girls were stranded in Reading. One of the other mothers went to get them and bring them home.

These two incidents of police overreaction would have

been annoying enough in any situation, but the timing, just as Lauren was beginning to calm down a bit and take more interest in ordinary teenage things, was catastrophic. I made formal complaints about both incidents and we received apologies, but the damage was done. Despite these apologies, Lauren decided the police were vindictive and arbitrary and out to get her. From that day on they became 'the fucking pigs'.

Whether related or not to the incidents with the police, Lauren started disappearing again, sometimes with Jennifer but just as often on her own. Most of this was local, as she would eventually stagger home drugged and drunk at about 3 a.m. or ring me from Cowley Road or one of Oxford's housing estates begging me to go and get her. However, there was a new and disconcerting phenomenon around this time: phone calls from heavily accented, foreign-sounding men in the early hours asking for her by name. I would explain that she was a thirteen-year-old girl and they would usually just hang up.

The name these men asked for was Lara. Lauren had adopted the name Lara when communicating with Jennifer, who would call herself Asianna. Later on they informed me that these were their street names and that everyone had to have a street name. Indeed, most of their circle did, names often influenced by black rap culture. Not all their circle, though, chose street names to add a touch of the exotic to their lives; one young boy actually called Fernando adopted the street name of Kevin.

The influence of rap or hip-hop or whatever it was on their lives was profound. Anything to do with black rap or music was venerated; the girls became fiercely anti-white culture and anti-feminist. White people were all deemed to be racist, and women, including themselves, merely bitches. Bizarrely, Jennifer even started to speak with a Jamaican accent. Their homes became their 'yards', days were spent 'chillin', and everyone was greeted with 'Yo, bro' or 'Respect, man.' The adult world apparently spent all its time 'dissing' them, and in return they had 'beef' with the adults and any authority figure. Every spoken sentence seemed to end with 'innit?' It might have all been a bit of fun, and of course every generation has to have its own slang, but the problem with this language was that it went hand in hand with profoundly disturbing misogyny, racism, drugs and the sexual exploitation of young women.

Despite Lara being Lauren's street name and therefore used in a lot of dodgy contexts, like men ringing her in the early hours of the morning, she spoke of it as a symbol of hope and change. Lara was the person she wanted to become – responsible, caring, lovable. She thought Lauren was none of those things: Lauren was a slag and worthless; Lauren was the unhappy past; Lara would be the future. She said she wanted me to call her Lara from now on. It took a little while, but I was determined not to slip up, given the associations the name Lara had.

Lara and I went down to Brighton one weekend for a large gathering at the marina to celebrate my friend Mary's birthday. There were several young children there, accompanied by parents trying to juggle feeding a baby, amusing a toddler and joining in adult conversation all at the same time. We had a large table in the corner of the restaurant and Lara started to organize a space between the table and the window into which the small children could escape the irritating rigours of sitting at a table. She collected up toys and colouring books, and set up a crèche. She almost single-handedly kept five toddlers amused for a couple of hours and they loved her. So did the parents.

On the way home, she said, 'I'd love to work with small children. I think I'm good at it. That's what Lara's going to be like.'

I had never heard her express any ambition for herself before. Could things really be changing at last?

But for the next few weeks it was back to the streets of London. No sooner did I get her home than she was gone again. Notting Hill, Leicester Square, Elephant and Castle, Peckham and numerous times places in Oxford. More and more these trips seemed to be without Jennifer.

About this time there was a trial of a gang of men who had kidnapped and tortured two girls in Reading and then brutally murdered one of them and severely injured the other in an attempt to murder her too. The Mary-Ann Leneghan case was all over the media. The girls were sixteen and nineteen, so a few years older than Jennifer and Lara, but there were many parallels, so I tried to talk to Lara about the case and show her the sorts of risks she was running. Lara responded that it was entirely different: the girls in Reading had got involved with a dangerous gang; she was only hanging around or going places with friends. Just because I didn't think they were nice didn't make them bad or dangerous; she didn't like a lot of my friends, come to think of it. And to emphasize her annoyance at my attempt to 'diss' her friends, she stormed out of the house, pushing her elbow through an antique stained-glass panel in the front door on the way out.

By the end of the summer term 2006, PRUIS had upped their game a bit and Lara was now supposed to be getting between two and four hours of education a day, three or four days a week. It wasn't enough, and some sessions were cancelled at short notice, but it was a lot better than it had been. Unfortunately Tier 4, the therapeutic part of the action plan, had failed to materialize, despite the fact that this was the key part of Lara's statement of special educational needs. Most of the support from education was peripatetic, some taking place at our house rather than in a school setting, as neither PRUIS nor Lara herself wanted her to be involved with other young people. This saddened me, as Lara had lost the skill of socializing with her peers, and the longer she was kept away from them, the harder it was going to get. The big plus side of this was that her key worker at PRUIS was a lovely young woman called Libby, who, in a very quiet, gentle way, developed a greater rapport with Lara than anyone else before her. Lara thought she was great.

Because Libby was going to be at the next case review meeting, Lara decided to come. She was always invited but usually declined. She coped amazingly well, holding her own with a group of nine adults all discussing her and her behaviour, something that wouldn't be much fun for anyone. When asked how things were going for her, she talked about her worries and problems concerning her birth family. Her half-brother, Jayden, had recently been jailed for his part in a child abduction, although we never knew the full details; Kirsten had been arrested for making threatening phone calls and trying to extract money with menaces; Terri, who had had her baby taken into care, was now in prison for drug offences; her birth father, who had beaten up his girlfriend, had just been released from prison and was hanging around with her sister, although he was only supposed to see her under strict supervision. Lara's meltdown seemed to be mirroring what was going on in her birth family. She feigned contempt and disinterest, but she was horrified and devastated by it all. It confirmed her view that somehow she was rotten, doomed by her genes, irredeemably different to the sort of person she thought should be my daughter. She had to reject me; she couldn't live in these two very different realities. Just as she'd told the Attach meeting back in January, Lara said that she hated them all but still worried about them and felt she ought to be able to help them.

At the meeting, we were informed that there might now be a place for Lara on a new programme being piloted by the Child and Adolescent Mental Health Service in Oxford. Known as dialectical behavioural therapy, or DBT for short, this was a therapeutic treatment programme designed to help girls and young women with intense and overwhelming emotional problems learn how to understand, control and ultimately change their feelings. It sounded ideal for Lara. She went along to meet the people running the programme and was offered a place, but she said she didn't want to change how she felt and declined the treatment. I was extremely disappointed because I knew about the programme and knew that if only she would engage, it would probably be very helpful for her.

Lara was extremely agitated after the DBT meeting, saying she wasn't a nutter and didn't need help. I think the real reason for her refusing the place was because she knew she would be around a lot of other very chaotic girls and she was finding it harder and harder to deal with people her own age. She disappeared that night and was gone for three days.

There was an extra layer of anxiety to this particular disappearance because we were about to go on holiday. We were going to Michael and Victoria's house in the South of France with Gerry, Hannah and Lottie, and my frail, elderly mother.

If we didn't make it, we would be disappointing a lot of other people, especially my mother. Lara rang me from London thirty-six hours before we were due to leave. I drove and picked her up from Paddington. We came home and I put her back together – bath, clean clothes, food and sleep over twenty-four hours. I packed our holiday suitcases while she slept, virtually carried her into the car and off we went.

We had glorious weather in France and Lara and her cousins spent most of the time in the pool. In the evenings we either sat outside looking at the stars and listening to the cicadas or inside playing Boggle, a favourite holiday game. One evening we all got out sketchpads and drew each other. Hannah, an art student, did a wonderful drawing of Lara, a pencil sketch of a fresh-faced young girl curled up in an armchair by the fire.

Sadly, my mother did not really enjoy the holiday. Despite being surrounded by all her family, she became very agitated and distressed. She was sleeping in a downstairs bedroom and I realized she was getting up at night and wandering around in the dark, not quite sure where she was. I decided I would have to sleep downstairs too to keep an eye on her and made up a bed on one of the sofas in the living room. Lara wouldn't hear of me doing that on my own, so made up a bed for herself on the other sofa. She and I shared the nights, waking up when my mother got out of bed, calming her down and settling her again. Lara, just turned fourteen, was magnificent with her, calm but firm and infinitely patient. She could rise to any occasion when someone else was in need. If only she could turn some of that care and concern on herself. Lara even pushed my mother's wheelchair through passport control and immigration at Bristol Airport.

Once we got my mother settled back in her home, she immediately started to relax. We stayed another night with her, we did a food shop, and Lara filled her fridge and put flowers in a vase. We left with heavy hearts and on the way home discussed whether Granny should come and live with us.

'I would love that,' Lara said. 'I could look after her while you're at work.'

The next day we were both in a post-holiday slump and feeling very flat and worried about my mother. Lara's phone started ringing early in the afternoon, and as I had resolved on holiday to renew my efforts to prevent her going out, I rushed around the house locking all the doors and windows and hiding keys in the pan cupboard.

Lara stormed into the kitchen. 'Why are all the doors locked?' she demanded. 'I'm going out to meet some friends.'

'Can we have a talk about this?' I asked. 'Why do you need to go out today? We are only just back from holiday.'

'It's none of your business. I have to go out, that's all, and you can't stop me.'

'Well, before you go, can we just talk about where you are going and when you are going to be back?'

Pow! She slapped my face, pushed past me and stormed upstairs. There were lots of bangs and thuds, which I assumed was her throwing things around her room.

After a few minutes she came running down the stairs in tears, sobbing and shouting, 'Now look what you made me do.' Her right arm was bleeding. She had stamped on a new mirror I had bought her for her room and cut her arm. The cuts were not very deep, so I cleaned them up and bandaged them and she calmed down. She then got the shakes, so I sat and held her. I asked her what she would do if she were a mother trying to keep her daughter safe.

She looked at me and said, 'There's nothing you can do. No one can – they're stronger than everything.'

'Who are stronger than everything?'

'No one. Er, I just meant my feelings.'

Who were these people, and how could they have such a hold over her?

I had kept her in that night, at some cost to both of us, but the next few weeks were awful. Her mood swings were more extreme and more frequent than ever. Her self-care was terrible; she wouldn't wash and hardly ate. She took to dressing in children's clothes out of a bin bag of clothes destined for a charity shop. One night she went out in stiletto heels someone had given her and a tunic that said, 'Aged 7–8 years', on the label. She was spending a lot of time with Charley, the young heroin addict I had talked to several times on the streets. I was in two minds how I felt about that. On the one hand, I knew that Charley was not wholly irresponsible and had shown some concern about Lara's youth and vulnerability, but on the other she was still a heroin addict living on the streets, and that was not what I wanted for Lara. When she was not with Charley, she was, on three occasions, in London, with a very dodgy-sounding guy called Marcus. Lara was vague about who he was, but from what she did say, he sounded like a drug dealer.

About this time our neighbourhood was becoming very concerned about the dramatic increase in drug dealing in the area, concern that accelerated rapidly after a shooting and stabbing on our recreation ground in broad daylight, fifty yards from both the local nursery and primary school. We were half a mile

from the city centre, on the river, with the towpath running in
either direction, open land to the south and west, and myriad
footpaths. It was, the police told us, an ideal drug-dealing area
because it was hard to patrol and there were so many ways of
escaping on foot. In fact there were very few patrols and the
dealers operated fairly openly even in daylight hours.

One figure was particularly memorable. Tall and thin and
wearing a hooded coat even on the hottest day, he was known
as Egyptian Mo. The likes of him and his desperate customers
were turning a wonderful green space, with recreation ground,
playing fields and nature park, into a bit of a no-go area. Two
dogs had become critically ill after eating human excrement
containing heroin; another trod on a needle and nearly died.
The detritus of drug and alcohol addiction – needles, crack
pipes, empty bottles of cheap cider – as well as excrement and
even two drug-related deaths were leading parents not to want
children to play out, and even adult dog walkers preferred not
to walk alone.

We set up a group of local residents to try and reclaim the
area. We organized working parties to clean up the rubbish,
and we met with police to discuss ways to reduce the drug dealing. The police said there was little they could do unless they
could catch dealers red-handed, so we decided to monitor activity and feed it back.

It appeared that five thirty in the afternoon opposite the
church on a footpath that led through to the nursery and school
were the favourite time and place. We decided to make a point
of walking the dogs at about that time and would ring the police
if anything was going on. We also hoped that if residents were
clearly visible out and about, and alert to what was happen-

ing, it might put the dealers off, especially if we were carrying cameras.

On one occasion Egyptian Mo was out and we walked slowly past him. I wanted to get a better idea of what he looked like under the hood so I could describe him properly to the police. As I walked by, I turned to face him and met a look of pure evil that made my blood run cold. His face was staring, mask-like and menacing.

One evening Lara was sitting in the garden with two friends discussing mutual acquaintances. There was much hilarity about who was a 'minger' and who was 'well fit' before Lara said something and the tone turned much more sombre.

'OMG, he is the scariest person I've ever seen,' said one of the girls.

'Who is?' asked the other friend.

'Egyptian Mo,' replied the first.

OMG, Lara knows Egyptian Mo.

It was slowly dawning on me that Lara knew an awful lot of the dodgiest people in Oxford. Despite living in the same house, we now inhabited two different worlds. One Saturday morning we walked into town together, about half a mile up one of the main roads into the city centre. As I walked, I smiled at a neighbour off to do his shift in the Oxfam bookshop, nodded at the vicar's wife, waved at a friend in her art gallery window and stopped to admire the new baby of a woman with whom I was on a local charity committee.

Lara, no more than a foot away from me, was walking through a completely different Oxford. A man looking like an elderly rapper in a baby-blue tracksuit gestured at her from across the street, tapping his ear with his fist. She then yelled a greeting to two scruffy young men coming out of the police station, a car with blacked-out windows hooted at her, and a young Asian man muttered something that sounded quite threatening as he walked by. I turned to remonstrate with him, but Lara said, 'Please, Mum, I beg you, don't.'

We now lived in parallel universes and knew nothing of each other's worlds.

About the only reality we shared, although Lara tried hard to deny their existence, was our dysfunctional relationship with social services and education, or Children, Young People and Families, as the combined service had now been rebranded. We hadn't had any contact with them for weeks, but in the middle of the summer holidays they contacted me and commanded us to go and see them. We turned up, only to be told that, in future as well as informing the police when Lara went missing, I should also inform them. I was then instructed that I should tell them if Lara was violent to me. There was still nothing they could do for us, but this information must be given for their records. The tone of the meeting and the letter that followed was one of slight menace.

Of course this sent Lara into a complete spin. She ran off as we left the meeting and at half past one the next morning the police rang to say she had been arrested along with several other young people on suspicion of criminal damage. She was too drunk to be interviewed, so she would be locked up until the morning. I went up to the police station at 8 a.m., as asked, and was there for nearly eight hours. Eventually Lara was bailed. It was alleged that she and a gang of feral children she sometimes hung around with had smashed windows in Brasenose and University colleges. It was all on CCTV. Kevin, aka Fernando, apparently always carried an emergency glass-breaking hammer, stolen from a train carriage, which they'd used to break the panes of ancient glass in the colleges. This wasn't Lara's normal style. She might break windows at home either out of anger or in an attempt to escape, but I had never known her go out and commit acts of wanton vandalism. I was appalled and told her so in no uncertain terms.

Lara, on the other hand, feigned amusement and appeared to regard the whole business of being arrested and locked up as a trifling irritation. She was bailed with conditions, including a 9.30 p.m. curfew. It was nearly 5 p.m. when we got home and we hadn't eaten all day, so I cooked some food and then said I needed an early night. I reminded her of her curfew and said I would report her immediately if she attempted to leave the house. I remembered it was bin day the next day and she offered to put the bins out on the pavement, saying she was feeling bad and wanted to make things up to me. She needed the keys to put out the rubbish, and I decided she wasn't likely to try and run off that night, so I let her have them and she brought them back to me almost immediately. She said she had put out the bins and was going to watch TV for a bit and then go to bed. And then I twigged and went downstairs. She hadn't put the bins out at all, just used the keys to unlock the basement door. She was obviously planning to go out later despite everything.

I locked the doors and took the keys up to bed with me. I did wonder if I would come downstairs the next day to discover that Lara had smashed a window to get out, but she hadn't. She did go out the next night and didn't make her curfew, so I phoned the police and reported her missing and in breach of her bail conditions. Eventually the bail was cancelled and the charges dropped and she was referred to the Youth Offending Team, run by the local council to help young people in trouble with the law, for an assessment of her behaviour and needs, but that was never carried out and in the end the YOT closed her case without even meeting her.

Despite looking forward to education starting again in the autumn, the reality seemed to disappoint Lara. It still was very little, just a few hours three or four days a week. She went most days without grumbling and really enjoyed Libby's company, but always came back in a foul mood, angry and frustrated. She would then try to engineer a fight by making demands that she knew I would refuse. At the first refusal she would become verbally very abusive, and then if I continued to refuse to buy her cigarettes, alcohol or new clothes, she would become violent. Her first target would be me; she would kick me, slap me, bend my fingers back and sometimes hold a knife or scissors to my throat. Next, as that didn't work, she would seek out my most treasured possessions to destroy: vases, ornaments, pictures. She seemed to know instinctively what I valued most. She would sometimes finish by turning the violence against herself, cutting her arms with whatever she had broken earlier. The cutting, if she reached that point, seemed to act as a safety valve, and although she would be upset at what she had done to herself, she would always calm down afterwards. If the violence didn't get to the self-harming stage, she would burst out of the house and disappear.

I came to realize that Lara's self-harming really did help to relieve some of her turmoil and tension, and although it used to terrify me when she did it, the damage was always super-ficial. At least when she hurt herself physically, I could see the wounds. When she was out on the streets, I had no idea what was happening to her. I could put antiseptic and bandages on her wounds, but her emotional damage was impossible to heal.

I was becoming quite frightened of Lara at times. The finger bending was absolutely excruciating, and when she had a knife at my throat, I didn't know where she would stop. I held off tell-ing the police or social services about her violence, as I knew their response would just be punitive and therefore unhelp-ful. I tried not to let Lara know I was becoming scared of her, and above all I never gave in to the violence. I made it clear she would only get rewards if she earned them.

But I knew I couldn't let it continue, so I mentioned the esca-lating violence at a meeting we had with the Attach Team. I had assumed that because this was a therapeutic service, anything we said would be confidential, but they reported what I had said to social services. I had valued the support and wisdom from the Attach Team and felt they were the only service that under-stood the issues we were facing and had the tools to help us, but I couldn't risk matters we discussed being fed back to social workers, so very reluctantly I had to terminate our involvement with them. What I needed was emotional and practical advice without the threat of action from social services or the police. I knew they thought they were just looking out for me, but the services they reported back to had only damaged our situation. It was a bleak moment when I felt even the Attach Team had let us down.

Meanwhile Kirsten was almost in a worse state than Lara.

Her children's home seemed to have given up on her and allowed her to do just what she pleased. She wasn't in any form of education, was regularly drunk and often out on the streets all night. She turned to us more and more, seemingly for a sense of belonging and family. She was constantly on the phone pleading for money or to come and visit, or verbally abusing Lara if we said no. We saw her fairly regularly for official contact visits, but she wanted more and more of Lara's time.

Lara, unsurprisingly, had very confused feelings about Kirsten. One day she was pleading with me for Kirsten to come and live with us, the next she never wanted to see her again. They were so close in age and had been through so much together, but their relationship had been severely damaged by all the abuse and disruptions they had experienced. It seemed their relationship was broken and yet codependent; it was tragic.

One evening in August Lara got a call from Kirsten saying she was on a train coming down from Stoke to see us and would be arriving in Oxford at about 10.30 p.m. I couldn't allow her to visit right then. Lara was very low and angry, and there was no way she would cope with having Kirsten around. Also Kirsten had to realize that unplanned visits were not on. I phoned the children's home where she was living and asked them to come and get her. The night staff said they couldn't leave and there was no duty manager they could contact. I felt I really only had one choice in that situation, so I drove to the station with Lara; we picked up Kirsten and took her straight back to Stoke-on-Trent, arriving at 2 a.m. The girls bickered and fought for the whole journey. Lara and I then turned round and headed back to Oxford, stopping for a couple of hours in a service station to snatch a bit of sleep.

'I'm glad Kirsten didn't come to the house, Mum,' Lara said from where she was curled up on the back seat.

But Kirsten had sown a seed in Lara's mind. Most of the way back to Stoke she had been taunting Lara with comments about her seeing their father a lot now he was out of prison. Kirsten said that he was good fun and took her drinking to his friends' houses. Lara was clearly jealous and told me she wanted to see him. I knew he wasn't a safe person to be around; indeed, he was a very violent man, especially to women, particularly of course to Terri, but also to other girlfriends and, once, a female police officer. Kirsten still did see him officially from time to time when he wasn't in prison, but these meetings were heavily supervised, in an open public space, and she was always accompanied by two members of staff, one of whom had to be a man in case her father got violent. There had been no agreement that Lara would have any further contact with him after she was adopted, and she had never before requested it. Now, when she mentioned it, I said no.

'When you're sixteen, if you still want to see him, I'll support you, but not before,' I added.

I should have known better. Lara never took 'no' for an answer. Two days later she stole some money and my debit card from my handbag, went to a cash machine, withdrew £100 and disappeared to Stoke. And this was after a really happy day when Lara had been praised at PRUIS and I had bought her a new mobile phone as a reward for coping so well with Kirsten and progressing with her education programme. I was beginning to see a pattern: if things had been going really well, especially if she had been praised or complimented, she then had to go and spoil everything. It was as though she couldn't cope with being seen as good.

Lara rang me a few times that night saying how horrible and scary her dad was and how she wished she hadn't gone to visit him. She was back at 7 a.m., but I knew there wasn't a train from Stoke that would have got her to Oxford that early, despite her insistence that there had been. Someone must have driven her. Who?

The Stoke social worker was very keen that the girls should spend time together officially and offered to rent a country cottage for Kirsten, two carers, Lara and me for a weekend. Lara said, 'OK, as long as you come as well, Mum.' I agreed and a date was set.

Two weeks of chaotic behaviour ensued. Lara was not missing for long, and certainly not overnight, but she kept going out and getting very drunk and picking fights.

One night she came home very distressed.

'Mum, I think I've just killed someone.'

'Oh my God, what happened?'

She started screaming and sobbing.

She allowed me to hold her and eventually calmed down enough for me to be able to talk to her.

'What makes you think that? Where were you? Who was this?'

'I don't know. I think I was in town. I think it was a woman.'

'Did you know her? Why do you think you killed her?'

'I don't know . . . It might have been me that got killed.' She started screaming again.

'But I promise you you're alive. You are here at home with me.'

In the end I decided that it was most unlikely and tried to reassure her. In the morning she didn't even remember saying it.

Driving home from work the next day, I suddenly felt most peculiar, as though I was going to pass out. My arms and legs went numb. I was frightened and pulled over to the side of the road. After a bit I began to feel slightly better, enough to drive very carefully home. When I got there, Lara had several friends in the house and was complaining there were no biscuits. I decided to make some chocolate-chip cookies. It was a recipe I knew well and I didn't need to look in a cookery book, but I found I couldn't work out how to weigh the ingredients or even what ingredients to use. I was standing at the kitchen counter feeling very befuddled when Jean popped round, as she often did when she got back from work.

'My God, what's happened to you? You look terrible,' she exclaimed on taking one look at me.

I explained and she said, 'I think you may have had a small stroke – your face is lopsided.'

She whisked me off to the hospital, leaving Lara and her friends still bemoaning the lack of biscuits.

At hospital, they did all sorts of tests and ruled out a stroke but said it might have been a transient ischaemic attack, sometimes called a mini-stroke. I was given an outpatient appointment for a CT scan and to see a neurologist. On the way home, we stopped to buy fish and chips for everyone as it was way past normal suppertime and I didn't want to have to cook. Lara and her friends were playing pool when we got back, and Jean explained what the hospital had said. Lara went berserk.

'You're not ill – you look fine to me. If you're ill, why did the hospital let you come home? You're just trying to scare me. You're so selfish. It's so unfair. How dare you? There's nothing wrong with you, is there? Admit it!'

Her friends looked totally shocked, and I was a bit non-plussed by the level of her vitriol, but I assumed it was because she was frightened and scared. She had never really seen me ill or vulnerable and it must have been very disconcerting.

I had been told not to drive until I had seen the neurologist and therefore the next day I had to break it to Lara that we wouldn't be going on the weekend we had planned with Kirsten, as there was no public transport we could use to get within twenty miles of the place in the middle of Wales. She went through the motions of being angry and upset, but in fact I think she was very relieved not to be going.

In the end all the scans and tests revealed nothing, so I was given the all-clear and told I could drive again. Thank God, because I had been quite frightened. A few days later I had to go out in the evening to a trustees' meeting for a charity of which I was part-time chief executive. I arranged for Lara to spend the evening with a friend of mine and drove off to the meeting. At 8 p.m., in the middle of the meeting, I had a phone call from a neighbour saying that there was a gang of youths smashing our front railings and trying to break into the house. I drove home in a panic. In twenty-seven years as a chief executive of three different charities I had not once missed even part of a trustees' meeting and I hated doing it, but I needed to get home. I picked Lara up en route and told her what the neighbour had told me.

'Martin says there is a gang outside our house, smashing things and trying to break in.'

'Oh my God, I'm going to kill them. I'll absolutely kill them,' she exploded.

'Do you know who they are?'

'Probably.'

Five young men in hoodies were outside our house as we turned into the street, but they ran off when they saw us. Lara picked up one of the broken pieces of iron railing and said she was going after them. I took the railing from her, but she ran up the street anyway. She returned a few minutes later.

'I know who's done this. I'm going to kill him,' she said, grabbing a kitchen knife.

'You are doing no such thing. Don't be a fool. What good would that do?' I got the knife off her and she ran out. I called the police non-emergency number to report the damage.

I couldn't believe it when a few minutes later Lara returned with the gang, laughing and joking, and they all turned on me. One of the young men picked up a piece of railing and threatened me with it. He didn't say anything, just made a lot of menacing noises and gestures. This time I called 999. That had no effect on any of them and they all, including Lara, stood in the street jeering at me and threatening to hurt me until a police car pulled into the street and they ran off. The police caught Lara and brought her home. She calmed down and told the police who the young men were. I realized that I knew most of them at least by reputation. They were a motley crew of tearaways from local families. As children, they had been responsible for many acts of minor vandalism and theft in the neighbourhood; now, as young adults, their interests had, judging by reports in the local paper, turned to minor drug dealing and car theft, although they had obviously retained an interest in vandalism.

It was a totally bizarre incident and very frightening. I have no idea why the gang targeted our house or threatened me, or why Lara turned on me the way she did. I can only think with Lara it was just the adrenalin. She was such an adrenalin junkie; once it kicked in, she lost all control of her reactions and didn't have a sense of guilt.

I was becoming very stressed and exhausted by this time, and our home being attacked really got me down. Being attacked within it by Lara was something I had got used to, but being attacked from outside by strangers was something else. I felt under siege. I didn't know whether my priority was to try and keep Lara in or her awful associates out. I wasn't sleeping, and life felt overwhelming at times. I went to see our very kind and empathic GP. She prescribed me an antidepressant, which was also supposed to help reduce stress and tackle insomnia. That evening I rang a friend and got the name of a counsellor she had seen after her father had died suddenly. I was beginning to feel I needed extra help to try and stay sane.

Little did I know that life was about to get even more difficult.

11

Sam the Rapist

———————

Although the weekend away with Kirsten didn't happen, the girls did see each other eventually. We arranged to meet up in the Birmingham Bullring Shopping Centre. We could get there easily on the train from Oxford, and it was a relatively short run down the M6 for Kirsten and a carer. It started off reasonably well. We did a bit of shopping, had some lunch and then the girls wanted a cigarette, so we all went outside. Out of nowhere, a gang of young men descended on Lara and Kirsten, and started chatting them up. The carer and I stayed fairly close but didn't interfere; they were, after all, fourteen and fifteen, and had to be allowed some latitude. The girls kept looking over at us and very gradually edging further away. Every time they did, the carer and I moved a bit closer to them again, and then, all of a sudden, the girls and the young men just took to their feet and ran off into the throng. We tried to follow, but they had evaporated into the Saturday-afternoon crowds. I'm not sure whether it was worry and panic or frustration and anger that I was feeling more strongly as we were led this merry dance.

After about half an hour we found the girls, or rather heard them. They were having a fight, and Lara had hurt Kirsten.

We separated them, but they ran back into the Bullring and started screaming abuse at each other again. Within seconds four large security men descended on them. They were really fierce, much more so than police officers usually are, and the girls stopped in their tracks. They couldn't believe it when they were evicted from the Bullring: nobody in authority had ever really stood up to them like that before. They were allowed no explanations or justifications; it was just 'Get out or we will have you arrested.' It was magnificent; oh, to be able to have that power. We went our separate ways home, and Lara stayed in that night.

Sadly she didn't stay in the next night and her phone was off. I reported her missing at about 11 p.m. and decided to go to bed, the house phone and my mobile on the pillow beside me. The pills prescribed by our doctor were beginning to have an effect and I was certainly sleeping better and managing to get some sleep even when Lara was out.

At about 5 a.m. I was woken by the phone. 'M-Mumm, M-Muuum, M-Mum.' It was Lara. She was sobbing hysterically. I had never heard her quite so distraught.

'Mum, I've been raped. Ohhh . . . Mum, please come. He wanted to kill me. I'm so scared.'

'Where are you?'

'One of the hotels on Iffley Road. I think it's the Nanford.'

'Who's with you? Whose phone is this?'

'It's the police's. They're with me.'

She's safe right now, I told myself, trying to force my heart to slow down so I could focus. I pulled on some clothes and got into the car. Iffley Road is a very long road, a mixture of mainly Victorian buildings, mostly residential, some run-down houses in multiple occupation, a lot of student accommodation and many hotels and B&Bs. I wasn't quite sure which hotel Lara meant and at first went to the wrong bit of the road. I turned round and drove back towards the city centre. There was going to be nowhere to park as I got closer to the city centre, so I parked the car and got out and ran. I could see a police car about 500 yards down the road, by the Nanford Guest House, which was from the outside a quite attractive white stucco building with wrought-iron balconies.

The front door was open, and a very scruffy man was walking through the hall with packets of breakfast cereal. There was a room with tables laid for breakfast on my right.

'My daughter's been attacked,' I said breathlessly. 'She's somewhere in here with the police, I think. Is this the right place? Do you know?'

He didn't say anything, just pointed down a short flight of stairs. There, halfway down the stairs on the left, in a large cupboard full of catering tins of marmalade and large packs of loo roll, was Lara. She was wearing nothing, but had a small, filthy hand towel wrapped round her. She was sobbing uncontrollably. There was a young female police officer with her. I put my arms around her and, as she was shivering, went to take my coat off and put it on her. The police officer asked me not to, explaining that Lara had agreed to be forensically examined, which meant we had to be careful not to contaminate evidence. The officer was waiting for colleagues to arrive and then they would take Lara to a special house. I said that, sadly, we already knew about these police rape suites.

As Lara had calmed down a bit, I asked her what had happened. She said she had been out with a friend and he had got drunk, brought her to the hotel and raped her. She started crying again.

'Oh, Mum, I thought he was going to kill me. He said he was. He tried to strangle me. He tried to drown me in the shower. Oh, Mum, I was so scared he would do it.'

I couldn't take in what had happened; I just felt numb.

'But who? Who is this person? What were you doing here in this dump?'

Several more police officers now appeared and said they were ready to take us off. The young female police officer was lovely with Lara, so I decided to let them leave in the police van without me and I would follow in our car. It was frosty outside, so I asked again about Lara being able to wear something more than the skimpy towel, but again they were worried about the evidence. They said the van was right outside and it was nice and warm.

This rape suite was in a house on a roundabout on the Oxford ring road. When we got there, it was nearly 7 a.m. and the morning rush hour was starting up. The road was quite busy and Lara, dressed only in a tiny towel, had to walk fifty yards up the road from the car park to the house, her bare feet crunching in the frost.

We were shown into a lounge. It wasn't very warm, but two police officers were already there and had turned on all the radiators. They said that as soon as they could set things up, they would take mouth swabs and bag up and label the towel so Lara could have a hot drink and put on a dressing gown. And then we just sat and sat. We attempted to look at some of the magazines on the coffee table, but they all just seemed so banal. The police kept popping in and out. They couldn't find a forensic medical examiner. There were none in Oxfordshire who were available. Eventually they found one in Northamptonshire, but he was thirty miles away and would have to travel over in the morning rush hour. We sat and sat some more. I tried to chat about inconsequential things, but Lara didn't want to join in, so we lapsed into silence.

Eventually someone arrived; we could hear a man's voice booming in the hallway. He and the police talked for ages outside the door of the lounge Lara and I were sitting in. After about fifteen minutes he came into the room. He nodded at Lara and then turned to me and said, 'Mother, I suppose.' And then to Lara, 'I'll call you up when I'm ready.'

Another fifteen minutes went by and we could hear all sorts of noises coming through the ceiling from the room above. It sounded like furniture was being moved. Finally a police officer came and got us. Lara had asked if I could be with her, so I went up too.

We went into a cold medical examination room with a trolley behind a curtain. There was a table laid out with instruments and specimen bottles. 'Sit there, Mother,' he said to me. He then asked Lara a couple of questions about what had happened before starting the examination. He didn't talk to her again but barked the occasional instruction to the two police officers in the room who were labelling and sealing the evidence.

Just as he began to examine Lara, his mobile phone went. Ravel's *Boléro* filled the room. I couldn't believe it when he actually answered it.

'Hello . . . Yes. I have booked us six three-day tickets, teeing off at noon on Monday.' He was organizing a golf tournament. I couldn't see Lara's reaction to this breathtaking insensitivity as she was behind the curtain, but she remained silent.

He said nothing to Lara, just returned to his examination. About five minutes later his phone rang again. The two police officers exchanged horrified glances.

'Hold on a moment. I need to get a better signal.' He came out from behind the curtain and moved towards the window. 'Well, I know that Bruce has booked a couple of caddies and hired a buggy. That should be enough.'

He returned to Lara. She was very distressed and I could hear her whimpering behind the curtain. I wanted to rush in and comfort her but knew that I would be stopped.

Eventually the examination was over, and with barely a word to any of us, the forensic medical examiner, handicap 28, left the house, still on the phone.

I looked at the police officers and said, 'That was appalling. He—'

'I know. Don't worry – we'll be making an official complaint, and we won't be using him again.' I wanted to press them further on that, but it would only have added to Lara's distress.

Next Lara was due to be interviewed on video.

'I'm afraid we have a problem,' said a new police officer who had just come on duty. 'There's a technical fault – we can't get the recording machine to work. We'll have to go down to Abingdon and use the other video suite down there. I'm so sorry.'

It was now 11 a.m. We drove to Abingdon. The video camera there was causing some problems too, but eventually they got it sorted out and Lara was interviewed.

We finally got home at 1 p.m., and Lara had a bath and

went to bed. I knew that whatever had happened that night was significantly different to the sorts of sexual assaults she had previously experienced because of the extent of her shock and distress. She was completely traumatized. She told me in horror that not only had he raped her several times, he had hit her, tried to drown her in the shower, urinated on her and attempted to strangle her.

Sam the Rapist, as she referred to him, was arrested at the scene and charged the same day. For the next two nights she insisted on sleeping in my bed. She didn't go out, but spent a lot of time on her mobile phone. Three days later, just as we were expecting the police to visit to ask more questions, she announced that she was going to drop her complaint.

'For God's sake, why? The police have got all the evidence they need and he's been charged. You've done the hard bit going through with the examination. Why drop it?'

'Because he has young children and he'll go to jail and I know what it's like having a dad in jail. I don't want to cause that to happen to anyone else.'

I tried to persuade her to go ahead, but she was adamant. When she told the police, I was a bit surprised at how little they did to dissuade her. I knew that my pushing her too much at that point would be counterproductive; she had made up her mind. At least, I comforted myself, they have the medical forensic evidence and she might in the future decide to press charges again.

Despite the awful rape, there were grounds for optimism at the end of 2006. Lara had not disappeared to London for several weeks, she had decided to take up the offer of the dialectical behavioural therapy to help her control her emotional swings, social services had closed her file, and I was getting support from the case review meetings with my struggles to get her some formal education. The December meeting had concluded that the lack of formal education and schoolwork might be con tributing to her very low self-esteem and that requests for some formal educational content in her sessions with the education outreach workers were to be made. Most importantly the multi-agency group continued to share the view that locking Lara up in a secure unit was not the answer and that what was needed was to try to find ways to support her and help me to keep going with her at home.

With her ability to turn things on their head, though, every-thing suddenly changed once more. We had gone to London for a Christmas tea with the same group of friends we had been with in Brighton earlier in the year. We went to a hotel in the old county hall on the South Bank by Westminster Bridge. Again Lara was fabulous with the small children and we had a lovely time, eating too much cake and exchanging presents.

I thought it would be nice to continue the Christmas atmos-phere by going to look at the Christmas lights on Oxford Street. We got the bus up Regent Street to Oxford Circus and then started to walk down Oxford Street. It was just ten days before Christmas and the pavements were packed with shop-pers. Christmas music was blaring out from almost every shop entrance, the lights were shimmering and flashing, and we were swept along in a vast human river. Lara had hold of my sleeve as we flowed past John Lewis, but by the time we got to Deben-hams, I realized my arm had gone slack. I turned. She wasn't there. I tried to stop, but that was impossible, so I moved sideways and through the eddies of people trying to get in and out of Debenhams. I found a calm bit up against the window and looked frantically up and down. She wasn't there. She had been swept away.

We had been heading down to Selfridges, and although I doubted she knew where that was, I thought she might have asked for directions, so I pressed on down there. I spent about an hour squeezing through from one Selfridges doorway to the next, looking and hoping. A couple of times I thought I saw her in the crowd, a flash of red coat on a young girl that then disappeared. I kept trying her phone, but it was dead.

Eventually the shops started to close and the crowds thin out. I walked from Oxford Circus to Marble Arch twice, stopping several times to ask police officers if they had come across a lost girl, but no one had. She had simply vanished. I rang Mary, my friend who had organized the tea party, on the off chance that Lara had headed back to her for some reason, but no. Mary agreed to be on standby if Lara did surface somewhere in London, and I tore myself away from Oxford Street and made my way back to Paddington for the train to Oxford.

Two days passed. Lara having disappeared from right under my nose like that was deeply disturbing. I was completely freaked out by it. How could it have happened? What was it about me that couldn't keep her safe even when she was with me, right beside me? I was terrified about what had happened to her and desperately ashamed of my failings as a parent. The police knew, and Mary knew, but I didn't tell any other friends or family she had disappeared from right under my nose. I thought we were having a happy day together, and it was almost Christmas. Why had she gone off like that?

The phone rang at 11 p.m. It was the police at Uxbridge in West London, miles away from Oxford Street. Was I the mother of a girl called Lara? The police wouldn't tell me much, but said they had been called to a 'domestic incident' between a man and a woman in Uxbridge following a 999 call from a neighbour. In a flat, which they described as a highly undesirable place, they had found Lara and taken her into protective police custody. I drove up to Uxbridge with John Rutter's Christmas music playing on the radio and sleet sliding down the windscreen.

And there she was, dirty, pale, thin and clearly very pleased to see me. We got in the car after she had been formally released into my care.

'Thanks for coming to get me. I wasn't sure you would this time. I thought you might've had enough. We're going to have a really good Christmas, I promise.'

'Lara, I *have* had enough, but I will always come for you whether you want me to or not. I will always be there for you. It's what parents do.'

'No it isn't.'

'Sorry, I mean it's what good parents do.'

The day before Christmas Eve we had a small Christmas party, an open house for friends and neighbours to drop in for a drink and some food. Lara had enjoyed helping me make mini-quiches, sausages on sticks and mince pies, and we had a great afternoon and evening. We had a lot of lovely friends and neighbours in Oxford and during the course of the party over thirty turned up. Lara was an excellent hostess, handing round food and topping up glasses. I was aware that she was having the occasional beer herself. I had bought a box of little bottles of 2.5 per cent French beer. I did let her drink a bit at home under supervision. I reasoned that she was fourteen and a half, and better to be drinking a beer or glass of wine at home than have her out God knows where, drinking vodka and taking drugs.

By the end of the evening there was just Lara, Jean and me left, sitting in front of the fire surrounded by party debris telling Christmas stories.

Suddenly Lara said, 'I want to say something important. Mum, I need you to know how much I love you. You've given me the life I always wanted. I now have everything I ever dreamed of. You stand by me no matter how awful I am. I love you very much, and I hate the way I hurt and abuse you.'

She was a bit tipsy, but she did really seem to mean it. To my astonishment, though, she then disappeared.

We were due to be going down to Wales the next morning, Christmas Eve. Would she really ruin Christmas?

At 11 a.m. on Christmas Eve she rang from a call box on the other side of Oxford. The car was already packed, so I just put the dogs in and drove over to pick her up and straight out of Oxford.

Christmas Eve on the M4. This year the CD player had Slade blaring out about a merry Christmas and everyone having fun. I mused as to whether travelling in hope was perhaps better than arriving.

12

It's Only Just Begun

In the end Christmas 2006 in Wales and New Year 2007 in Cornwall were happy and fairly uneventful and offered some rare relief from Lara's difficulties. However, all hell broke loose in January 2007, when Lara went into free fall.

She had made a new friend, a mother with three small children, who unfortunately lived round the corner from us. Venus was a young woman with attitude, big attitude. A heavy drug user herself with a drug-dealing boyfriend, she decided to make Lara her protégée and part-time babysitter to her children. She also plied her with alcohol and drugs. I spent most of January going to Venus's house to look for Lara. Often Venus would lie to me, saying she hadn't seen Lara, while knowing full well that Lara was lying paralytic on her sofa. On one occasion when I went round to try and extricate Lara, Venus came out into the street shouting and threatening me. Lara was captivated in every sense by this woman and her associates. She was persuaded to part with her PlayStation and mobile phone, and she stole from me to fund their drinking and drug taking. She even took food from our kitchen for the children, who she worried were not getting enough to eat.

One Saturday morning Lara, who had been at Venus's overnight, came home demanding money and cigarettes that she said she owed Venus. I refused. Lara was coming down off skunk, which always turned her psychotic, and she went crazy at my refusal. She grabbed my hand and did that excruciating thing of trying to break my fingers by pushing them back on themselves; she punched and slapped me and then tried to push me down the stairs. When hurting me failed to bring about my capitulation, she turned on the house, smashing a clay angel she had made me for Christmas and kicking in panels on my locked office door to try and get my purse. She then grabbed a piece of the broken angel and started hacking at her arms. Fortunately the pieces were too soft and crumbly to have much effect. Next she said she was going to take an overdose and went into the bathroom, coming out with two packets of pills. One was aspirin, which she handed to me saying I might need them. The other packet was multivitamins, which she tore open, putting a couple in her mouth.

'Yuck, they're disgusting. How many would I need to kill myself?'

'About two hundred.'

'What? I can't swallow two hundred. What else can I kill myself with?' she said, eyeing up the light flex over the top of the stairs. 'Show me how to hang myself,' she demanded.

Only the excruciating pain in my nearly broken fingers stopped me laughing. When she had first kicked off, I had been worried that she really meant to harm herself, but now I knew that she wasn't really serious.

'What else can I kill myself with?' she repeated, running up and down the stairs.

'God, what kind of a home is this,' she demanded at last, 'where there is nothing to kill yourself with?' I didn't see any flicker of a smile, but I was certain she was now sending herself and the situation up.

Lara then slept for nearly twenty-four hours. The next day we went to a car boot sale with some friends and out for lunch, and had a very nice, companionable day. On the way home, we stopped at B&Q. I wanted to quickly look at paint for the kitchen. Lara was just down the aisle from me and there, right under my nose, a middle-aged man, a B&Q employee, started chatting her up and asking for her phone number. She was about to let him have it when I intervened.

'For goodness' sake, she's fourteen years old. What are you doing? She is young enough to be your granddaughter, you dirty old man!' I shouted.

What was it that Lara gave off that drew all these perverts out of the woodwork, and where did they all come from? She wasn't even wearing make-up or provocatively dressed on that occasion and was clearly a young teenage girl. It was always the same wherever she went, even with me – men would appear from nowhere within seconds and try to entice her away, often from under my nose.

It wasn't always from right under my nose. On every occasion when we met up with Kirsten, which we were now doing every couple of months, men would appear and spirit the girls away, despite both the carer and me being there and often giving chase. After two further incidents when the girls had given us the slip and got into harm and trouble with men and drugs, once ending up in hospital and once in a police station, I had said that we should stop meeting in such public places as shopping centres, which were so hard to control.

The next time we were due to meet up was to be an early evening after I had taken Lara to see her two younger brothers with their adoptive mother in Stoke. So the carer and I arranged to meet in a country pub just outside Stoke at 6 p.m. A small country pub in the early evening with me and a carer – what could possibly go wrong?

It was dark and raining when we arrived at the small, whitewashed pub. We were the only people there apart from three businessmen in suits sitting in the bar having a drink. We went straight into the restaurant and ordered our food. While we were waiting for the food, the girls went and played on a pinball machine between the restaurant and the bar, about twenty feet from our table. The men started to play on a fruit machine nearby. I was watching carefully, but apart from the odd jocular exchange when someone scored on one of the games, the girls and the men didn't speak to each other. There could be nothing in common between two young teenage girls and three middle-aged businessmen. This was a good choice of venue and we could relax and enjoy the meal, while the girls could spend time with each other without the distraction of flirting with and competing over men.

The businessmen left, we ate and got the bill, and were preparing to leave. Kirsten and the carer had a twenty-minute drive back into Stoke, but Lara and I had 120 miles of motorway ahead of us. The girls went off to the ladies', while us adults sorted out the bill. They didn't return.

They weren't in the ladies', so I assumed they had gone

outside for a cigarette. When I went out to check, Lara and Kirsten were on the far side of the car park smoking and talking to the businessmen who had left the pub about forty minutes earlier. I called to the girls and they squealed in wild excitement and ran off towards the road. I ran after them down a pitch-dark country lane, only to be overtaken by a car. It pulled in by the girls, who jumped in. I could see that the car was driven by the men in suits. It roared off into the night.

The carer was dumbstruck, and even I was fairly amazed as to how the five of them had managed to pull that off. They had barely spoken to each other and I was certain it wasn't pre-arranged, as some of the other incidents with Kirsten and men had seemed to be. They must have communicated by some secret sign language. I rang the police and waited for them to arrive. The carer was due to go off duty, so she rang in the news to the children's home and then left. I was a bit surprised she was just going to go off and leave me to cope, but I suppose it was just a job to her. I waited for the police to arrive and then accompanied them back to the children's home. I gave the police all the details they wanted about Lara and, in the end, about Kirsten too, as the staff on duty knew next to nothing about her.

The staff were on a sleep-in shift, not a waking shift, and they wanted to go back to bed. They couldn't let me stay in the house unsupervised, so I had to leave. Where on earth could I go in Stoke at 10 p.m. where I could keep warm? I needed coffee to keep me awake, and a telephone box because my mobile battery was dying. I drove down the M6 a few miles to a service station. The services were virtually empty, just a few travellers zombie-like with tiredness wandering around looking for coffee and toilets.

At 3 a.m. I got a call from the children's home. Kirsten had rung them demanding a lift and had given a vague description of where she and Lara were. Unfortunately the carers couldn't leave the house and were not prepared to send a taxi. Could I go and look for them? Another children's home that couldn't organize the proverbial in a brewery.

Kirsten had said they were somewhere near the botanical gardens. I had never been to that part of the city before, but fortunately I still had in the car the Stoke A–Z that I had bought when I was spending time getting to know Lara almost exactly four years ago to the day. I drove up and off the motorway and found the botanical gardens. That was the only information I had, so I just drove up and down some of the local roads looking. Amazingly, after about twenty minutes, I saw them. They were both dancing up the white line in the middle of a main road, except that at 4 a.m. there wasn't much traffic, just me and a night bus that hooted at them to get out of the way. When I managed to persuade them to get in the car, they were as high as kites and told me they had been snorting cocaine with the men in their hotel. I took Kirsten back to the children's home and drove Lara, fast asleep, on the long journey back to Oxford.

Although there were many incidents like the one in B&Q or the restaurant near Stoke, where men would spontaneously appear from nowhere, I was now convinced that most of the time Lara was being sold by a pimp or pimps. There was no way she could be getting to all the places she was, which recently had included Leeds, Wolverhampton, Gloucester, Thamesmead and Kilburn, on her own initiative. She had little, if any, sense of geography, no transport of her own or the money to get to all these places. She would often reappear in clothes that were not hers: someone must have given them to her. And the drugs and alcohol? Who was supplying all those, and why?

I put it to her on several occasions that I thought she was being used and sold by someone. She was furious.

'Are you calling me a prostitute?'

'No, but I am calling you a very vulnerable young girl who is being used by men for their perverted pleasure.'

'So you're calling me stupid, then? I know what I'm doing. These are my friends. Just because you don't approve doesn't mean I don't like them. I need friends. I don't have any others. I'm not like you and other people. I'm different and always will be. There's nothing you can do about it. Just leave me alone. I wish you'd all just fuck off and leave me alone.'

The violence towards me increased dramatically during this time. It usually followed a calm and happy time, maybe as little as a few hours, but time when we had had fun together and felt closer. I was beginning to see a bit of a pattern. We would have fun doing things together, which usually involved going out with friends, going shopping, to the cinema and of course away on holiday, but somehow it was never enough for Lara. Her need for attention, gifts and entertainment was insatiable at times: the more she had, the more she would demand, with menaces if necessary. She was not by nature a greedy person, despite often going hungry for hours on end as a small child. I knew she was expressing something much more complex than the need for distraction, novelty and entertainment. More fundamentally, I knew she needed to fill a huge void inside herself. A space that should have held a sense of self, of worth, of being loved and loving in return was just a void to be filled with thrills, presents and treats.

In February 2007 the police asked for a special meeting of the case review panel and four police officers attended. They wanted to discuss the risks to me of Lara's violence. I suppose it was reassuring to know that they were concerned, but it struck me as so odd that everyone was concerned about the risks to me, a fifty-something professional woman who understood how the world worked and who could make decisions for herself, but was so unconcerned about the risks a skinny, vulnerable fourteen-year-old was facing. Nor did they ever show any real interest in who was subjecting her to the risks, despite my repeatedly saying there had to be a pimp behind it somewhere. They wanted to treat me as a vulnerable victim in need of protection, while Lara was merely a delinquent making informed choices to be violent and hang around with dangerous people.

Even the social workers in Children's Services tried to suggest that their concerns for my safety were reason enough for them to reopen the file on Lara. I told them I was quite capable of making judgements about my own safety and the only justification for reopening their file on Lara would be if they had something to offer that would help her. Help her, not judge or punish her.

The case review panel advised me to report all incidents of violence against me to the police and to get out of the house and call 999 as soon as she started to kick off. The next night I decided to put this advice to the test. It had snowed heavily the previous evening, and as happens in England when there are more than a couple of inches of snow that lasts more than a couple of hours, everything had shut down: no education, no transport and, for a while, no power. The perfect excuse for us to skive off and play in the snow with the dogs. The dogs turned into snowballs as the snow clung to their coats, and Lara made snow angels all over Christ Church meadow. We got soaked by snowballs as they melted all over us. The power was still off at home, so we went into town in search of some warmth and food and ended up in the cinema. We had a lovely, totally unplanned day.

And then out of nowhere, back at home, it all changed. Lara announced she needed cigarettes and demanded I go and get her some. I said no, she had had the quota I allowed her every day. She started threatening and pushing me, and then she slapped me on the side of the head. Mindful of the police advice, I walked out of the house, telling her that I would call 999 if she came after me or hit me. Of course she did come out, pushing me and hitting me as I walked away up the street. I slipped in the snow and fell over. I don't know quite why, but I didn't try and get up; I just lay there in the snow curled into a ball to protect my head and let her kick me. It seemed so much easier than trying to deal with the situation, trying to stop her, attempting to look into her eyes and make some contact, trying to fend off the consequences of her behaviour. I said and did nothing. Just let it happen. It's too hard to try and deal with all this.

Someone rang 999 and the police were there in seconds. Lara ran off, they gave chase and arrested her, and I just let them take her off to the police station in handcuffs, screaming for me and imploring me to help her. This time, though, they couldn't call on me to be the appropriate adult, because I was the victim. In a way, it was a relief to let someone else deal with it all for a bit.

I wasn't badly hurt, but I did have an enormous swelling and bruise on my arm that took weeks to clear and a few smaller ones on my legs. But my pride and self-confidence had taken a real hammering. I thought there was nothing I couldn't cope with as far as Lara's behaviour was concerned. How could I just lie there and let her kick me without even trying to regain control or reason with her? I felt both deflated and completely overwhelmed.

I had perked up by the time they released her five hours later. She had seen a solicitor, who got her bailed when she was charged with assault. I walked up to the police station and she was released into my care. She was calm and apologetic, and I wasn't angry with her. I almost never did feel angry for more than a few minutes, no matter what she did. A lot of people could never understand that, but although I was sometimes quite frightened of her rages, I never felt they came from the real Lara, or that they were directed at the real me. Several people told me I should be really angry with her and show it; some even went so far as to suggest I should threaten to ask social services to take her away to give her a wake-up call, but I knew that no amount of wake-up calls would make the slightest difference. Any threats from me would simply confirm to Lara that eventually everyone had their breaking point and would abandon her. What I hoped would eventually help heal Lara was my unconditional commitment and love, no matter how bad things got.

She stayed in bed all the next day, missing education. I went to work and came home exhausted. I had to go to bed, although Lara was just getting up. She promised me she would stay in and watch television. I wasn't convinced, but I couldn't stay up with her. I was worried I was going to have another mini-stroke; I had to get some sleep. I locked up the house and went to bed with all the keys under my pillow. Sometime later I was aware of her in my room reaching under the pillow for the keys. I caught hold of them and she swore and left my room. She must have come back later when I was more deeply asleep because when I woke at 2 a.m., the keys had gone and so had Lara.

She was gone for twenty-four hours, ringing me the following midnight. Please could I come and pick her up because she was feeling really ill? She was at the Plain, a large, tree-covered roundabout, complete with a covered Victorian fountain, at the bottom of Cowley Road. A strange scene greeted me when I arrived. At first I couldn't see Lara, but then I spotted her lying on the wet pavement outside a pub that boasted a huge reproduction of Edvard Munch's painting *The Scream* as its sign. She was moving, but there was a young man standing beside her looking panicked. He was on the phone dialling 999. There was also another person who looked a bit like a gremlin but without the big ears. He was running up and down swearing and then trying to grab at her.

I parked and ran over. The gremlin was trying to pull her up by her hair.

'Leave her alone. Get away from her!' I shouted.

'Fuck off,' he spat back at me, while the earnest young man on the phone visibly flinched at the language.

'What's happened to her? What have you done to her? How has she got into this state? Have you given her something?'

'Fuck off, you cunt. I'm her friend. Who are you?' he said, trying to pull her shoulder bag from round her neck and nearly strangling her.

The young man looked as though he might pass out.

'I'm her mother, and I'm going to call the police if you don't leave her alone and go away.'

'You're not my fucking mother. You stole me from my mother. I hate you.' Lara had come to.

That got the gremlin very excited and he ran around trying to hit me as the young man and I got Lara to her feet. As we did, she grabbed my hair, twisted my head round and smashed it into the stone windowsill of the pub. She started screaming abuse at me, saying I had ruined her life. The gremlin got even more animated and started attempting to kick-box me. Just at that point, fortunately, the police arrived and the gremlin ran off. I suddenly realized who he was: he was a local figure often seen going through rubbish bins or begging aggressively from tourists in town and was implicated in the theft of bikes from our street. The kids used to call him Gizmo.

The ambulance arrived and the paramedics took one look at Lara and summed up the situation. She didn't need them; she needed to go home, sober up and come down off whatever it was she had taken. My head was sore, but I knew it didn't require emergency treatment. The police helped me calm Lara down and get her into the car. I thanked the earnest young man, who looked absolutely shell-shocked by everything he had witnessed.

Apart from Jennifer, who was a one-off, Lara's associates fell into three distinct groups. There were still a few girlfriends she saw, mainly girls she had known from school. While by and large they were not model pupils and had their wild sides, they nevertheless managed to stay in school, and while they might get drunk occasionally and stay out too late, they did not get into the state Lara did and did not go missing.

Then there was a group of almost feral children, mostly younger than her. These children roamed the streets day and night, engaging in petty theft and minor acts of vandalism. No one seemed to care for them, and by and large they cared for no one. Two or three of them had parents who had serious drug problems, but mostly they had parents who just couldn't be bothered. Lara would often bring some of them home, and I would end up cooking large dishes of macaroni cheese or cottage pie that would get wolfed down in seconds. Two little waifs, a brother and sister, ate at our house several times a week for a couple of years. They would even come round when Lara was out or missing 'just to keep you company', they said. The little girl referred to me as Mum sometimes until Lara turned on her in fury. 'She's my mum, not yours. You're not to call her that. I'll never let you come here again if you do.'

The third group were much less distinct: older, shadowy and sinister. There was obviously Egyptian Mo and Sam the Rapist, but who were the others? I constantly listened out for any hints or clues, but Lara rarely dropped any. There was someone called Jay, who drove an Audi TT, and Lara told her educational support worker that he wanted her to work for him as a receptionist. She mentioned Jermaine, who worked at the Vodafone shop at Paddington Station, and then there were various names like Sharky, Snake, Ripper and Riccardo that kept cropping up. There were several unpleasant and menacing young men who lived close to us who Lara loathed but who clearly knew or thought they knew a lot about her. They were apparently associates of Egyptian Mo. One day Jean and I were outside the houses cutting back Jean's hedge when two of these young men, Abs and Ali, walked by and as they passed us, they said, 'That bitch's daughter is a whore who gives head for crack.'

I turned to Jean, horrified. 'Did you hear that?'

''Fraid so.'

'My God, do you think that's true? How do they know?'

I had had a couple of late-night phone calls from a very foreign-sounding man with a speech impediment telling me the same thing. I have no idea why he rang other than to try and cause trouble between Lara and me.

And a couple of weeks after the incident in the street, a reporter from the *Oxford Mail* contacted me. Somehow he had come across a video on YouTube of an unconscious naked girl being sexually assaulted by a man. The video clip gave Lara's name, address and phone number, and referred to her as a 'crack whore'. The young reporter asked if he could come and see me, and when he did, I told him what I knew of these men and the risks and threats to Lara from them and the abject failure of services to do anything useful to help us. He wanted to run a story but was warned off by the *Oxford Mail*'s lawyers. If only we could just shrug it all off so easily. The abuse and distress Lara was suffering was now public property on the internet. I told the police, and so did the reporter, and the video was removed, but I was disappointed that nothing was done to try and find out who had posted it in the first place. I tried as gently as possible to raise this with Lara to try and find out who could have done such a truly evil thing. She feigned ignorance and disinterest, but a couple of years later said that Mo had filmed her and that Abs and Ali had put it up on YouTube to teach her a lesson.

Lara disappeared up to London ten times in February 2007. Sometimes I would go up to bring her home when she surfaced, and sometimes if I had friends in the vicinity, I would ask them to pick her up and hang on to her until I could get up. Sometimes Lara would try and get to one of our friends, but her terrible sense of direction would usually mean that she ended up travelling the wrong way on the Tube. Either I or one of my friends would end up tearing across London trying to catch up with her. Once when I was trying to catch up with her going the wrong way on the Bakerloo line, we came to a shuddering halt in a tunnel. After about fifteen minutes the driver informed us that there was a person under the train ahead of us. I convinced myself this must be Lara. When thirty minutes later we crawled into Oxford Circus Station and it became clear it wasn't Lara, I was so relieved, but then appalled with myself that I was relieved that someone else had lost a loved one, not me. I eventually caught up with Lara at Waterloo.

The next Saturday, in an attempt to keep her close to me and entertained, I decided to take Lara with me and two friends, Jane and Joanne, to have a meal at a new noodle bar in town and then on to the cinema. Lara chose the film, and as it was likely to be popular, I bought the tickets before we went to eat. I was rather dismayed that Lara chose to go out wearing hideous stiletto boots someone had given her, a tiny skirt and filthy T-shirt, and a poncho full of holes, clothes she usually kept for going to meet her 'friends', but I decided to say nothing for fear of provoking a fight and her running off. We had a nice meal, and as I was paying the bill, Lara said she was just going outside for a cigarette.

When we went to join her, she wasn't outside. Perhaps she had walked over to the cinema, I thought, but no, she had gone. I should have seen it coming, especially seeing how she was dressed. Jane, Joanne and I decided to go to see the film anyway, and I left Lara's ticket for her at the desk, not really thinking she would turn up, and she didn't.

At 5.30 a.m. I got a phone call from St Mary's Hospital in Paddington. Lara was in A & E. She had collapsed in the street having taken crack and a 'friend' had called an ambulance. I went up on the first train with a bag of clothes, wet wipes, snacks and drinks. I was greeted in A & E by a nurse, who ushered me into a little side room off the main waiting room. My heart missed a beat. Oh God, it must be really serious: no one in any of the A & E departments I had turned up to collect Lara from before had ever wanted to talk to me. She said Lara had definitely taken crack and told me how addictive it is. One dose can be enough to get someone addicted, she explained.

She then looked at me and said, 'You have to look after yourself, you know. You're trying to cope with the impossible. Lara knows what she's doing, and only she can decide not to.' It sounded as though Lara had told this woman quite a lot about the sort of life she was leading. The nurse told me, 'Lara can see two quite distinct divergent paths into the future, but can't decide which one to take.'

Lara and I had already talked about that. One route was signed 'Lauren', a dangerous path to a future of criminality and drugs; the other road was the road to Lara and a good future as a loved and lovable, responsible adult.

I found Lara on a horrible dark, crowded and very claustro-phobic children's ward so cramped that parents were sleeping on the floor under their child's bed. For an awful moment it seemed that they might want to keep her in, but eventually she was allowed to leave. Lara changed into the clothes I had brought with me and we left. She was still pretty out of it as we walked down the street to the station. She was swinging the bag with her old clothes in by just one handle and I didn't tell her when one of the stiletto-heeled boots fell out in the street or when the hideous poncho got left behind on the luggage rack of the train. I shoved the strip of fabric she called a skirt into a rubbish bin on the train, so by the time we got to Oxford, all that was left of the get-up was one boot and a T-shirt for an eight-year-old child.

'No point in hanging on to those,' I said. 'We'll get you some new things tomorrow.' And I slung them into a bin in the car park.

Later that week Lara started work experience in a local nursery. She had always wanted to work with young children and was really looking forward to it. The work experience was half a day a week and was an integrated part of the education programme that had been drawn up for her. Her first day went well and she was very proud of herself. As part of her induction, she was talked through their various policies and procedures. There was one she referred to as the abandoned child procedure, which dealt with situations when a child was not collected at the end of the day. She was in tears, recalling more in raw emotion than words the times when she got abandoned at nursery.

Although the work experience at the nursery began well, after a couple of weeks Lara started to refuse to go. I couldn't work out why, but she just wouldn't. With their unerring ability to get it wrong, someone in the PRUIS unit decided that if Lara wouldn't go to work experience, they would withdraw any other education planned for her that day and maybe the next day too. It was another vicious circle that didn't give Lara a chance. They should have started with what she was able to do and built on that. They should have taken every opportunity to hang on to her rather than yet again looking for excuses to start to reject her. They knew how disturbed and chaotic she was, but they also knew she was engaging well with Libby, her education key worker. It felt like they were removing the part of the education programme she loved out of pure spite.

With Lara now receiving less education, she was at home even more. As the disappearing was now happening on virtually a daily basis, I didn't dare leave her at home on her own too much. I felt I was neglecting both of my jobs as a freelance consultant and part-time chief executive of a small charity and certainly couldn't take even more time off to make up for the lack of education. I talked it over with colleagues and we decided Lara could do work experience at the charity. She started coming out with me about once a week and helping out with fundraising, mailings and data inputting. She got easily distracted and frustrated at first and found it hard to concentrate at times, but she didn't do too badly. Her skills and confidence grew, and she started to see a different world, the world beyond education, the world of work and responsibility. She admitted she was proud of what she achieved, although she would usually quickly add that I shouldn't think that she was going to become 'posh' and work in an office long term! The charity worked with very profoundly disabled children and adults, and as ever Lara was always able to put her troubles behind her when there was someone in need of her help and support.

13

Lock Up the Victim

In April 2007 the most unpleasant police officer I have ever met entered our lives. I shall call her DC Nasty. Lara actually called her much worse.

The previous evening Lara had been brought back very distressed by the police saying she had been abducted and raped by a taxi driver. The next morning a woman in a rather glamorous long green mac banged on the door as though she was trying to knock it down. I opened it and she tried to push in past me. I put my foot in the way and asked her who she was. She said she was a detective from the child abuse team, and when I still didn't move my leg, she reluctantly produced her warrant card from inside a very large Gucci bag.

Her first comment to Lara was, 'Well, Lauren, you just can't keep out of trouble, can you.'

Lara said, 'I'm Lara now.'

'You may have changed your name, but you haven't changed your ways, have you? Your name is still legally Lauren, so that's what I'm going to call you.'

Lara just clammed up and refused to say anything more.

Lara was understandably extremely distressed by this latest

attack, which was obviously very different to her from the abuse that she seemed to be suffering on an almost daily basis at the hands of God knows who. But distressed though she was, she would not accept that there was anything she could do to lessen the chances of such things happening by not hanging around with dodgy people and disappearing all over the place.

'You don't understand, Mum – it's just how life is for me. It's never going to change.'

Two days later DC Nasty returned with a social worker in tow. The social worker spoke little English and insisted on standing throughout the one-hour conversation in our living room, which made for a particularly awkward dynamic, especially as she stood behind Lara and me. Both went out of their way to be as unpleasant to us as possible.

'Please could you tell me your name and what your involvement is? We've not met before, have we?' I said to the social worker.

She had a very long name, which she muttered so indistinctly I couldn't catch it. As to her role, 'invention assessing' was as near as I could get to it.

When I asked her what her involvement with this police inquiry was, she told me in very broken English that it was none of my business, adding, 'Mrs Moderu, I here to ask you and Linda questions. You do not ask me questions.'

The detective constable sneered at Lara's choice of friends, lack of education and frequent involvement with the police, accusing her of wasting their time and saying she should watch it because they could get her locked up.

This was new. We had encountered plenty of indifference from the police and social services, and a few veiled threats, but never before had their approach felt as though it was fuelled by animosity. The pair of them sat, or in the case of the social worker stood, in our living room and threatened that if Lara didn't tell them who she was associating with, they would have her taken away and locked up. It was a horrible experience. I was beginning to feel quite frightened

Afterwards Lara just said, 'Well, they can all fuck off.'

About four weeks later at 5.30 p.m. a young woman called Sophie rang from what she called Team 1. She wanted to come and talk to me first thing the next morning about the incident with the taxi driver. To begin with, I thought she was from the police, but it emerged that Team 1 was something to do with social services. I explained I had an important work meeting the next morning and that at this late stage of the day it was too late to change it, but I could meet her later in the day or the following one. That did not suit her. In fact, she said she would be on leave for a week. We agreed a date just after her return and she said she wanted to come to our house. I said I would allow no more meetings in our house after the last one had gone so badly. Our house was our home and Lara's sanctuary, and we would not be threatened and bullied there. We therefore agreed to meet in the social services offices.

On her return from leave, Sophie rang once more, again trying to insist the meeting must be in our house because the police were coming and they wanted it to be there. Again I said no and she threatened to force me to have the meeting in our house. I said you can't force me, and at that point Lara, who was in the room, unhelpfully took the phone.

'Who the fuck are you, and what do you want?'

I couldn't hear the other end of the conversation, but Lara

responded, 'What would help would be for you all to fuck off and leave me alone. You're all crap. I'm fine.'

Again I couldn't hear the other end, but 'And don't give me that secure unit shite. Don't you get it? I *don't care!*' was Lara's parting shot before throwing the phone at me.

I picked it up and ended up feeling quite sorry for the woman, who sounded as though she was close to tears. She seemed young and inexperienced and uncertain, presumably firing someone else's bullets. It turned out she knew nothing about Lara, or of any previous social services involvement with us, not even the visit from a colleague just four weeks before. Someone had simply given her Lara's name and our phone number, told her that the police wanted social services 'to do something' and left her to it.

Realizing that we were being discussed behind our backs by nameless people who had never even met Lara or me but who had virtually total and unaccountable power to lock up children and break up families was deeply troubling. I rang my solicitor, who suggested I take out a formal complaint against social services for failing to do anything constructive to help us. She said she would be very happy to represent me if it came to formal proceedings, but she would have to charge her standard fee and I should expect to have to pay about £2,000 for approximately seven hours of her time. I was broke and already at the point of selling some jewellery my grandmother had left me in order to keep us afloat. The twelve or so hours a week I was able to work were not enough to live on, even with the adoption allowance. I knew my family would help me out if I asked them, but at this point I hadn't told them just how dire things were, and I didn't want to worry them unnecessarily.

Another desultory meeting took place with DC Nasty from the police and Sophie from Team 1. As ever, they did a lot of tut-tutting at Lara's risk-taking behaviour, which they saw as purely wilful and delinquent. They frowned at me for failing to control it and then completely backed off when I asked them what they were going to do to help us. I was learning that the way to deal with threats and challenges from both the police and social services was to threaten and challenge back. Quick to judge the inadequacies in others, they repeatedly turned a blind eye to their own shortcomings. The same was true of education. I knew of parents who were being threatened with prosecution for failing to ensure their child attended school often enough, even though their child was in fact in school receiving several more hours a week education than Lara was being offered, despite my battles to get a proper education for her. It was very much 'Do as we say, not as we do.'

The worry over Lara's risk-taking, the abuse she was clearly suffering at someone's hands and her increasing violence to me was at times quite terrible; nevertheless it was almost easier to cope with than the threats and callousness of the statutory services. Having to juggle both was almost too much to bear. I knew that as things stood, Lara was in danger, but I knew she would be at even greater risk if social services took her into care again – either from her own hand, neglect or from the criminals who clearly preyed on girls in care. Although I knew I was not able to protect her properly, even in the darkest hours of self-doubt I knew I was doing a better job of it than social services ever could.

As was usually the case, after I had issued a challenge to either the police or social services to do something useful to help us, it all went quiet for a bit and there were no more threats, despite the fact that Lara was disappearing nearly every night and turning up in terrible states in terrible places. Lara's disappearances would always follow a call to her mobile. I started to think of these calls as the 'call of the wild': something inaudible to me but irresistible to her that had the power to pull her out of a happy and comfortable situation and propel her into danger and harm.

At this time Jane, an old friend from Australia, was staying with us. She was working part-time as a supply teacher and was happy to offer me help and support with Lara or take care of the dogs while I pursued Lara across the country. She could cover times at home when Lara was on her own and I was at work. She gave me a huge amount of moral support, and perhaps most importantly, her presence in the house changed the dynamic a bit. It wasn't just Lara and me locked in our battles over her safety. Jane was pretty much halfway between Lara and me in age, and as a secondary-school teacher, she was probably more aware of the ins and outs of everyday life for teenagers in 2007 than I was, although she was as much at a loss as I was to understand what was going on.

All three of us went to London in April during the school holidays and stayed with our friend Mary at Elephant and Castle. The next day Jane and Lara went to the London Dungeon while I had a work meeting with clients. Lara was glowing with pleasure that afternoon. She had loved the scariness of the London Dungeon.

Jane was staying on in London, but Lara and I were going back to Oxford. When we got to Paddington Station, I went to Sainsbury's to get some food for supper, but Lara insisted she wanted to go to the Vodafone shop to see if her friend Jermaine, who worked there, could get her a good deal on a new phone. The Vodafone shop was right by the platform for our train. It was three thirty in the afternoon, but yes, when I got back to the shop, Lara was nowhere to be seen. I went inside and asked for Jermaine. They denied knowing a Jermaine or a girl answering Lara's description, but after a few minutes someone called Gabriel, who also worked in the shop, came back and said that he did know Lara and would go and find her while I waited on the shop floor. He brought her round from the back of the shop, but she immediately ran away. Jermaine was nowhere to be seen.

I rang the police, told them about the Vodafone shop and also gave the young men in the shop a lecture about Lara's youth and vulnerability. I asked them not to give her shelter or cover again. I was now making a point of letting people know as much as possible about Lara and the police involvement with her to try and put them off having anything to do with her. I hung around Paddington for a few hours in the forlorn hope she might reappear, but in the end I had to go back home.

The next day Lara turned up at Mary's flat in Elephant and Castle. She was tired and dirty but not too distressed, so Mary, who had an important meeting to go to, judged that she could make her own way home, bought her tickets, gave her money for lunch and saw her on the Tube to Paddington. I said I would meet her from the train in Oxford, but she didn't arrive.

The next day there was nothing, and the following day was Good Friday and we were due to be in Wales for a family Easter. Lara's mobile phone was dead, so I decided Jane and I would go to Wales as planned and await events down there, where there were at least distractions and company. I put our house phone on divert to my mobile, and we got to my brother's house just after lunch. I tried to make light of the absence of Lara, especially to my mother, but I couldn't disguise the fact that I had no idea where my fourteen-year-old daughter was.

At about 5 p.m. Lara rang my mobile. She sounded very disorientated. She said she had woken up in a flat in Hampstead in strange clothes and with £27 in her pocket. She claimed to have no recollection of how she'd got there. It would take me at least three hours to get over to Hampstead, so my brother and sister-in-law offered to get a long-haul taxi firm that they sometimes used for work to pick her up and bring her down to Wales. I told her to get out of the flat, find a cafe, have something to eat and wait while we sorted that out. We got hold of the taxi firm and I rang Lara back, but she didn't answer her phone. An hour later she rang again, this time from Golders Green, saying that she had been raped. She became very distraught and started to threaten suicide, so I rang 999. There was then an agonizing two-hour wait for news until a police officer rang from Collingwood Police Station to say she was safe and with them.

I packed a bag with a change of clothes for Lara, wet wipes and snacks, the usual items. Victoria made us a large flask of strong coffee, Michael fitted his satnav in my car, and Jane and I set off for North London. Lara had flatly refused to give the police a statement of what had happened, or even a description of the man who had attacked her. They just let her leave with me, clearly glad to be relieved of the responsibility. It was a 350-mile round trip and Lara, Jane and I got back to Wales at 3 a.m.

The next morning was a lovely spring day with lambs skipping and daffodils in the fields. Lara woke up a child again and spent the rest of the day helping Mike, Michael and Victoria's farmer neighbour, to bottle-feed some orphaned lambs. She was deeply embarrassed about what had happened, knowing that it was the first time our wider family had experienced first-hand her disappearing acts. The family, who knew some of the difficulties we were having, were nevertheless shocked and baffled by what had just occurred, but at my request said little directly to her. She said she didn't deserve Easter gifts, but she got them anyway.

We stayed in Wales until Easter Monday and had a happy time, but as usual as soon as we got near Oxford on our return journey, Lara started to get twitchy. Luckily her phone didn't ring that night and she stayed home, sleeping in my bed. The next day she wouldn't let me out of her sight, even sitting on the floor outside the bathroom when I went to the loo.

On Wednesday we drove down to Surrey to stay a couple of days with a friend on her smallholding. Life was now only manageable when we were outside Oxford, so I took every opportunity to get away. I had been thinking about trying to move away permanently for some time, but the logistics seemed overwhelming. Lara was dead set against the idea, and each time I broached it with her, pointing out how much happier she seemed when we were away, she went berserk. I tried again in the car.

'I've moved so many f-ing times. I'm not moving again. You're just trying to wind me up.'

'But moving this time would be different because we would be moving together. We could choose a new home together and have a fresh start.'

'I am not moving again ever!' she screamed, and started to

try and climb out of the car window. She became so agitated that I had to stop the car. She got out and started running across a busy dual carriageway. I decided not to follow in case it made her take even bigger risks and eventually she came back to the car sobbing and choking.

'I need a fucking fag.'

I agreed to get her a packet if she calmed down and got back into the car.

In any case, where would we go? I would have to give up work and we would lose our friends and the little support we were getting from the statutory services. And Lara's fundamental problems would still move with us. No, we were stuck, locked in this unresolvable misery and locked in Oxford, a city I used to love but was coming to see as a place where there seemed to be only grief, disinterested services and, beyond that, just anarchy.

Despite the tricky start to our trip, we had as usual a great time away from Oxford. We helped build and light a huge bonfire, and Lara was in seventh heaven surrounded by so many animals.

But we had to go back, and on the way home Lara engineered a row (this time over my refusal to let her smoke in the car) and stormed off as soon as I pulled up outside the house. She rang later to say sorry and that she was with friends on Cowley Road and would be home by 11 p.m. But she wasn't, so at midnight I drove to Cowley Road to look for her. It was some time since I had been down Cowley Road stopping people and asking if they had seen Lara and I was shocked at the difference. This time I showed them a photo Lara had taken of herself on my phone, wearing exaggerated eye make-up and with pouting lips, and at least half the people I spoke to said they had seen her around. Several added that she was usually with some older Asian men and that they were not very nice people for a young girl to be with. This was further confirmation of my suspicions that there was something fairly organized going on, but who were these men?

Lara came home late morning in a foul mood, clearly coming down off something, and went to bed. At about 5 p.m. some girlfriends were knocking on our front door wanting her to go skating with them. I was always pleased when she wanted to do ordinary things with pretty ordinary teenagers, so I agreed to give her the money to go and to run them all to the ice rink. I said I would pick them up at 8 p.m. Just as I was leaving to pick up the girls, Lara rang to say that they were all going back to the home of a friend of one of the girls for an hour or two.

Lara missed her curfew, but at least she was home before midnight and in a fairly reasonable state. She said her friend Kim had a boyfriend who had a friend with a flat and they had all been there together. They had each had a can of lager, but that had been it.

'I've left my phone there, but it'll be OK. Ricky, who owns the flat, will definitely look after it for me. He's really nice.'

I asked as casually as I could what Ricky did and how old he was.

'Oh, he's about eighteen or nineteen, and he's a builder and earns lots of money.'

Young to have his own place, then, but stranger things have happened.

The next evening Kim called round for Lara. They were going to go to Ricky's to get Lara's phone. An hour later, though, a man rang the house phone.

'Uh, yeah, Lara's left her phone at my place. Uh, I, er, want to give it back.'

'Are you Ricky? I thought Lara and Kim had gone round to yours.'

He sounded surprised I knew his name, and he didn't sound anywhere near eighteen. I offered to come over to get the phone, but he said no. He wanted to meet somewhere and give it to me. We agreed on Folly Bridge. It was dark and he was wearing a ubiquitous hoody, but it was clear he wouldn't see twenty or even thirty again.

'Do you know how old Lara is?'

'She said she was nineteen.'

'No, she tells everyone that. She is actually only fourteen.'

He looked genuinely shocked and promised he would have no more to do with her. And at least, I suppose, he had acted responsibly over the phone.

It was spring 2007 and Lara hadn't seen her birth mother for quite some time. After the last 'contact', when Terri, who had been pregnant, had ignored all the children and Lara had been so upset and angry, none of the children had wanted to see her again. Terri's baby, born just after she came out of prison, had severe disabilities and had been taken away from her after just a couple of weeks. Kirsten and Lara were curious about what had happened and had been asking to see Terri again, so we drove up to Chester and met in a Little Chef. It was so small it was not possible to all sit at one table, so Kirsten's carer and I sat on a separate table. It was even more awkward than previous contacts, as the girls kept telling the carer and me that they didn't want us there; they just wanted to be a family again. They even tried to demand that we go and sit outside in our cars! I felt terrible and didn't really know how to react. I knew Lara found it difficult to have her two worlds, her two families, her two realities overlap, but I wasn't prepared to pretend I didn't exist or that it was possible for them to play happy families as though nothing had ever happened. Kirsten's carer was absolutely furious with the girls and told them so and we refused to budge.

Lara was in a terrible mood when it was time to leave.

'Why did you take me away from my real mother, you fucking cow?' she demanded as soon as we were in the car. 'She's the one I want to be with, and I would be with her if you hadn't taken me away. I love her, and I hate you for what you've done. You've broken my heart. I want to kill you.'

She punched me in the side of the face and I stopped the car. It was almost dark and we were on a twisting, narrow country lane. She grabbed my hair and slammed my head down on the steering wheel, shouting, 'I hate you. You've ruined my life. I wish you'd die so I could go back to my real mother.'

I completely lost it. 'If she's so wonderful, then go back to her. Go on – get out of the car and go back and see what reception you will get. I'm fed up with being treated like dirt. Go on – go back to her.'

I regretted it the moment the words were out of my mouth, because of course she did get out and ran back up the road in the dark. Oh God, what had I done? How could I have been so stupid?

I sat in the car for about twenty minutes, then tried ringing her. Every time I did, she just hung up. I turned the car round and tried to retrace our steps. It was pitch black by now. Eventually she rang me.

'Where the fuck are you? I'm going to get killed walking in the dark. There're no pavements.'

I found her and she got in the car. I turned round and headed back towards Oxford. She was quietly seething for a bit, but on the M42 near Warwick she suddenly exploded again.

'What I really want to know is if you love me and think you're such a good mother, why did you let all those awful things happen to me when I was little? I was only tiny and all those awful men my dad used to bring back from the pub hurt me and you just let it happen.'

For a moment I was lost for words. What she was saying was ludicrous but clearly born of such pain and anguish and confusion that I had to try and find the right words.

'But, love, I didn't know you then. I didn't know what was happening to you. If I had done, I'd have done everything I could to try and stop it,' I attempted lamely.

It wasn't the right response. Sobbing hysterically, she screamed, 'You should have known, you fucking bitch. If you really cared, you'd have known.'

She grabbed the steering wheel and we careered from the fast lane to the hard shoulder before I regained control of the car. Fortunately, we were only about half a mile from some motorway services. I crawled down the hard shoulder at about twenty miles an hour gripping the wheel as hard as I could and parked.

'You nearly killed us both. We're not going anywhere until you calm down and have stayed calm for at least twenty minutes,' I said as steadily as I could. Then I sat impassively, car keys clutched tight, while blows and abuse rained down on me, trying hard not to show her how shocked and upset I was.

Eventually the blows subsided and I suggested we go and get something to eat and drink before continuing our journey. God, she really could end up killing one or both of us.

The next evening she rang Terri using a very false sugary voice that she only ever seemed to use for her birth family. After a bit she became very distressed and rang off. She said Terri had been telling her how good drugs were and that she should try crack. She obviously hadn't told Terri that she already had. She started to weep uncontrollably. Jane and I both tried to calm her down and comfort her, and just as we were getting somewhere, her mobile went and she said she wanted to go out and meet a friend. I had no fight left in me, so I just let her go. She didn't, of course, come back that night.

The next morning I went to work, while Jane waited for her at home. Lara rang me from home at 5 p.m. swearing and demanding that I return immediately to buy her cigarettes. I reminded her that I would do nothing under threat and hung up. When I got home, she was running up the road in tears. She turned round and came back when she saw me.

I was hardly in the door when she announced between screams and sobs, 'I'm pregnant.'

'How do you know?'

'I've done two pregnancy tests and they were both positive.'

I had to tell myself to breathe. I had been half expecting this, but if it was true, it was a disaster. There was no way Lara could even begin to manage with a baby, and I knew instinctively that she would never cope with competing with the baby for my attention if I took on the care. But nor would she cope emotionally with yet another loss, either through abortion or adoption. This pregnancy could completely destroy her.

That night was not the time to try and have the necessary conversation about options, and she spent the next day in bed refusing to engage with anything, including a conversation about the pregnancy. It was possible that she wasn't pregnant even if she really had done two tests. In her chaotic state, she might well have not done them correctly or judged the results accurately. In order to know what we were dealing with, I asked her if she would do another test, but she refused, accusing me of calling her a liar.

It was hard enough dealing with Lara's existing problems . . . How would we cope with this as well?

14

Who Are They?

Over the next couple of weeks Lara did suddenly look pregnant. She was blowing up like a balloon. How had I not noticed something earlier? I did manage to have a bit of a conversation with her about her options for the pregnancy and the pros and cons of each.

'Sweetheart, I know it's difficult, but we do need to talk, you and I, about the pregnancy and what's going to happen, what you want to happen. You do have choices, you know, and you need to think about them and decide what's best. It's your decision, and I will support your decision as long as I know that you have thought about it and made an informed choice.'

She became quite calm and mature as we talked, suddenly hugging me and saying she loved me and asking what she would do without me. 'You've literally saved my life, Mum. You know that, don't you? Don't listen to any of the crap I say when I'm angry. I love you.'

And then the phone rang. It was Kirsten to tell Lara that Terri had attacked their grandmother and that she was in hospital as a result. In an instant Lara was incandescent with rage, as if assaulting one's mother was something completely foreign to her. She stormed out of the house and was gone all night.

The phone went at 6 a.m. 'Mum, hurry up and come and get me. I'm on Cowley Road. I look like a prostitute, I'm having a miscarriage, and I need a fag,' she screamed hysterically.

When I found her, she was clearly coming down off something and not making a lot of sense. In the car, she told me she had killed her baby, then, bizarrely, that Jane had killed her baby. She refused to let me take her to the GP, but wanted to see the therapist who was working with her on the DBT programme about managing emotions. She had been due to see her that morning anyway, but when I rang her, she came to the house early and persuaded Lara to see a doctor at the child mental health unit that was running the programme. Of course I was not allowed to know what she told the doctor, or if the doctor thought she was or had been pregnant, but the pregnancy just disappeared. Lara refused to discuss it at all. I suspected she hadn't really been pregnant, but then again, she could have lost the baby without very obvious physical symptoms that early in the pregnancy, and the life she was leading would have greatly increased the chance of an early miscarriage.

In the middle of all this the police rang asking if they could have my laptop to see if they could find out whom Lara was associating with on the internet. Having broken her own laptop, she often used mine to go on Facebook and other social networking sites. I agreed, but as I used my laptop primarily for work, I had to borrow another one and copy all my work files onto it first.

Then late in April 2007 I was officially informed that there was to be a child protection conference to discuss Lara and the risk she was under with a view to putting her on the Child Protection Register. Ironically this was something I had requested a couple of years ago but had been refused. I had thought that by being on the CPR, Lara would be more on the radar and more likely to get help, but I was told by both the police and a social worker that really it was little more than a paper exercise and would simply mean that I, as her parent, would be more marginalized and she would actually be more likely to be sent away.

Over the intervening two years the services and I had changed our positions. Seeing how little any of these services were able to do for a child like Lara, I was convinced that having my role removed was not in her best interests. Meanwhile, being unable to provide practical help, the police and social services at least needed to ensure all the procedural boxes had been ticked and now wanted a child protection meeting in order to do that.

The meeting was convened and chaired by someone who described himself to me in person and in a letter on headed notepaper as the independent chair of the Oxfordshire Safeguarding Children Board. I was to discover later he was simply another social worker. It was a deeply humiliating experience for me, as the first thing that happened was that dozens of letters were sent out to all sorts of statutory and voluntary bodies asking if they knew anything about Lara. Some of those were people I knew professionally, some personally, and some were clients. I suppose that embarrassment would have been a small price to pay if the child protection conference had achieved anything, but it was just a protracted exercise in hand-wringing. Nothing new came up at the meeting, which was attended by all the same people who met regularly at Lara's bi-monthly case reviews, and we just went over the same ground that we had been over and over now so many times in so many settings over the past two years. In the end the meeting agreed not to put Lara on the Child Protection Register, saying it would achieve nothing, and we all went home. Another wasted meeting that had achieved nothing but raised anxiety for both Lara and me.

The next few weeks were absolute chaos. Lara disintegrated further. She was constantly missing, once for five days. Shockingly, she was now taking crack quite openly. I found a crack pipe and little wraps of substances in her room, which I handed to the police. Weed or even skunk had been one thing, but she had now moved into a different and truly dangerous league. To an extent, though, having the tangible evidence of the crack smoking was helpful: it provided an explanation for at least some of the further deterioration in her behaviour, and it gave me another possible source of help to pursue – the addiction services.

She was arrested for assault on another girl and admitted it, although at least one police officer didn't think she had done it but was covering up for a man called Sharky. He was a vile local drug dealer who I had twice had to chase away from our house, once with a broom when he came round menacing us for money he said Lara owed him and I happened to be sweeping the front steps.

In early May we were subjected to a drugs bust. I was alone in the house and opened the front door to rather insistent knocking by a man with a large toolbox. For a moment I thought he had come to service the gas boiler, but he waved a police warrant card and a piece of paper at me. The piece of paper was a warrant issued that afternoon in the magistrates' court authorizing him to search our house for drugs. I was shocked and hurt. There was no need for a warrant, as I had always cooperated with the police. They could have searched the house at any time; they only had to ask. What made it more hurtful was that the warrant had been applied for by the police officer who had headed the Missing Persons Unit and had been such a support to me – and who was now here as part of the search team. We were on first-name terms; it seemed like such a betrayal. The ante was certainly being upped now, all round.

Apparently there had been a drugs raid on a house in the next street and, along with drugs and weapons, they had found Lara, who had been taken into protective police custody. While the police were crashing around in Lara's bedroom, the phone went. It was a duty social worker who had been called as a matter of standard practice when the police had taken Lara into protective custody.

'Mrs McDonnell, I am at the police station with your daughter, Lara. I am sorry to have to say I have been ringing round but can't find anywhere to place her tonight.'

'But why does she have to go anywhere? Unless she is going to be charged with something and they keep her in the cells, why can't she come home?'

'Oh, you will have her home, will you? That's a relief. A lot of parents wouldn't after something like this.'

'Of course I will have her home. She hasn't even been charged with anything yet.'

The search took two and a half hours and they brought a dog and took away some old foil and bits of cling film. The sergeant in charge of the case brought Lara back, told her how lucky she was to have a good home and told her not to be so stupid in the company she chose. She was not charged with anything.

The next morning Libby, the educational key worker, rang to say that because Lara had missed another work experience session at the nursery (they had recently been restarted), she had to cancel her education for two days. She said her boss wanted to cancel next week's education as well, but she was trying to resist that.

So that it wasn't left to me to tell Lara, Libby said she would come the following day to explain to her that she might be losing more of her education programme. Lara went crazy when Libby told her, her face turning bright red and contorted, and she became very rude and threatening to Libby before turning on me. She stamped on my foot, headbutted me, grabbed me by the throat and then did her usual twisting of my fingers before heading for the front door, picking up a glass vase on the way. She threw the vase at Libby, but it fell short, smashing into a thousand shards on the tiled floor. She then ran out into the street.

Seeing how violent she was, I locked the door, and Libby rang the police. Jean came out from next door and managed to calm Lara down a bit, who started begging to be allowed back in the house, but I refused. Libby was in tears. I think it was the shock of Lara turning on her like that. She could have been seriously hurt. There were little daggers of glass embedded in a cupboard door that could easily have cut her. The police arrived and took Lara away in handcuffs. She waved tearfully at me from the back of the police car. I just stood in a daze and stared after her.

The police took statements from both Libby and me, and

filled in what they called a domestic violence risk-assessment form. Again I was told that the police regarded me as high risk and would be ringing me every day to see if I was OK. They said I should refuse to take Lara back. I tried to explain that this was not some drunken partner we were dealing with but a very damaged and disturbed child who needed help, not yet another rejection. They didn't get it.

Lara came back after five hours in the police cells, having been bailed until the end of June for criminal damage and common assault. She was fairly calm for the rest of the day, but there was no sign of remorse or an apology. I felt a rare moment of real anger towards her that day. To do that to Libby of all people was inexcusable.

I realized after that morning that I was at the end of the road of trying to keep Lara at home with an inadequate package of support services. No one could contain her, and the way things were heading, she was going to end up killing herself or someone else. I had heard about a unit at St Andrew's Hospital in Northampton that provided a secure therapeutic setting for adolescents with mental and emotional health problems and challenging behaviour. Unlike a secure unit, it aimed to understand and treat underlying psychiatric and psychological problems, and provide appropriate treatment. It offered a fantastic education programme and all sorts of recreational activities. Needless to say, it was very expensive.

The normal way of funding a placement in such a place – unless, I suppose, you were a multimillionaire – was to secure tripartite funding, with education, health and social care sharing the cost. That night I wrote to the Mental Health Trust, the education officer and social services to formally request they consider jointly funding and referring Lara to St Andrew's.

Before going to work the next morning, I printed off the letters and put them in envelopes. I also put on a load of washing. Emptying the pockets of Lara's jacket before putting it in the machine, I found a condom. In a rush and not wanting to leave it on top of the washing machine, as our cleaner was due any minute, I shoved it in my pocket and went to work. I only remembered it when I got back home, but it wasn't in my pocket. The pockets were very shallow and it must have fallen out, probably under my desk. I wondered what our caretaker would think when he cleaned the next morning.

Lara was in the house when I got home because she was now banned from any education. Jane had managed to keep her entertained, but she was clearly planning to go out, judging by the amount of make-up she was putting on. I suggested she come and walk the dogs with me, but she sullenly refused and left the house.

When I went out with the dogs, it was clear that a drugs drop was due, taking into account the number of haunted-looking people hanging around the footpath from the church to the primary school. Doubtless Egyptian Mo would be round soon. On my way back, there were still people hanging around, and then suddenly a large black jeep-type car with blackened windows pulled over to the kerb. As I glanced in through its front passenger window, a figure ducked down and the car pulled sharply away and sped off. Lara?

I didn't hear from her for two days; then she rang in hysterics saying she was on Cowley Road and a man was trying to attack her and kidnap her. When I got there, there were two police officers with her. She was clearly genuinely frightened and kept pointing to a man who was hanging around a hundred yards up the road, watching us and ducking back behind a wall when we looked at him. The police saw him and I assumed they would go after him, but they didn't; they just got back in their car and drove off in the other direction. Everyone had given up on her, even the police.

We got a similar response the next day when a man stole her bike and rode off on it when she was hanging around on Cowley Road. We were able to give the police full details, including who had taken it, but they didn't want to know. Stolen bikes were, of course, ten a penny in Oxford, but this would have been such an easy hit for them.

And then Lara was off again. Firstly she rang saying she was in Birmingham. The next day she rang from London. I met her off the train; she was in a terrible state – filthy, dirty and hardly able to walk because her feet were so blistered and swollen from a pair of stilettos she was carrying. Despite the state of her feet, as we were walking to the car she ran off, saying she knew where the bike was and would just go and get it.

She shouted back at me, 'Don't worry, Mum – I won't be long. I can't go very far in bare feet.' But she could, and was gone for two days.

The next time she rang, she was in London again, completely off her head. Eventually I managed to talk her back to Oxford and she came through the station barriers looking even more awful than last time. She was drawn, skin so pale it was almost translucent, dark purple streaks under her eyes. In the car, I was overwhelmed by the smell, a mixture of unwashed body, stale perfume and alcohol. When we got home, she had a hot bath and fell into bed. I went into the bathroom to tidy up after her and found blood-soaked jeans and a T-shirt on the floor, no underwear. She had obviously been quite violently sexually assaulted, presumably selling herself for drugs, but she wouldn't have organized that on her own. Who was pimping her?

A nice, kindly, older police officer came to sight her and she told him she had been clubbing in Leicester Square. He smiled, told her she was too young to be doing that and left.

The next day she was exhausted and stayed in bed. There was no education for her to get up for anyway. I managed to keep her calm and at home until 5 p.m., when two workers from a drugs project were due to visit. I had contacted them after finding the crack pipe in her bedroom. I didn't tell her they were coming until just before they were due and tried to keep it light.

'Oh, I just thought they might be able to give us some general advice – you know, after the drugs raid and things.'

'Well, you can talk to them; I'm not. They'll just be wankers like all the others.'

A young man and young woman knocked on the door. I took them into the kitchen, and after a few minutes Lara walked in, saying she was just going to make herself a cup of tea. She stayed and eventually sat down at the table and joined in the conversation, which at that point was still about the weather. They started asking general, very gentle questions, but Lara dismissed everything.

'I used to do drugs, just a bit of weed, but I don't anymore. Drugs are for losers. Anyone who does drugs is a twonk.'

I couldn't just let this opportunity for some help end there with a pack of lies from Lara.

'But, Lara, what about the crack pipes I have found and the

ones found in your bedroom in the drugs raid? And anyway, you've told me you have been taking crack.'

She stormed out of the room. The drugs workers explained that was a fairly typical response often indicating someone felt caught out.

After a few minutes Lara returned and said very emphatically, 'I don't do drugs, but I do drink a lot of alcohol.'

To which, quick as a flash, the young man said, very matter-of-factly, 'Oh, I help a lot of people who drink a bit too much. Shall we meet for a chat?'

Lara positively beamed at him, and they arranged to meet the following week.

Before then there were two meetings looming that we were both dreading. Lara refused to come to the first one, which was the bi-monthly multi-agency care plan review hosted by the Mental Health Trust. The education representatives, I suppose not surprisingly, wanted to focus on the violent outburst when the vase had been thrown at Libby. They now deemed Lara too dangerous for most staff to work with. I tried to explain that their tactic of depriving her of education because she wouldn't go to work experience was totally counterproductive. A child who had experienced deprivation at a young age would be immune to responding to deprivation as a punishment. It just sent her into a spiral of shame and incandescent anger.

After much hand-wringing, the meeting concluded that there was nothing to be done to save Lara from herself except lock her up. With a very heavy heart, I was party to that decision, although I never accepted that there was nothing the services could have done, rather that what they did do was too little and now it was too late. We had all failed.

We jointly agreed that Lara should be told at the education meeting scheduled for the afternoon, which she would hopefully be attending, that if she went missing again or was aggressive or violent, she would be sent to a secure unit. But who would be the one to tell her this? The social worker said it should really be her, but she didn't want to because it might ruin her (non-existent) relationship with Lara. Everyone else had similar concerns, so once again we went round the table and it landed in my lap. I actually didn't mind – it felt like it should be my responsibility as her parent to tell her this – but it made me smile despite myself, because I was probably the only one who did have a relationship with Lara to ruin. We agreed that each of the professionals would outline to Lara how they saw the situation from their organization's point of view and then I would say that we had all decided that the only way now to keep her safe was for her to go to a secure unit.

Feeling utterly despondent, I went home and together Lara and I went to the meeting. As soon as it started all the professionals started to waffle evasively – so much so that although I'd been at the earlier meeting, I still didn't recognize what they were on about. There was very little chance that Lara would understand anything. Simone, Lara's mental health key worker, and I took control of the discussion.

'Lara, you know that we had a review meeting this morning and discussed what has been going on and the even greater risky situations you are putting yourself in?' Simone opened, and then looked at me.

'And you know that we all said some time ago that if you carried on like that, there would come a time when if you couldn't stop yourself, then steps would have to be taken to keep you safe even against your will?' I continued. I drew a deep breath, 'Well, we all feel that we have now reached that point, and we have to tell you that the next time you go missing, you will be sent to a secure unit for your own protection.'

Simone backed me. Lara took it all quite well and managed to remain in the meeting and stay surprisingly calm. She actually remained calmer than I did throughout the rest of the meeting, while the officer in charge of organizing the programme designed to meet Lara's statement of special educational needs apologized for the lack of notes from the last meeting, regretted the absence of the promised new plan and waxed lyrical about the ideas they had for new programmes next year – they all seemed to have names like Jump Start, Spring Forward, Bounce Back, Leap in the Dark.. They had decided to plan new programmes for the next school year as none of the ones for the current year had actually come to fruition.

On our way home, we stopped at TK Maxx to look for some new clothes for Lara. She gravitated, as she usually did, to the glittery party wear and insisted on trying on some long, sparkly evening dresses. She was upset when I said I wouldn't buy one, and on today of all days I didn't want to see her disappointed, but the poshest event we were ever likely to go to wouldn't require a shimmery chiffon number. Lara, my love, I thought to myself, where you are heading, a tracksuit is probably all you will be allowed. We did buy quite a lot of more day-to-day clothing and she cheered up. But the new clothes and the stark warnings at the meeting were not enough to keep her in that night. Some force stronger than all that was clearly at work and she disappeared at about 8 p.m.

The next morning, still having heard nothing, I realized this was now it. Lara would be locked up when or if she surfaced this time. I made another desperate attempt to follow up my letters about tripartite funding for the adolescent unit at St Andrew's Hospital. None of the key people were available, so I left urgent messages. As I was doing this, I got a phone call from a police officer in the Domestic Violence Unit at Cowley Road Police Station wanting to see me urgently to finish my statement about Lara's attacks on me.

'I don't want to pursue those,' I said, hardly even able to think about something that now seemed so unimportant. 'Lara has gone missing again, and when she returns, she's going to be locked up. I've got bigger things to worry about.'

'We don't need your consent to prosecute a case of domestic violence,' she told me, 'but it might go better for Lara if the statement is in your words. That way, you could put in all the mitigating factors.'

Reluctantly I agreed to go and was taken by the police officer to her shared office, where I could overhear phone calls her colleagues were making about other cases. Was this normal? I sat by her desk, which was covered with notes and witness statements about other people. Trying to avert my eyes while she took phone calls, I turned to the noticeboard above her desk and there, alongside a notice about the fire drill, a note from personnel about booking holidays and a few postcards, was an internal memo. My name jumped out at me from it. I was officially categorized as one of the top ten of those most at risk of domestic violence in the county. My name was third on the list. Bloody hell, that was ridiculous.

Once home, I got calls from Simone, the mental health key worker, and Sophie, the social worker. I asked whether Lara's secure unit might be a place that offered some therapy. Sophie was very nice to me, quite kind and gentle, not the usual social worker tone. She said she would do her best, but it would depend on what was available when Lara turned up. I mentioned again the possibility of St Andrew's, but she said there wasn't time to get all three parties of education, health and social services together to agree tripartite funding. Apparently that can take up to a year.

Two days later Lara rang from Finsbury Circus in London. She told me she had taken a lot of drugs and felt awful. I rang Missing Persons and social services, but it was Friday afternoon and I didn't get an answer from either. I got hold of Mary, and as luck would have it, she was just finishing a meeting not far from Finsbury Circus and offered to go and find Lara and keep her safe until I could get there. Friday afternoon on the roads would be painfully slow, so I got the 4 p.m. train to London, thinking, Thank God it's Friday – it may give us a couple more days.

As I walked towards Carluccio's at Smithfield, where Mary had got Lara pinned down, Lara ran towards me and very affectionately threw her arms around me. She looked quite sophisticated, like a high-class hooker – black skinny jeans, black off-the-shoulder top, pink stiletto sandals, hair down and wavy. She hadn't chosen those clothes. I wondered who had. She said she had woken up that morning in a posh flat near the Barbican with £10 in her pocket. She had no idea where the money had come from, or who she had been with. We went home.

For the next few days Lara, the police and I played cat and mouse. She would disappear, either the police or I would find her, and then she would disappear again. Meanwhile social services found a secure unit for young girls that looked reasonable. They had used it before and said it was one of the better ones. I researched it on the internet and didn't come across anything awful about it. Peterborough was a long way from Oxford, but perfectly manageable once or even twice a week. I didn't know how often I would be allowed to visit her.

On the Wednesday afternoon Lara returned home, after disappearing for a few hours, while I was trying to pack some clothes for her.

'What are you doing with my clothes? What's the suitcase for?'

I told her that she would now be going to a secure unit and she went berserk, kicking and screaming and dragging the clothes back out of the case. In the middle of this the social worker rang back to say the place at Peterborough had gone, but there was a secure unit at St Helens in Merseyside, called St Catherine's, that had a vacancy. There was no time to check it out, so I just had to say OK, as Lara was trying to climb out of a Velux window in her bedroom, four floors up. Sophie rang the police while I held on to Lara's legs. Three police officers were with us in minutes and Lara started to calm down.

We had a bit of a party in the kitchen, the three police officers, Jane, Jean, Lara and me, while we waited for the special escort to arrive. I made several pots of tea, and Jane went out for chocolate biscuits. Everyone tried to be light-hearted and jolly; we even went on the internet and looked at St Catherine's Secure Unit, which was marketing itself like a three-star hotel.

We were sitting on the front steps when the security people finally arrived so Lara could have a last cigarette or two: she wouldn't be allowed them in the secure unit. Lara freaked out when she saw the security people. As luck would have it, one of them, a woman, was familiar to her, as she had been involved in the forced eviction from the care home in King's Lynn and the deportation in the early hours down to Devon nearly two years earlier. We calmed Lara down and got her into the car, then sobbing, she slipped away into the night.

We went back indoors and I started shaking uncontrollably. Jane poured me a large brandy and stayed with me. I felt utterly desolate but hugely relieved at the same time. And such a failure. How had it come to this?

15

The Prisoner

While we'd had a laugh looking at St Catherine's online before Lara left, when I had a chance to research it further, I was shocked. It was run by a charity called Nugent Care, a Roman Catholic organization founded in the nineteenth century, and as with so many childcare organizations of that pedigree, the internet was full of stories about child abuse and cruelty, including a current case in the courts. However, when I spoke briefly to Lara the following morning, she didn't sound too bad, except for the fact that she couldn't smoke. She said it was just like a prison but that the staff seemed nice.

Bizarrely we saw each other the next day back in Oxford at the magistrates' court, when Lara was dragged back from Merseyside for the magistrates in Oxford to confirm that she should have been sent to a secure unit in Merseyside in the first place and order her to be dragged back again. Cruel, stupid, costly. Three words that seemed to sum up every aspect of the childcare system as we experienced it.

As I walked up the stairs of the dismal 1960s court building to the waiting area, I heard Lara call, 'Mum.' She ran towards me with her arms outstretched, two enormous prison escorts chasing her. They tried to stop her hugging me, but I shouted furiously at them to back off. She had been sent down with a prison guard detail of three, two men and a woman. There was no member of staff from the unit with her.

They had wanted to keep her locked in a cell while we waited to see the magistrates, but that had been opposed by the solicitor acting for the guardian ad litem, so she was allowed to wait with me, with our every move glowered over by the prison escorts. They even tried to go to the loo with her. I was appalled; they were treating her like the criminals we were surrounded by.

We waited and waited, sitting in the communal area along with that day's selection of Oxford's petty criminals awaiting their just deserts. Lara knew several of them. But she wasn't a criminal; she was a vulnerable fourteen-year-old child. This was a family hearing that shouldn't have been taking place in such a setting. The escort service each had their own packed lunch, but there was nothing for Lara. She had left Merseyside at 6 a.m. with no breakfast. It was now lunchtime, she wouldn't be back until the evening, and no one had thought about food or drink for her. I couldn't go out for something in case the magistrates suddenly called us, so I just pumped money into the snack and drinks machines and kept her going on crisps, chocolate and fizzy drinks.

After nearly four hours' hanging around, we were finally summoned into court. My legs felt like lead as I stood up to go in. The guards tried to stop Lara and me walking in together, and in court we were not allowed to sit together. The guardian ad litem wasn't there, but the solicitor who was officially representing Lara's legal interests sat with her. Sophie the social worker was there with a solicitor from the county council, who outlined the reasons they were seeking a court order to lock up Lara. I said I wasn't opposing it, but that it would never have come to this if Lara had been given help earlier. And that was it – in less than fifteen minutes the rather bewildered looking magistrates had made an order that Lara be detained under a secure accommodation order until 3 July, eighteen days later. I had been expecting the order, if made, to be for three months, not less than three weeks. What use would three weeks be?

Lara was distraught: she had been hoping they would release her. I asked if I could take her back to St Catherine's myself. I was told no, but only afterwards did I think that as I still had parental responsibility, I could have insisted. As it was, I didn't think and so I could do nothing but watch her go, virtually dragged off by the two male guards. The social worker and the two solicitors stood together chatting and laughing. They were obviously old friends.

I left court feeling annihilated, humiliated, very angry with myself and utterly alone. I should have handled it better; I should not have lost my temper with the guards. I should have better argued the case for taking Lara back to St Catherine's myself, as it was such a long journey up to Liverpool. I should have taken food for Lara. I felt I had totally let her down. I was completely overpowered by the system.

I was summoned to go and meet the guardian ad litem the next day. She was a woman about my age wearing a T-shirt and tracksuit bottoms. She had sounded quite understanding on the phone, so I wasn't prepared for her attack when I got to her offices. She was quite pleasant to start with, but I had hardly sat down when she laid into me.

'What have you done to Lara to make her so unhappy and angry?' was her opening shot.

I was completely stunned.

'I don't think it's really me she is angry with; it's everything that's happened to her.'

'Oh, come on – she seems to hate you,' she retorted in a very antagonistic way. This from someone who hadn't met either of us before and who had just admitted she hadn't had time to read the file yet.

I hadn't expected this kind of interrogation, but I tried to explain everything I had been told by the various therapists and psychologists. I talked about the anger Lara felt about all the abuse she had suffered and how that was now surfacing and she was projecting a lot of that onto me.

'Oh, you don't like being challenged, do you?' she sneered.

'I don't mind being challenged,' I said coldly, 'but I won't put up with downright rudeness. If you aren't prepared to treat me with basic courtesy, I'll leave.'

She actually looked a bit shocked at that, blinked and moderated her tone slightly, but she continued to harp on about me wanting to be in control.

I said, 'Somebody has to try to be in control: Lara isn't in control of herself, and the system has shown itself utterly unable to get a grip on things, so yes, I am doing what any responsible parent would do in trying to keep Lara from harm, including harm from the system.'

She said I shouldn't have asked to take Lara back to the secure unit. They would simply remove my parental responsibility if I raised objections to anything again. I tried to explain what it felt like to see your child with people who were little more than jailers, but she wasn't interested.

Her parting comments to me were, 'Don't go wasting your money on getting legal representation – it won't do you any good. You have no rights or role in this anymore.' And this was the person who in the eyes of the law was supposed to represent Lara's best interests. Poor Lara.

The following day was my birthday, something I didn't particularly want to celebrate in the circumstances, but I was persuaded to go down to Michael and Victoria's in Wales. Lara rang me twice, which was lovely and really made my day. She didn't sound too bad, but again it was not being able to smoke that really bugged her. She said she didn't want to make friends, as most of the other girls were psychos and kept trying to kill themselves.

I drove up to St Catherine's the next day, the dogs with me in the car; it was a grim journey, rain all the way. I was early so decided to stop at some local shops and buy a few things for Lara, but there were really no shops to get much in. All I could find was a Bargain Booze and a Costcutter. Although I grew up in Merseyside, I had forgotten just how poor that part of the world can be. The main saving grace was a park right next to the secure unit, very handy for walking the dogs.

The first part of St Catherine's that you encounter when turning in off the road is absolutely grim, a huge, dark, semi-derelict institutional building of which there are so many in Merseyside. You could almost hear the misery of generations of abused children wailing from the walls. Though it had teemed with rain the whole journey, just as I parked the sun came out, meaning that I had to leave the car windows open for the dogs, banking on the grimness of the place to put off any local criminals.

Sophie arrived as I did. Again she was nice, even apologizing for the type of escort that had brought Lara down to court on Friday. She said they were an adult service and should never have been used for Lara. The outside of the secure unit itself wasn't too bad, about ten years old, single storey and in a light brick. There were, however, rolls of razor wire on the tops of the walls and cameras and searchlights on metal towers.

The public reception areas were light and brightly painted with pictures and tapestries. We had to leave all our bags and papers in lockers, and Karl, the unit duty manager, who came to reception to meet us, searched what I was bringing in for Lara and removed the staples from the magazine. He seemed nice, warm and welcoming, but very much in charge. I felt myself relax. I can trust this guy to take control of the situation, I thought. He knows what he's doing.

He took us through several locked doors down a corridor to a meeting room. As we sat down, he said, 'I need to tell you that we did a pregnancy test on Lara this morning and it was positive. We haven't told her yet, as we thought it might come better from you.'

'Oh God!' I gasped. 'I don't know how she'll cope with that. Are you sure?'

'Yes, pretty certain, but to be on the safe side we've done another test. We don't have the results yet.'

As Karl and I went through the public reception towards the residential area, the environment rapidly deteriorated. There were no curtains, no ornaments, no pictures, and the walls were white. We never went into the part that the girls and young women actually lived in, but I did catch the occasional glimpse on different visits and it was really awful: crumbling walls, hardly any furniture and the most basic of cells. Walking through on that first visit, I caught a glimpse of Lara through a vision panel in a locked room; she was in tears. Apparently she'd just had an argument with a teacher.

Eventually Lara joined us in the visitors' room, but there were many interruptions and distractions, as alarm bells rang, children screamed and staff came in and out.

'Mum, I think I'm pregnant,' she blurted out.

So she does know. 'Yes, I'm afraid it looks as though you are. Karl said the test you did this morning was positive,' I said.

She ran out of the room crying before I could say anything else.

However, while she was out, another member of staff came in to tell us the second test was negative. When Lara returned, she'd had a complete change of heart and seemed happy with the prospect of being a mum. I had to tell her she wasn't pregnant after all and she became hysterical, blaming me for everything, including killing her baby. I tried to pacify her, but everything I said just made it worse and she stared at me with hatred in her eyes before picking up a mug from the table and going to hit me with it. Karl tried to restrain her, but before he could get a grip, she smashed the mug onto his hand, breaking his watchstrap in the process. As he dragged her out of the room, she was screaming in absolute despair. Her last words to me were, 'Why have you done this to me?'

I sat feeling shaken until Karl returned and told me Lara had calmed down but wouldn't be allowed to spend more time with me that day. He walked me to the car to see the dogs so he could report back to Lara on how they were doing, and then I drove home, 200 miles, again in the teeming rain. Lara rang me when I got in, sounding much better and apologetic.

Every time a child is sent to a secure unit, a reviewing panel is set up consisting of three independent experts drawn from different parts of the country, one to chair, one to nominally represent the child and one to represent the local authority perspective. Their job is to consider whether the justification for locking up the child in the first place still applies, whether the care being provided is appropriate to the child's needs and whether those needs could be met in a less confining setting. The panel appointed to oversee Lara's incarceration met, with us all in attendance, up at St Catherine's just two weeks after Lara was secured and wow, they were good! Each of the three panel members was informed, knowledgeable and tough but also warm, articulate and insightful. It was the first time in this whole grim process that Lara and I had been treated like human beings and I had not been made to feel like a damaging failure as a parent. Instead of being a minor party, they treated me like a key player, even *the* key player in Lara's future.

Lara was brought back to Oxford Magistrates' Court on 3 July. She was desperately hoping they would release her because she had been making such good progress and the order that had been made was about to expire. Knowing that I would again feel totally outnumbered by the massed ranks of social workers and their solicitors, I got a solicitor to represent me. I had borrowed the £2,000 that a solicitor for half a day in court would cost me from my mother. I had thought of asking someone to come with me but decided not to, fearing what a grim experience it would be.

It felt very different to the last time, partly because I was legally represented and therefore felt I had some support for Lara and me, and partly because this time Lara was brought down and looked after by a specially trained escort service designed for children. They were lovely and even got her a private room so she didn't have to sit and wait in the main waiting area. The guardian, who did turn up this time, tried to bait me again, but knowing I had legal representation, I ignored her.

The outcome of this hearing, however, was devastating for Lara. The magistrates, who looked even more nonplussed the second time round, decided to send her back yet again, this time for five weeks, saying that she hadn't been there long enough for them to know whether the reported improvement was permanent. She was removed from the court sobbing hysterically and all I could hear was, 'Mum, Mum, please help me,' as she was led away. But there was nothing I could do. I just had to pray that the staff at St Catherine's had the expertise and compassion to help us survive this.

The process was cruel; if they were going to keep sending her back, why make the orders for such short periods in the first place? It just got her hopes up each time. It felt like a game of cat and mouse, but it was clear that in fact the magistrates didn't really understand what would be in the best interests of the child, or perhaps they misguidedly thought they were being kind in making the orders for such short periods.

The magistrates had told Lara they were hopeful she could be released by mid-August so she began to pin all her hopes on that, even starting a countdown calendar, which she told me she had put up on her cell wall.

Realizing that there was no possibility of her being released for at least five weeks, I decided after much soul-searching, but still totally selfishly, to continue with a holiday that Jane, Lara and I had planned: ten days in the South of France at Michael and Victoria's holiday home. I didn't want to let Jane down, and I was also desperate for a break. I was so stressed that I was beginning to fear for my sanity. I reasoned that I could still ring Lara every day, and as I was only able to visit her once a week, she would actually miss just one visit from me. The big cause of my guilt was that I would be away for her fifteenth birthday.

We filled the car boot with books and swimming things, and drove off to catch the ferry. It was a glorious break, warm and sunny. And 800 miles away from Oxford and further still from Merseyside, there was nothing I could do about anything that might be happening there. I got into a wonderful routine – an early swim followed by breakfast by the pool, the morning spent sitting in the cool of the beautiful old French farmhouse dining room, French windows open wide and voile curtains blowing gently in the breeze, transposing the various diaries, journals and notes I had kept over the past few years onto my new tablet computer.

I had kept diaries on and off for most of my life, ever since someone gave me a five-year diary for my tenth birthday. I don't know why, but I felt really driven that holiday to get the diaries of the recent years into a more coherent whole. I didn't then know that these diaries would be used as evidence in two separate criminal trials, or as material for a book, but I needed to be able to try and pin down some of the chaos of recent times, to see if I could bring some order to it or make sense of it. Just having it all set down in black and white seemed to help somehow.

Lunch would be followed by another swim, and the afternoon was usually spent reading lying on the grass under the trees. I had always been a keen reader, but the worries and distractions of the past three years or so meant that I now struggled even to keep up with the bi-monthly book for my book group. That week, though, I devoured four books, losing myself for a few hours at a time in other people's lives and imaginations. Each evening we dined under the stars on wonderful local food bought from the market in a small town nearby. It was an utterly indulgent, carefree and child-free break, and my enjoyment of it far outweighed the guilt that I felt for being so self-indulgent at such a time.

I rang Lara every night. She tried to give me grief about being away in the sun while she was locked up indoors for twenty-three hours a day, and even when let outside, it was just into a small yard with thirty-foot walls that only got the sun for twenty minutes a day, but on the whole she seemed OK. On 17 July Jane and I sang 'Happy Birthday' down the phone and she said she had received not only the card and presents I had left for her but also many from friends and family, and staff and other girls in the unit. I was so pleased she hadn't been neglected.

It was with a heavy heart and increasing trepidation that I set out to drive the 600 miles to the ferry at Saint-Malo. With every hundred miles we drove, the sun grew less bright and my mood gloomier. We spent the journey over the Channel listening to reports of flooding across many parts of the UK, including

Oxford, and before we docked we had a phone call from Jane's sister, who was staying in the house dog sitting, to say our house was starting to flood and the fire brigade had been round telling everyone to be prepared to evacuate. Would we make it home?

We did, just, driving through water about five inches deep and rising. What a brutal return to reality. The house wasn't too badly flooded inside, just puddles of water where the ground-water had risen, but the front and back gardens were under water. I built a bridge from the cat flap up to the garden for the cat, then we got the washing machine and tumble dryer up on bricks, and I drove the car to a car park on higher ground to make sure I would be able to get up to see Lara the next day. As I did so, the police were closing the main road, effectively cutting off our part of Oxford to motor transport.

I had come back to a letter from the guardian's solicitor saying they wanted to delay the next hearing to consider when Lara could be released for no better reason than it didn't suit their diaries. Oxfordshire County Council were also dragging their feet, citing distance and the summer holidays as reasons why they could not visit Lara as often as they were required to nor set up education and other services for her in Oxford so she could return home. In order to buy themselves more time, they kept trying to raise the bar of what Lara had to achieve before she would be allowed home. But Lara had already more than achieved what the court and the panel had required of her by way of behaviour and compliance with things like the education programme.

It seemed incredible that a child could be left locked up

when they no longer fitted the legal criteria to be locked up simply because bureaucrats couldn't be bothered to do what was required of them. I appealed to the chair of the review panel, who agreed that it was incredible and also would not be tolerated. He said he would chase them all. I said I would produce a detailed project plan of what we each had to achieve to get Lara home as soon as was appropriate.

To take the pressure off Sophie, I took over coordinating the actions of the different agencies, including education and health. We still didn't know when Lara would be out, but given the vagaries of the Oxford magistrates, we had to plan for it possibly being as early as 14 August.

I was not sure that mentally or emotionally she could have coped with another let-down. Lara needed predictable, clear structures and cause and effects. She had now ended up in a legal system that was even more chaotic and unpredictable than she was. She would have fared better as a criminal; at least she would have known how long her sentence was from the outset. All the time Lara had been with me, I had tried to convince her that life could be different for her and it was not her destiny to live the sort of life her parents had. She struggled with that notion, but I thought there was always a glimmer in the back of her mind that she could have a good future. But stuck in the secure system with officials constantly moving the goal posts, she was losing all hope. She spent most of our nightly phone calls sobbing bitterly. I had never known her so low and despondent. Taking away someone's hope is a terrible thing to do to anyone, but especially to a fifteen-year-old with her whole life ahead of her.

Whether it would have happened anyway or was because

pressure was building I don't know, but suddenly both mental health and education came up with detailed planned programmes for her, both to start in September. For the first time in three long years, full-time education was being offered. At the next review meeting, on 7 August, the panel determined that Lara had made such good progress that she no longer met the criteria for being locked up and that when the present court order expired the following week, she should be released.

So Lara left St Catherine's the following week, after an eight-week stay. Overall the secure unit itself was a positive experience for her, despite the privations. The staff were all excellent with her and very supportive of me. Trained, motivated and focused, with very clear frameworks and outcomes planned for everything they did, they were so different to most of the social residential care and education staff we had encountered in other settings. To be fair to those others, it must be a lot easier to provide support or education to someone like Lara where they can't keep running off, but in addition the secure-unit staff seemed to have a much higher sense of commitment to and interest in their charges as individuals. Ironically the secure unit, which I had so feared, had been a good thing for Lara.

We drove away from St Catherine's with the car full of tangible evidence of Lara's achievements there – art projects, schoolwork and good-luck cards and letters from other girls and staff – and our ears ringing with praise for Lara's performance of 'Amazing Grace' at a unit concert the previous night.

The first thing Lara wanted to do was stop for a cigarette: eight weeks' enforced abstinence sadly had not broken the habit. It was great to have her back, but I knew our problems were far from over.

16

Friends In Their Infinite Variety

I got a last-minute booking on a package holiday to Lanzarote. It was a pleasant, if somewhat dull hotel in a fairly nice resort, but it was good for Lara and me to be able to spend time together. There were, as I had hoped, plenty of young people holidaying with their parents and Lara joined a group of about eight teenagers who hung around the pool and were allowed to walk down to a bar on the beach early each evening to play pool. I joined in the anxiety of the other parents about what might happen if they were five minutes late back and whether there was any risk someone might serve them a beer. Ordinary life was really quite unexciting but a welcome change. Would it last, though?

Once we were settled back in Oxford, a much better package of services was put forward. Lara was offered a place (paid for by the county council) in a private tutorial college mainly used by overseas students wanting to get into a British university or by those needing to resit exams in order to get higher grades. It was hoped Lara could, with a lot of one-to-one support, get at least five GCSEs by the end of the year. Social services provided a support worker to help Lara once or twice a week, and monthly family support sessions were set up with Lara's mental health key worker.

We settled into more of a routine than we had had for years, until one day in late September Lara rang me at work. Screaming hysterically, she spluttered out, 'Terri's dead! Mum, she's dead.'

Our neighbour Joanne came on the phone; she had heard Lara running screaming up the street, 'My mum's dead. I need my mum!' Lara was now in her house sobbing uncontrollably. To begin with, I was not certain whether it was true or not: there had been previous rumours that Terri had died, mainly put about by Kirsten to wind up Lara, so when I heard that this news had come from Kirsten's children's home, I remained sceptical.

I rang the home. It was true: they had received a phone call from Terri's father. It hadn't been Kirsten who rang Lara but a care worker, without bothering to find out if there was anyone with Lara when she got the news. I rushed home.

Lara was the most agitated I had ever seen her, certainly when not under the influence of drink or drugs; she paced around and pulled at her face. We talked about how Terri might have died and, as we had no information, assumed it must have been a drug overdose.

Over the following days I didn't quite know how to play it with Lara. Most of the time she seemed just to want plain talking about death and funerals in general from me, backed up with comfort and reassurance, but every so often, especially after talking on the phone to Kirsten, she would clam up, tell me I didn't understand and retreat to her room.

The funeral was grim. How do you grieve for a mother who

neglected and disowned you but nevertheless gave birth to you, while you are sitting beside her coffin with her bereft parents? How do you feel when there is someone whom you now call 'Mum' sitting in the chapel with you, but the priest taking the service describes the woman who has caused you so much pain as 'warm' and 'loving' and a 'wonderful mother to all her children'? Lara did it by disowning me. I wasn't allowed to sit with her or comfort her or attend the wake afterwards, which was held in the homeless hostel were Terri had been living until she was found dead in a drugs house nearby.

Two days after the funeral Lara said, 'Well, I guess you really are my mother now. I didn't love her, you know. She was a stupid druggie.'

Sadly I knew it wasn't that simple for her.

Within a month the honeymoon period at college was over. Lara couldn't cope with the expectations that she would be able to work largely on her own and motivate herself. Apart from the fact that she was still reeling from the turmoil caused by Terri's death, the last time she had been in a real educational programme was year seven. She had never developed the skill of self-discipline and the application needed to learn. The private tutorial college tried, but they didn't have the right experience or resources to motivate her. Above all, I suspected that a fear of success was holding Lara back. If she ever demonstrated success or talent at anything and it was remarked on, she would immediately stop doing it. With success would come responsibility and increased expectations from other people. Lara set herself against succeeding at anything.

She spent a lot of the daytime and several evenings a week with Ricky, the thirty-something man who had returned Lara's phone to me on the bridge and who had virtually sworn an oath when I told him how old she was that he would never see her again.

'It's OK, Mum – we don't have sex,' she said when I challenged her about their relationship. I didn't believe that and I told her so, and that I would be reporting him to the police the minute she was gone beyond our agreed curfew of 9.30 p.m. However, it was true that for many weeks she was always back on time and I was pretty sure I knew where she was. Bizarre as it may sound, I even ran her to his flat on a couple of occasions so I could be certain where he lived. Compared to what had been happening to her earlier in the year, this seemed relatively safe, and I didn't want to push her to the point that she started lying to me again and disappearing overnight.

But it wasn't long before the curfew was breached and she started to spend the night with Ricky. I had his telephone number, so I rang him again. Again he feigned shock when I told him her age. I reminded him we had already had that conversation, but he pretended not to have understood me. He promised once more that he would not see her again and that he was deleting her number from his phone straight away. Lara and Ricky continued to see each other, although whenever I confronted him, he said it wasn't possible that he was seeing her as he no longer had her mobile number on his phone. I couldn't quite decide whether this man was wicked or downright stupid. I decided both, and utterly shameless to boot.

Every time Lara was not home on time, I rang the police, told them who she was with and gave them his name and address.

When I told him what I was doing, he retorted that he was going to report me to the police for harassment.

To add to my concern, Ricky's flat was the subject of a drugs raid, although he was never charged, and even more worryingly, I realized from things Lara was saying that he was a close associate of Egyptian Mo and Sam the Rapist. Astonishingly Lara was now consorting with both of them on the phone and also at Mo's flat and other places, although she was clearly frightened of them. I couldn't understand it, but she said they were friends and they had good parties. I was gradually coming to realize the profound damage that the very early abuse she had suffered had caused her. She really couldn't distinguish between abuse and affection when it came to men; they were one and the same to her.

We were seeing even more of Kirsten since Terri's death. She was now sixteen and therefore pretty much out of care and increasingly expected to fend for herself. I desperately wanted to be able to help and support her, because without us she was now essentially alone in the world. She was down with us at least once a month and Lara started to introduce her to Egyptian Mo and his associates.

One weekend when Kirsten was staying with us and she and Lara had failed to return at the appointed time, I went to see if they were with Mo. I knew he lived in a block of flats near us. Originally built by the council for people with support needs, they now housed a motley assortment of young families, people with obvious mental health problems or learning disabilities and, increasingly, drug dealers and other criminals. Walking past one day, Lara had pointed out his flat from the outside. I decided to go and try and find him, either to reason with him or, if necessary, threaten him with the police. Once inside the block, I couldn't work out which flat was his. The building was shaped like a hexagon with a central courtyard and different staircases, making it hard to relate the external features to any particular front door. It was like a maze in there. I knocked on a few doors and finally got an answer from a young man I had seen around and who had come to our house a couple of times with messages for Lara, presumably from Egyptian Mo. This man told me he didn't know anyone called Mo and hadn't seen Lara round there for weeks.

I went home and later that night got a withheld-number call on the house phone from a man with a really rough, menacing voice. 'Yer fucking bitch, don't go round causing trouble. Yer daughter's a slag and a crack whore, and she ain't here. Come here again and yer gonna get hurt.'

'Mohammed, I know exactly who you are and where you live and what you get up to. Don't think you can threaten me. I'm going straight to the police.'

I was shaking so much I dropped the phone, but hopefully he didn't realize that. He uttered some obscenities I couldn't quite make out and hung up.

Later that weekend I walked up the towpath towards the block of flats, still looking for Lara and Kirsten, and I spotted them on the footbridge over the river. When they saw me, they started to run over the bridge and jumped into a waiting car, an old BMW with blacked-out windows, which sped away as I shouted futilely after it.

They were gone for three days. On her return, Lara said they had gone to Leeds via Wolverhampton, and had then dropped Kirsten back in Stoke before returning to Oxford. I discovered much later that they had been snorting cocaine with the girls' birth father in Stoke. Whatever was really going on with Egyptian Mo and his associates, Kirsten was clearly getting dragged in too. I knew she had had issues with drugs and alcohol for some time and she saw this gang as a ready supply.

Apart from that incident Lara was not disappearing to other parts of the country as often as she had been. Ricky and Kirsten were her main companions, and although neither was good for her, they were less harmful than the menacing, shadowy figures who used to spirit her away all over the country.

I was, though, very concerned about her relationship with Ricky, especially as he was now trying to get her to stay away from home for longer and longer. I rang him one Sunday morning suspecting Lara was with him.

'Is Lara there?'

'No, I haven't seen her for ages.'

In the background a girl's voice was shouting, 'Who the fuck is that? Is it my mum?'

'I'm not that stupid, Ricky – I can hear her shouting. I know she's with you.'

'No she's not. You're harassing me, you stupid cow. I'm going to report you to the police.'

'Please do,' I said. 'I'm going to do the same.'

Christmas 2007 was spent in Oxford, not Wales. My mother, brothers, sister-in-law and nieces, and Kirsten all came to us. Together with Lara, Jane, her brother and me, it was a jolly squash. On Christmas Eve Lara and Kirsten announced they had been invited to a party. Probing got little information out of them, but I gathered Ricky was involved. I reasoned to myself that they were not likely to get so wrecked they would risk ruining Christmas Day for themselves, and in any case there was not much I could do to stop them. Some of the rest of us decided to go to midnight Mass at the cathedral.

Walking home, we bumped into Nick, a friend who was a part-time curate at our local church, who said Lara was very distressed and looking for me. Apparently, not knowing we had gone to the cathedral, she had run into the church, which was just round the corner from our house, in the middle of the service, shouting, 'Where's my mum? I need my mum. My sister has stolen my boyfriend and I need my mum to come and sort it out.' I rushed home while the others tactfully followed slowly behind.

At home, I found a very distraught Lara. At the so-called party, which included not only Ricky but also Egyptian Mo and Sam the Rapist, to whom Lara now referred by his real name, Bassam, Kirsten and Ricky had disappeared and had sex together.

'But he's my boyfriend,' she sobbed. 'I hate her. Why did she want to steal him?'

'But he's at fault too. I'm afraid it shows what sort of a man he is, and he is more than twice your and Kirsten's age.'

'No, it's her fault – men can't help doing things like that. She threw herself at him. I could kill her.'

Kirsten turned up in a terrible state at about six in the morning and spent most of Christmas Day in bed. The two girls disappeared again on Boxing Day, this time to Mo's flat, and didn't return for twenty-four hours.

As most of our family gatherings were in Wales, where Lara

was usually very relaxed and well behaved, my family had not really experienced first-hand her wilder, chaotic side. I tried to play it down, but they could see what was going on, and my mother in particular was appalled at what Lara and Kirsten were getting up to. I had to work very hard to persuade her not to say anything to Lara. I did not want to antagonize Lara and make the situation worse.

We survived Christmas, celebrated New Year in Cornwall, and 2008 started fairly peacefully. After a lot of grumbling Lara went back to college, but found it hard to attend for more than a couple of hours at a time, which was never going to get her the five GCSEs everyone was hoping for.

Then early in January Lara came home with three new friends. An unlikely trio, Ben and Brian were two young men from a homeless hotel, and Becky was an undergraduate at the university. Apparently the three Bs had been friends for a bit. Our house was quite full most evenings with the three Bs, plus Kelly and Will (the little brother and sister from round the corner who I had been feeding for a couple of years). To this group Lara added Amy, a very young disabled girl from the other side of Oxford, and another couple of young men, Tyrone and Dale, who lived somewhere near us. They were a motley crew, and with the exception of Becky all had significant social disadvantages. The dishes of macaroni cheese or cottage pie had to be scaled up, but it seemed a small price to pay for having Lara at home and starting to make some new friends. It was touching to see how she was drawn towards those she saw as needing help and protection. It also seemed significant that she brought all these people home to me.

A few weeks later Lara was complaining of feeling unwell.

As she was always a bit of a hypochondriac, I didn't take it too seriously until she started being sick. After a couple of days I went to Boots and bought a pregnancy testing kit. Yes, she was. Oh hell, just when there was a suggestion that things were settling down a bit.

Lara was insistent that she wanted to keep the baby and would not even allow me to broach the topic of abortion.

'You can't make me kill my baby,' she screamed at me.

But I knew that there was no way she would cope with a baby; she was, after all, only fifteen. She seemed to have no idea who the father might be, and whoever he was, he was unlikely to be the sort of man who would help and support her. I could see only a future of heartache, with the baby possibly disabled, given the alcohol and drugs Lara took, and taken from her by social services. It would be history repeating itself. But if she really wouldn't consider a termination, then I had to do my damnedest to ensure that both she and the baby got the best care they could and that she minimized the harm she might do to either of them. We got her signed up with the doctor and midwife, and onto the folic acid.

Knowing Lara was pregnant, I became less tolerant of all the hangers-on she kept bringing round, not the kids but the older ones. Apart from anything else, they were clearly smoking in the house, something I had always banned. Ben and Brian brought their washing round without asking and clogged up the machine with mud. They left old clothes and beer bottles everywhere, charged up an astonishing number of mobile phones from every available socket, forgot to flush the loo and consumed vast amounts of coffee, milk and biscuits. The final straw came when I found a knife down a sofa in the living room; it had dropped out of Ben's jacket. I don't think he had any intention of threatening us with it – as a young homeless man, he probably felt he had to carry a knife; I knew that many of them did for protection – but I wasn't going to risk it. So a couple of months after they first moved in, I told them I was not going to be allowing them in the house anymore. They took it with reasonable grace. I heard a couple of weeks later that Brian had gone to prison.

Becky, the Oxford undergraduate, was a much harder nut to crack. Young, black and very angry, she greeted everyone with a 'Come on if you think you're hard enough' attitude. From an Inner London comprehensive, she must have worked very hard to get a place at Oxford University and was clearly extremely bright. I couldn't fathom out the basis of the friendship between her and Lara, or how she had come to know the two young homeless men. There isn't usually much mingling between town and gown in Oxford, certainly not when the students are living in college, as Becky was. It was a mystery what either girl was getting out of the relationship. I smiled at the thought of Lara eating in college with Becky: Lara, who had dropped out of school at twelve, who had steadfastly refused to acquire any education ever since, chatting away to some of the most educated young people in the world. I asked what they talked about.

'Oh, you know, Mum, just politics and philosophy and stuff. It's really quite interesting.'

If only things had gone differently at school, Lara too could have been at university in a couple of years.

A few times when I had come back from work or shopping a bit earlier than expected, I had found Lara and Becky shooing older men out of the front door. When I remonstrated, I was told they were fellow students of Becky's who had just dropped round. Must have been mature students, I thought.

The events of one summer evening finally made me realize what Becky was gaining from their friendship. I was in the kitchen preparing supper for the usual assortment of family and Lara's protégés. My brother Gerry was staying and we had opened a bottle of wine. Lara and Becky were three floors up, in Lara's loft-conversion bedroom. I called up the stairs that supper was ready and the girls came down, told me that they were going to eat in college and more or less ran out of the door. A few minutes later I was sure I could still hear noises coming from upstairs. Gerry came up with me and we climbed the stairs to Lara's bedroom. As we entered the room, we spotted some legs underneath Lara's bed. We shouted to the legs to come out and for a few minutes they just tried to crawl further under the bed. Eventually, as we started to lift the bed frame, not one but two men clambered out, both wearing just boxers. They were black and probably in their late twenties or early thirties. They claimed not to understand English, but clearly got my meaning when I ordered them out, because they got dressed in lightning-quick speed and fled down the stairs.

When Lara came home, I challenged her about them. 'Oh, thanks for getting rid of them, Mum. Becky brought them round and they wouldn't go. We didn't know what to do, so we just went out.'

It now all started to make sense: Becky was on the game. Wishing to eke out her student loan, she was prostituting, and because she was unable to do that in college, she had sought out and cultivated someone vulnerable with a view to using his or her home. I didn't know whether she had got Lara involved as well, but given there were two men, it seemed highly likely. In the morning I rang Becky's college and spoke to the dean. He was not surprised at what I told him, virtually finishing my sentences for me. We did not hear from Becky again, and rumour had it that she had been sent down. That incident made me realize that it wasn't just men who could take advantage of Lara; she was also vulnerable to being preyed upon by women.

Though we didn't hear from Becky, we did hear from her clients for a bit longer. Twice I answered the door to men with little English asking for 'B-eac-kee'. Once, at 4 a.m., concerned about a noise downstairs, I went to the living room to discover a man lying on the sofa. Lara said he had come round looking for Becky and she hadn't known what to do with him so had put him in the living room.

'Oh, thanks, Mum – I knew you'd know what to do with him. You always make me feel safe because you know what to do with these people. I don't know what to say.'

Just say *no*, Lara! Lara who didn't bat an eyelid about saying no in the most uncertain terms to every authority figure – parent, school, social services, the police, mental health workers – couldn't, to save her life, say no to all these bits of lowlife.

Protection for Lara came from a most unlikely source, from the two new friends Tyrone and Dale, young men living in the local bail hostel. I realized that because they were in a bail hostel, whatever they had done must have been quite serious. They were only allowed out after 11 a.m. and were subject to a 9 p.m. curfew, and were clearly very anxious not to break any of their parole conditions. They were exemplary in their attitude to me and the house, never abusing my hospitality. They usually refused food and if they accepted coffee would often turn up the next day with some milk. I never saw them drunk; they didn't even smoke. And they escorted Lara around town as though they were guarding the most precious possession, a prize jewel or film star.

And then one day I got a phone call from the local police station. Did I know that Lara had been seen in town on several occasions with two sex offenders just out of prison and on parole? It was a shock. Out of all the things I imagined they had done, I hadn't anticipated that. But strange as it may sound, I was confident from the open demeanour of all three that neither of the young men was abusing her in any way, so I let them stay around, although I did keep an even closer eye on things. The police probably thought I was mad, but I knew these two young men were not the villains as far as Lara was concerned, and if I had tried to ban her from seeing them, it would just have gone on in secret. Better the devil you know. And better to be keeping a pregnant girl at home or near to home even if that meant having two registered sex offenders in the house.

And so the pregnancy went on. Despite my best efforts Lara was still smoking and drinking, but since she found out she was pregnant I saw no evidence of drug taking. I was starting to have panic attacks about what would become of them both, this child mother and child. I would often wake up in the middle of the night from nightmares in which the baby was dragged away from Lara by social workers, or in which Lara disappeared forever, leaving me to bring up her baby, or even just took the baby off into her murky underworld. These scenarios played out endlessly and without resolution in my dreams and I would wake struggling to breathe. I simply couldn't get my head round what would be best for Lara, best for the baby and best for me. I decided that what was best for me was what was best for the other two, but what was that? And what about the father? Would some ghastly child abuser rear his ugly head and try to claim paternity rights? Lara didn't know or wouldn't say who the father was, and whoever he was, he was clearly an abusive paedophile.

One day, about four months into her pregnancy, I managed to have a serious conversation with Lara about what would happen. It was very difficult to get her to engage with and stay in a discussion about a contentious topic, but this time she did. I think even she was beginning to realize that we really did need to work out how we would cope.

'Love, we must talk about what is going to happen when the baby is born.'

'I'm not going to let anyone take it away.'

'Well, whether you like it or not, social services will have to take a view on the baby's safety, and the best way to reassure them is if we can show them that we've made plans for everything and that you're going to let me and others support you.'

'OK, but I'm not going to let anyone take it away. It's my baby.'

'Well, then you need to show that you can do what's best for it.'

The deal Lara and I made was that for the first few months at least I would take the main responsibility for looking after the baby and that she would let me do that. We would employ a live-in maternity nurse for the first month to show us how to care for the baby. Michael and Victoria generously offered to pay for that. Lara also agreed that she would go back to college in September after the baby was born so that she could try and get into something approximating a normal life for a sixteen-year-old and catch up on some education and that I would find a long-term childminder to enable me to keep working two or three days a week.

Having reached that agreement, I felt we could now both start to feel a bit excited about this new life, which we had nick-named Spuddy for some reason. We started to collect together bits and pieces from car boot sales and charity shops. Various friends donated a Moses basket, a cot and a high chair. One friend who lived in London and loved ferreting around in charity shops posted us three huge parcels of baby clothes. My mother, who had come to terms with the fact that her fifteen-year-old granddaughter was pregnant remarkably well, gave us the money to go and choose brand-new bedding for her first great-grandchild. And a maternity grant paid for the pram and car seat. I had to vacate my office, as it would have to become the nursery, and Lara and I decorated the room together. Jane found some Winnie the Pooh curtains in the Oxfam shop, and Jean spotted a matching baby changing mat on top of a skip that looked brand new.

We felt very cared for and supported, and Spuddy, who we now, after Lara's second scan, knew was a little boy, went from being something of a worry to a source of love and optimism. There can't have been many babies whose birth was awaited with such excitement by so many people. The utter dread I had first felt at the potential grief of the situation started to be replaced by anticipation at the prospect of new life, one that might help ground Lara and give her a sense of purpose and a reason to start to take some responsibility.

The support we got at that time also came from some of the statutory services. Yvonne, Lara's outreach worker from social services, who started seeing her once or twice a week after Lara returned from the secure unit, was fantastic. Someone who had experienced a lot of life both personally and professionally, she was warm and kind and fun, but no fool and she put up with no nonsense from Lara. Lara thought she was fab.

The family support sessions with representatives from the Attach Team and Lara's mental health key worker met every six to eight weeks at the Mental Health Trust. To begin with Lara found every opportunity to take exception to something I said and to storm out of the room, but gradually she found it easier to focus on how life was for us and how we could make it better. A key part of this group was about assessing how we would cope with the baby. They must have provided some positive feedback to social services because a couple of months before Spuddy was due, we received confirmation that providing both Lara and I agreed that I should become the main carer, they would not consider removing him. That was such a relief to hear and something I knew I could use with Lara if there was ever any question of her trying to challenge me in the future.

I went back to the Attach Team for advice and support on dealing with Lara's issues and behaviour. I had mistrusted Attach once I'd realized that everything I said in what I had thought were confidential sessions had to be fed back to social workers who were looking for negative things about Lara and possibly me and were likely to interpret everything in an unhelpful way. But now that Lara was nearly sixteen, they were unlikely to try locking her up again, and we had already been told that Spuddy could remain with us as long as I was the main carer, so I didn't think I had too much to fear and potentially a lot to gain from seeing an expert from the team.

In my monthly meetings with Gillian from Attach, we talked about how both Lara and I would manage our relationship in the future, which would be so altered by the arrival of a baby. Almost before Lara and I had established a proper relationship between just the two of us, there was another person coming along to make things even more complex. I was also concerned that if I was doing most of the caring, I would inevitably become very attached to the baby and vice versa. I worried that Lara would resent that attachment terribly and that the resentment would be fuel for major rows. Gillian helped me sort out my concerns and fears, and find ways forward, giving constant positive feedback and support. She also helped me find more effective ways to communicate with Lara. For the first time since everything went into meltdown, I really started to feel I wasn't doing such a bad job. More or less everything the Attach Team did was predicated on the importance of the relationship between Lara and me, something I had always felt was fundamental but which seemed to be dismissed or denied by other parts of social services. Through my involvement with them I felt some of my self-confidence return, along with my enjoyment of the role of parent and soon-to-be grandparent.

Another positive was the start of some music therapy for Lara. I had a colleague who was a very experienced music therapist and he had met Lara on several occasions when she'd come to work with me. He offered to do some songwriting work with her to see if she could find a way through music of expressing some of her anger and grief. The Education Department agreed to fund it as part of the therapeutic element of her statement of special educational needs. Lara went every four weeks and produced a CD with a lovely song for me, but ultimately she couldn't allow herself to go any deeper into her pain. As the pregnancy advanced, she had to give up these sessions and sadly, with that, her interest in music and singing.

Out of the blue on our way back from one of these music therapy sessions, I got a phone call from a police officer. They had just arrested Ricky and wanted to charge him with sexual activity with a child due to his relationship with Lara. I was gobsmacked. I had regularly given Ricky's name and address when reporting her missing, but no one had ever asked for any further information about him. I didn't even know anyone had read the information I had given, let alone built up a case against him. It came as a complete surprise to realize that after all these years when Lara was clearly having sex, drinking and taking drugs with adult men and coming to all sorts of harm, the police were now prepared to act against one of her abusers.

I was delighted; Lara was, of course, furious. In her opinion, it was none of the police's business who she saw and Ricky hadn't done anything wrong. We both gave statements. Lara's initial reluctance changed as she started to see what Ricky was doing through other people's eyes and gained a growing realization of how manipulative he had been. Her reluctance completely evaporated when he and his new girlfriend, Anna, a girl Lara had known for years and loathed, started trying to intimidate her by bombarding her with abusive and threatening phone calls.

On 17 July 2008 we celebrated Lara's sixteenth birthday with a meal out in town accompanied by ten of our closest family friends. Lara didn't want to include any of her own friends, pre-ferring to keep a distance between what she still saw as Lauren and Lara, bad and good, old and new. At nearly eight months pregnant, there were not many ways she could mark her birth-day other than by doing something fairly sedate. Nevertheless we were quite a jolly group as we walked up the hill to town.

Lara slipped her arm into mine, and with a huge lump in my throat I managed to choke out, 'I never thought we would reach this day. I thought you'd be dead long before now.'

'Oh, Mum, you didn't really, did you?'

From behind, Lara was still so small and skinny you would not have known she was pregnant, but from the front it was a different story. She was now reaching the beached-whale stage and Spuddy was sticking way out and proud. Fortunately the summer of 2008 wasn't too hot, but Lara still felt very uncom-fortable at times. But shepherded everywhere with devoted care and attention by her two sex-offender minders, she managed to keep fairly calm and relaxed, at least by her standards.

As Lara's due date approached, we spent over two weeks going to and from the hospital on an almost daily basis. She had several scans and we saw many midwives, but it was only on the eighth visit that we saw one who raised an alarm. The baby, who a month earlier was predicted to weigh seven or eight pounds, had clearly lost weight and was in some distress. She made an urgent referral to an obstetric consultant, who con-firmed the midwife's fears and said the amniotic fluid had dried up. He assessed the baby as being at least ten days overdue. He would arrange for Lara to be admitted the next day and be induced.

When we turned up the next day at the white, modern

Women's Centre at the John Radcliffe Hospital with supplies for Lara, who was terrified and excited in equal measure, and the baby's bag, complete with vests, hats, mitts, Babygros, nappies and a tiny teddy bear, we were told the consultant had made no such referral. I was about to knock seven bells out of the hospital by ringing all my friends and contacts in senior management positions or on the board.

'No need!' exclaimed a sister. 'We have rung the consultant at home and he says he is very sorry but he forgot to make the referral. Nevertheless Lara must be admitted and induced today.' Phew.

We were moved into a delivery room at about 5 p.m. Lara was offered an aromatherapy footbath, which smelt lovely but did nothing to hurry things on. They put Lara and the baby on a monitor at about 8 p.m., and at eleven they put Lara on a drip, followed by gas and air. The gas and air made poor Lara terribly sick, vomiting her guts up between each contraction, so in the end she opted for an epidural. I was amazed and so proud of how well she was coping with all this. There were no hysterics, no self-pity. I don't think she even swore!

The midwives were rather concerned at the lack of progress and at what the zigzag lines were telling them, but the doctors saw no cause for alarm. One doctor repeatedly tried and failed to take a blood sample from Spuddy's head.

As the night wore on, we both attempted to get some sleep. I curled up on a beanbag and, although I only slept for an hour, awoke feeling very refreshed. Lara, too, managed to doze. It was nearly 11 a.m. the next day when a new midwife came on shift, looked extremely concerned and summoned a doctor. The doctor studied the printout, checked how dilated Lara was and said there was still some way to go. She was about to leave the room again when the midwife shouted out, 'Doctor!'

She turned back, looked at the readout, where one of the lines had suddenly run off the top of the paper, turned and said, 'Lara, you and I are going to deliver your baby right now. He's in distress and it's too late for a C-section. I'm going to have to cut you and use something called a ventouse to pull him out,' and she crashed down to the end of the bed.

Within seconds several midwives and a resuscitation team, complete with a baby life-support unit, were in the room. Some of the midwives were in full-blown panic mode, chaotically running around and kicking over the bowl of aromatherapy water, and then slipping all over the room until I mopped it up. Of course, I had never given birth or even seen a baby being born, and in spite of the preparation I didn't know what to expect. It was barbaric and shocking. It was honestly the worst thing I have ever experienced, including watching people die. Lara was so ill, so distressed, and it went on for hour after hour, and Spuddy, who had been starved for at least a week, nearly died. It was terrifying.

With so many people now hovering around, I couldn't see anything. I just sat at Lara's head trying to comfort her as she dug her nails into my arm. The doctor cut Lara and with the ventouse pulled out a tiny bluish-grey creature, who was handed straight to the resuscitation team. Spuddy was breathing but very cold. After a few minutes they wrapped him up in towels, put on his little blue and white hat, briefly showed him to Lara, who gasped when she saw him, and then handed him to me as she was still being stitched up. As I held him, his colour started to change and he began to take on a pinker hue.

He was tiny and very wrinkled, his skin like dry parchment as a result of Lara's amniotic fluid having dried up, but he was perfect and in that instant I fell completely, utterly, totally in love.

A short while later, as I handed him to Lara, being careful not to slip in the mess that was all over the floor, he opened and rolled one little eye.

17

New Life

Noah Frederick McDonnell was born on 29 August 2008 at 11.44 a.m. He weighed in at five pounds fourteen ounces, possibly two pounds less than he would have been had he been born at the right time. His skin hung in horizontal folds across his legs, back and bottom because of the weight loss. His head, apart from a black silky down, was covered with bloody scratches from the attempts to do blood tests, as though his hair had been combed with barbed wire. He was tiny and looked a bit like ET, but he was gorgeous.

'Look what you've made,' I said to Lara.

She stared at him with such an intense look of awe, wonder and maternal devotion I thought, Maybe we will be OK. Maybe this tiny scrap, with his bloodied head, his ET wrinkles, his unknown father and chaotic child of a mother, can change us all.

The nurses brought us tea and toast. I couldn't get Lara to eat much, but I devoured it. I would never have thought hospital toast and marmalade could taste so good. We were left alone for half an hour and rang family and friends with the news. I also left a message for the maternity nurse saying we would be needing her within the next few days.

Then a nursing assistant came in. Noah's blood tests showed his sugar levels were a bit low and he would need to be taken to the Special Care Baby Unit, or SCBU. Lara sat in a wheelchair with Noah and I pushed them down the corridor while the nursing assistant regaled us with her credentials in childcare and how she didn't believe much in paper qualifications.

Noah was crying as we put him on a special bed under a heat lamp. It was an odd room, because apart from this bit of high-tech medical equipment, it was full of office equipment – a photocopier and printer, piles of office stationery and a bicycle wheel. Lara started to stroke Noah's head as the nursing assistant busied around and after a bit he stopped crying.

'See – he knows his mummy's touch already and you've been able to soothe him,' I said.

'Oh no, it's nothing to do with that. It's the lamp that's calmed him,' retorted the nursing assistant. Clearly her university-of-life course hadn't covered human psychology.

Lara started to cry, but fortunately at that point we were handed over to the SCBU staff and Noah was admitted to a ward full of tiny babies, many in incubators.

Lara went outside for a cigarette and I for some daylight, as we hadn't seen any for nearly twenty-four hours. As I sat in the warm, bright August sun, the whole world felt new, full of excitement and optimism. I was now a grandmother, just over five years after becoming a mother for the first time. But I was also now the main carer of a newborn baby at the age of fifty-eight. I was living my life backwards.

One of my first practical jobs was to rush to Mothercare and buy some extra-small baby clothes. All the newborn clothes we had for him were far too big and would swamp him, with the risk of suffocation. There was no time for the frugal purchasing from charity shops that we had been doing and I spent £100 on clothes that Noah would wear for just two weeks.

When I got back to the hospital, Lara's friend Billie had arrived. They'd met a couple of years earlier, both hanging around on the streets. Billie, who was fifteen, had been in and out of care all her life, was totally chaotic, unreliable, interfering, infuriating and one of the most sweet-natured people I have ever met. She had bought Noah a little silver bracelet. Jean and her daughter dropped by with presents and a card, and Lara's two minders turned up to check on her.

As Noah was in the SCBU, there was no question of anyone other than Lara or me seeing him, which avoided the awkwardness of saying who could and could not meet him. I went down with Lara so she could feed him. She was determined to try breastfeeding, although the staff had said they would probably need to supplement it at least to start with as he was so underweight. That done, we went up to the ward on the maternity unit where Lara would spend the night. All the other women had their babies with them, but I just hoped Lara would be so tired she would sleep and hardly notice.

I went home, and as I parked, several neighbours came out with good wishes and congratulations. I slept like a log, but of course Lara didn't sleep well at all. The other babies kept her awake, and every physical and emotional fibre in her was aching for her own baby, five floors away. She went up and down all night to check on him.

In the morning they said Noah was now well enough to leave the SCBU and come up to the ordinary maternity ward. Lara was overjoyed. They also said that there was a spare private room, and if I could stay with Lara to support her, they would let us have it so we could all be together. That afternoon Lara and Noah held court in our private room to several admiring visitors who seemed to regard it as a privilege to be allowed to change his nappy and mop up dribble.

And then we were on our own. I had a confession to make.

'Lara, I've never changed a nappy before.'

'What, never?'

'No. I've watched other people, but I've never done it myself.'

'Well, it can't be that hard, can it?'

'No. Let's have a go.'

We had to discard the first couple of new nappies because I got the tapes stuck together, and he weed all over the third one before I got it on him, but finally we did it. We rearranged the furniture so his plastic cot was in between our beds and we settled down for the night.

'Do you think he's OK?'

'Yes, I think so.'

'Can you hear him breathing?'

'Not sure.'

'Shall we check?'

'Yes, turn the light on.'

'He's fine. Let's go to sleep.'

'Do you think he's OK?'

The next day we were allowed home. Noah was tucked into his little car seat by one of the nurses and off we went at a sedate twenty-eight miles an hour. June, the maternity nurse, wasn't due till the following day, so we would have to cope on our own for thirty-six hours. It was a bit scary, but we managed quite well. Even so, it was a relief to hand over to June the following evening. She got us into a routine and helped Lara get to grips with breastfeeding, although she wasn't enjoying it.

There must be some advantages to giving birth at sixteen, because three days after a twenty-hour labour, an emergency delivery and twenty internal and external stiches, Lara and friends went to Oxford's St Giles' Fair to go on the rides. I was pleased that she was going out to have some fun, but slightly concerned about what we would do if she wasn't back by the time Noah's next feed was due. But she was.

June was with us for four weeks, during which time Noah put on two pounds. She was so proud of herself and of Lara for that achievement. Lara had decided to give up on the breastfeeding after three weeks, and I was in some ways relieved because now if Lara was late home or even disappeared, I wouldn't have to worry about how I was going to feed him.

We tried taking it in turns with the nights, but I couldn't rely on her waking up. Noah's cries didn't always rouse her, and when they eventually woke me in the next room, I'd have to get up to wake Lara, and then we'd row about whether she was going to feed him or not. It was easier and a lot less stressful to just do it myself. I was trying to keep rows and stress to a minimum for everyone's sake, particularly of course Noah's. I was also anxious to get Lara feeling rested and relaxed and willing to start at the local college of further education to try and pass some GCSEs.

The autumn of 2008 was the most exhausting period in my life. Noah was a lively little chap who woke every two hours throughout the night and was in no hurry to go back to sleep after a feed. I had his cot beside my bed and his pre-prepared bottles of milk and bottle warmer on the other side. While I hadn't looked after a baby before, I ended up using a lot of my forty years' managerial experience to organize his care and my day. I wrote a work plan in twenty-minute slots.

I would get up at 5.30 a.m. and, while Noah still slept, shower and dress. Then I'd get Noah dressed and downstairs for his daily exercise routine – baby gym and tummy time – while I got the washing on and sterilized bottles. Next I'd squeeze in twenty minutes on work emails and feed the dogs, cats and other animals. Then I'd put Noah into a bouncy seat inside a playpen, just to be on the safe side, while I started the daily struggle of running up and down three flights of stairs half a dozen times to persuade Lara to get up and ready for college.

The next job would be making Lara some breakfast (otherwise she wouldn't eat) and preparing a packed lunch for her or, if I was feeling flush, counting her out some lunch money. While Lara held Noah, I would pull his pram up the basement steps. Then I'd get the dogs on their leads to combine one of their walks with the operation of walking Lara to college. If I didn't walk her, she wouldn't go, because she said she was scared of whom she might meet on the way. The route to college went right past the homes of several of her abusers and tormentors, aka friends, including Egyptian Mo and Ali and Abs, the men who had put the video of her on YouTube. All this before 9 a.m.!

Back home, I would breathe a sigh of relief if it was one of the days Noah's childminder was due because I could hand him over for a few hours and escape to work, otherwise I would pack him, his pram, changing bag, a bag of clean bottles and pow-dered milk, and my briefcase and laptop in the car and head off to work. While he was still tiny, it was doable, just, to have him at work with me. A small organization with most staff working out in the field, there were often only two of us in the office. Noah would sleep in his pram, wake after about two hours for a feed and change, have a short play and then go back to sleep. If necessary, I could jiggle his pram with my foot while still working at my desk.

At 5 p.m. it would be home via the shops to get something for supper for however many people were due to turn up that evening. Kelly and Will from round the corner still ate with us most nights, and I didn't discourage them because it helped to keep Lara in. They adored Noah. A week after Noah came home from hospital, ten-year-old Will turned up with a pillow he had hand-embroidered for him, complete with his name and a dolphin swimming in the sea. He had started it at school the previous term, and his teacher had helped him finish it off. As he handed it over, he was bursting with pride.

If Lara was home and in a reasonable mood, I would leave her with Noah and give the dogs a quick walk. Failing that, I would put Noah in a sling and he and I would both walk the dogs. Then it was supper, getting Noah bathed, which I hated until he could sit up, but Lara was good at, so if she was around, that became her job. After settling Noah, I'd do two hours at my desk on my freelance work, then prepare bottles for the night, turn off the phone and collapse into bed. If lucky, I would get two hours' sleep before he woke for his first of three nightly feeds.

The sort of daily routine I have described will, I'm sure, be familiar to many young working mothers, but I was fifty-eight and I wasn't sure how long I could keep it up. But I had no choice if we were going to stay together as a family. Lara had become very chaotic again after Noah's birth.

There was one particularly grim patch when I began to wonder if, for Noah's sake, I should try and persuade Lara to put him up for adoption. We had descended into a wet and dark autumn, which made all tasks seem harder, especially dog walking and the early starts. Lara was missing regularly again, often for days on end. Now she was sixteen, neither the police nor social services were very interested in her welfare, so unless I had specific concerns, I was told not to report her missing. Nonetheless I was very worried. I knew sometimes she was with Kirsten, who now had her own bedsit in Stoke, but on other occasions I had no idea where she was. I had told Lara in no uncertain terms that if she got herself into difficulties far from home after the baby was born, she would have to make her own way back. I would not be dragging a baby out of his bed at 3 a.m. to drive halfway across the country to pick her up from some godforsaken place. To be fair, she didn't ask me to, but there was still the anxiety to cope with, and the loss of even the small amount of childcare she was doing felt like the last straw.

The absolute low point came in late November. Lara was missing, I had an evening trustees' meeting to attend, and there was a lot of flooding around Oxford. The plan had been that Lara would look after Noah at home that evening with one of her sensible friends for support. In the end our childminder agreed to have him at her home. I drove through inches of floodwater with Noah, who hadn't been very well, his bag and Moses basket in the back of the car. I handed him over in the teeming rain, worried he might catch pneumonia, and drove twelve miles through flood water to get to the meeting. The journey back was even worse. It had been a somewhat difficult meeting, made worse because I wasn't able to fully concentrate. The windscreen wipers could barely cope with the downpour, but I made it to the outskirts of Oxford when the car stalled in the water. It was 10 p.m. and Noah was still five miles away. Two young men in soaking hoodies came swaggering over to me. Getting mugged was clearly going to be the grand finale to this day.

'You stuck? D'you want help?'

'Oh yes, please, but I'm not sure what will work. I think water's got into the engine.'

'We'll push you out of the water first and then see if the engine will start again.'

We pushed the car onto dry ground and waited five minutes. Then I turned the ignition. It worked and, very grateful, I was off again. Never judge a book by its cover or a young man by his hoody.

I got Noah back to our house at 11 p.m. Still no message from Lara. As I sat and held him close, rocking this tiny, fatherless and pretty much motherless baby to and fro, trying to figure out what was best for him, I thought I was going to have a heart attack. I felt as if I couldn't breathe. I decided that night that if something didn't give, I would have to abandon work altogether. In the end, though, I simply got used to the crazy routine. It is amazing what the human body and soul can adapt to in time.

As well as tightening up my daily schedules even more, I also delegated furiously where I could to whoever was willing. Our childminder was wonderful, but I needed more than the time she could give us. Ruth, our cleaner of fifteen years and one of Noah's godparents, was wonderful too, helping out with

Noah fairly regularly. Several friends would offer to walk the dogs or fetch shopping.

I could just about manage if things ran to plan, but there was no slack for anything going wrong, especially Lara disappearing. One Sunday afternoon Lara, who had been gone since the previous evening, finally came home. She had promised she would have Noah for a couple of hours so I could go shopping, but now the shops would be closing and I was cross. I was even crosser when she said she wasn't feeling well and would have to go to bed. So cross, in fact, that I walked out of the room in disgust without really looking at her. I heard her go into her room and close the door. I must have been slightly aware that all was not well, though, because something made me go up to her room to check on her. She was lying on the bed struggling for breath. I called an ambulance and the paramedics took one look at her and said she would need to go to hospital. I put Noah into his little carry seat, threw some nappies and a bottle of milk into a bag, and got into the ambulance with her. Oh my God, what now?

In A & E she admitted she had been given crack by Egyptian Mo. The staff told her she'd had a bad reaction and could have died. We were there for hours. The one bottle of milk I had brought with me for Noah was woefully inadequate, but a nurse kindly went and got me another. It wasn't the same brand we used at home and I worried it might upset his tummy, but it didn't.

At midnight Jean, who had been away for the weekend, came and picked up Noah and took him back with her. Lara was eventually discharged at 7 a.m. and we got a taxi home. We barely spoke. I had run out of words.

Somehow we made it to Christmas and went to Wales. Noah was now a round, noisy, cuddly four-month-old, far from the tiny scrap he'd been a mere sixteen weeks earlier. He marked Christmas Day with his first mouthful of baby rice, which he rolled around his mouth and then spat everywhere just for the fun of it. He loved the lights and all the attention and cuddles he got. He wasn't a baby who went in for a lot of smiles, but he seemed happy, bright and alert, and very chatty. Looking after him was beginning to get a bit easier and become quite fun, but Lara sadly was in a very bad space again by New Year 2009. She was refusing to go to college, slept all morning, spent the afternoon watching *Jeremy Kyle* and then went out most nights. When challenged either to go back to college or get a job, she said she couldn't because she had a child to look after.

We had some terrible rows and she was often foul to Noah, whom she accused of ruining her life. She would scream abuse at him and he would just smile back at her; he adored her. I knew she loved him very much too, but also resented him and me and our easy, uncomplicated relationship. She would accuse me of trying to come between her and Noah.

'You're trying to make him love you more than he loves me.'

'No I'm not, but he needs total love and attention all the time, and if you can't or won't give him that, then I will. He is not going to lose out.'

'Well, I didn't have it when I was a baby and I'm fine.'

'Lara, you are not fine. You missed out on so much when you were little and that's a lot to do with all the problems you have. But you're sixteen now and unless you want to start to help yourself, there isn't much anyone else can do for you.'

During one particularly loud and violent row, I asked Jean

to come and take Noah round to hers. However, when I talked that over later in a session with the Attach Team, Gillian said as long as he wasn't at any physical risk, it was probably best for Noah if he could see us together, especially if Lara and I could work through the argument in front of him. Small though he was, he would probably be much more anxious about seeming to have lost both of us than in witnessing our row.

The most difficult situations to manage were when Lara threatened to just take Noah off somewhere. 'You'll never see him again,' she would say, sometimes adding, 'I know you love him more than me.'

I felt so disappointed with the downturn Lara had taken recently. It seemed such a setback after the relative calm of her pregnancy. She was, I was sure, doing drugs a lot more and seemed to spend three or four nights a week with Egyptian Mo.

Life would have been altogether easier if Noah could have gone to nursery. As a single parent attending full-time education, Lara was entitled to have any nursery costs met, and just round the corner from us was what many regarded as the best nursery in Oxford. People actually moved to our area for the nursery and primary school. However, the nursery operated in an ideal world and their policy was that a baby should be at home with one main carer until thirteen months old, so they wouldn't take any child under that age. Unfortunately we didn't live in an ideal world, but they wouldn't relax their rule for us.

We rented a cottage on the Gower Peninsula for two weeks at Easter. As usual Lara was a different person away from Oxford and seemed to quite enjoy doing some of the baby-care stuff as long as it wasn't the nights. It was a lovely, gentle break, and

Noah had his first experience of sitting on a beach, eating sand and whacking everything in sight with a spade. Lara still says it was her best ever holiday, and it certainly seemed to strengthen her bond with Noah.

We were gathering strength for Ricky Krong's trial, which was scheduled for mid-May 2009. He was being prosecuted for sexual activity with a child. Apart from the police, there were to be just two prosecution witnesses – Lara and me. We were both dreading it, and Lara felt very conflicted about the whole case. On one level, she understood that he had taken advantage of her and had tried to set her against me; she knew he was highly promiscuous with many girlfriends and had children by different women. At the same time he had been less obviously abusive than most of the other men she had been associating with, and she had such a profound mistrust of the police that she felt drawn to support anyone the police were taking action against. All in all we were hoping against hope he would plead guilty. He didn't so we spent three days in Oxford Crown Court.

Lara went first, giving evidence by video link from a separate room in the court building. She was very distressed afterwards and refused to discuss what had happened. I wasn't called until the next afternoon. They questioned me about the times I had reported Lara missing and the occasions when I spoke to Ricky and reminded him of her age.

The defence barrister asked me, 'Mrs McDonnell, this must have been a very difficult and confusing time. How can you be so certain of the dates and times of the incidents?'

'Because I keep a diary.'

The prosecution barrister was on her feet addressing the judge. 'Your Honour, it would seem that these diaries might be very helpful to the court in this case.'

The judge sent the jury out and I was asked to bring in my diaries the next morning. I wasn't even sure I would be able to find the right ones, with all the moving and reorganizing that had gone on in our house since Noah was born.

I arrived at the court the next morning with a bag full of old diaries, which were taken away and read, and then I was called in to give more detailed evidence on anything that related to Ricky.

We didn't hang around the court and listen to the rest of the case, and it was one of the police officers who rang us the following day to tell us Ricky had been found guilty and sentenced to two and a half years. Lara went very quiet. The verdict certainly didn't seem like any cause for celebration, but at least that was one of Lara's abusers out of the way for a bit. I don't know how Lara really felt about Ricky being locked up. Although she gave evidence against him, she didn't seem that certain that what he had done was wrong.

The judge wrote me a personal letter after the trial apologizing for requiring me to bring in the diaries and wishing the three of us all the best for the future.

On 30 May 2009, the day after the trial ended, Noah was christened at our local church. Friends and family came from London, Surrey, the Midlands, Wiltshire and Wales. Our friend Nick officiated and we made a big party of it. Neither Lara nor I was religious, but having a christening was a way of celebrating this new life openly with friends and giving Noah the option in the future of whether to continue his life as a Christian. It would also give him, I hoped, some roots in the local community. The main significance of that day to Noah was the discovery of cake.

We held the party in the church hall, a lovely big room to scoot around in a baby walker. Noah and Lara cut the cake together, and he had his first taste of sugar. His eyes as wide as saucers at this wonder, he scooted off around the room, a sticky lump clutched firmly in each fist. I wanted the day to be a celebration for Lara as well as Noah. Her life had never been celebrated like this at its start; her name had never been emblazoned on a cake; she had never been the centre of attention. She was lucky if someone noticed her often enough to change her nappy.

I also wanted it to be a celebration of them, mother and son, and their future together. Noah had adored Lara from the start; even when she shouted at him, he would giggle and wave at her. Lara loved him too but had struggled to really bond with him to begin with and understand what it was to be a mother. If you were neglected as a baby, you have no inner model to guide you; there is nothing innate about being a good mother. I tried to model it for her, but of course the attachment between Noah and me was the cause of some resentment and jealousy on her part. Increasingly, though, there were moments when she could do it, could love and care for him and take responsibility for his well-being. In short, be a parent.

Of course, Lara rose to the occasion of the christening magnificently as both the attentive hostess and adoring mother. But perhaps the most significant aspect of the day for Lara and me was a moment before the party started. That morning our kitchen had been a frantic hive of activity, preparing the food for later. Our friend Mary took charge of that and I focused on Noah and my mother. Someone needed to go into town to the cake shop and pay for and collect the christening cake we had ordered. Lara said she would go. I hesitated for a moment, but then realized this was an opportunity in so many ways. I gave her my bank card, which I had been forced to keep under lock and key in a safe, and told her the PIN.

'Do you trust me?' she asked with bated breath.

'Yes. Please don't let either of us down.'

'I won't. Thanks, Mum!'

She rushed out of the door beaming from ear to ear. Half an hour later Lara returned with the cake, flushed with the exertion of running up and down the hill, but also, I sensed, with pride at having been trusted. I never locked up the card again, and she never stole from me again.

In June we had the last of the family support meetings that had started in 2007 after Lara returned from the secure unit. Noah, Lara and I attended. After the meeting one of the members of the review from the Attach Team wrote to us as a family to say goodbye and tell us he had enjoyed being part of our 'journey'. He finished the letter:

> Who would have believed a couple of years ago that we
> would have a meeting where Lara would actually remain
> in it and calmly state her point of view with her son sat
> smiling on her lap? Thinking about that now, I think there
> was always part of me that believed that would happen.
> Elizabeth, I think your belief and hope for Lara must have
> rubbed off on me along the way!

Lara was able to celebrate her seventeenth birthday in a more normal teenage way than she had been able to with her sixteenth. She had a group of friends round and I provided beer and pizzas. Judging from the smell wafting up from the garden later, someone had also provided dope, but in the main it was a pretty orderly affair and she seemed to enjoy it. The next day she had her first driving lesson.

Noah's first birthday, six weeks later, was altogether more rowdy. Four toddlers, several teenagers and a few adults, and of course cake. The birthday boy was resplendent in a tiny blue and black Man U strip with 'Noah' and the number '1' on his back, a present from Lara's new and surprisingly nice boyfriend, Tyler, someone she had met in a nightclub. Noah was now able to cruise around the furniture independently and shout loudly and enthusiastically at anything that caught his fancy, especially dogs, balloons and candles. We had made it through his first twelve months and I dared to hope we were beginning to function a bit like a family.

18

Death Threats

At last Noah was able to start at the nursery and Lara went back to college in September 2009. I thought the upward turn might continue and allowed myself to take on new freelance work that involved monthly trips to London, Birmingham and Manchester. Selfishly, I loved having the bit of time and space for myself that the new work afforded me. Providing I knew all was well at home and Noah was in safe hands, I could luxuriate in being inaccessible while on the train and entering the different worlds of the projects I was working on. Providing services for offenders with mental health needs and female sex workers or housing for vulnerable groups such as care leavers or young asylum seekers may not sound a million miles away from the sorts of issues I was dealing with at home, but there is a world of difference between the personal experience and the professional. I was fired up and stimulated by issues that came to me through my work that merely ground me down at home.

At home, things were a little easier, as Lara and I were not fighting as much. I had given up asking her to do anything as far as childcare was concerned, which had reduced the number of rows considerably. I got myself into a mindset where I would expect nothing and therefore anything she did was a bonus. I told myself that she genuinely couldn't do more than she was doing and therefore being angry and resentful was pointless, emotionally draining and bad for all three of us. She was much less jealous of and angry with Noah as a result and didn't shout at him nearly as often as she had. She still competed with him for my attention, though. One evening Noah was sitting on my knee and we were playing 'this little piggy' with his toes when Lara came in from college. She looked at us, walked over, picked Noah up, put him in his high chair and handed him a rusk. Then she came back, sat on my knee, put her thumb in her mouth and closed her eyes. She didn't say a word; she didn't need to; she was still a baby herself.

Lara's boyfriend, Tyler, was five years older than her, so there was still a bit of an age gap, but considering most of her other 'friends', this was a big improvement. He worked at the BMW factory, he wasn't afraid to meet me, and he was very fond of Noah. He also worried about Lara – she couldn't fully shake off the 'call of the wild'. I simply couldn't understand why she continued to see Mo, who she now tended to call Mohammed, a couple of times a week. I knew he gave her drugs and that he would take money from her or steal her mobile phone as payment. On one occasion, I'd allowed Lara to borrow my mobile. When she came back without it and very upset, I rang it.

'Yeah?' Mo answered.

'Who's that? What are you doing with my phone?'

'It's not your phone, bitch. That whore of a daughter of yours sold it to me.'

'It is my phone. You must have stolen it and I intend to go to the police.'

'Do that and you're dead, bitch.'

I would have gone to the police – I wasn't frightened, and I certainly wasn't going to be threatened like that – but Lara begged me not to. Instead I ended up allowing her to earn money by doing tasks at home to buy back my own phone from the creep Mohammed. It seemed insane.

I was certain Mohammed and others were still using and abusing Lara, but every time I put that to her she denied it. She said there were no other men, and although Mohammed did abuse other girls – indeed, she knew he had raped other girls – he had never touched her. I was devastated that I still couldn't get her to see what was happening to her or to feel that it was wrong, but she was seventeen now and her denial was so deeply entrenched there was little anyone could do unless or until she was able to see for herself what was going on. All I could do was what I had always tried to do – be alert, challenge, inform the police and, above all, be there to pick up the pieces.

One horrible foggy evening in November at about 10 p.m. I was sitting in the living room. Lara had been missing since the previous night, when she had said she was going to see Mohammed. I had reported her missing and the police call centre had somewhat reluctantly logged her as a missing person, but they no longer made house visits or went looking for her. I was getting really anxious; she hadn't even rung me, which by now was very unusual. Whatever was going on, she did keep in touch and would always ask how Noah was. Jean was sharing my vigil for the umpteenth time when we heard the noise of a car pulling up quickly outside the house and then a pause, followed by heavy acceleration as it pulled away again. I heard a bump on the front steps and went to the door. Lara fell into the house, barely conscious. We got her onto the sofa and she started mumbling incoherently. Her pupils were like pinpricks, and she was hardly breathing. I dialled 999 in a panic. I had never seen her this bad before.

The ambulance was at the house in a few minutes. The paramedic clearly knew what was going on.

'Lara, what have you taken? Have you taken heroin?'

Lara managed to nod. They had some sort of antidote to heroin in the ambulance and gave it to her. It had an almost immediate effect. Her breathing improved, her colour came back, and she became more coherent, although she was clearly very traumatized. She managed to tell us she had been locked in a flat and raped by several men almost continuously over the past twenty-four hours. She was rushed away in the ambulance, blue lights flashing.

Jean stayed at home with Noah, and in a state of shock I followed behind the ambulance. They kept her in hospital for six hours to check everything was back to normal; then I drove her home. She made a statement to the police, who came to the house later that morning, then went to bed. She told the police she had been abducted by one of her so-called friends and held in a house in a street about four roads away from ours. She was in a terrible way physically and emotionally, there was no doubt about that, and yet she kept walking into these situations time after time, and neither I nor anyone else could find a way to stop her. I simply couldn't comprehend how she could still have no sense of how to keep herself safe from these awful people. What hold did they have over her? Was it drugs?

We heard the next day that the police had arrested the man Lara had named as having abducted her. He was an odious man who lived in the next street, a pimp who had thought nothing of trying to proposition her in front of me while we walked into town together a few weeks earlier. He had sauntered off when I shouted at him, but Lara said he'd continued to plague her. In the end, because Lara refused to record a video interview, the police had to let him go. She had, I think, been leaned on by someone, but she wouldn't say. Every time I gently tried to probe, she flew into a rage and threatened to run off, so I stopped asking.

Inevitably, I suppose, given her inability to keep herself safe and to stop seeing these terrible men, Lara was drugged and raped yet again a few weeks later, but this time was too confused to be able to name her attackers. A detective came to see her at home to try and get a bit more information from her. Lara refused to say anything.

After the detective left, Lara turned to me. 'I can't tell you who those men were. They'll kill us if I do. You don't understand how dangerous they are. They're much stronger than the police. They're not scared of the police; the police are scared of them.'

Despite refusing to talk about what had happened, she seemed a lot calmer for a week or so after the last assault.

Over supper one evening she said, 'Mum, you can stop worrying. I've decided never to see Mohammed again. He's an evil piece of shit.'

I was banking on that resolve a few days later because I had to go to Manchester for a meeting. I arranged with Bev, our childminder, that she would take Noah to nursery at 9 a.m. and all Lara had to do was pick him up before they closed at 5.30 p.m., get him home and wait for me. I was catching a return train that would get me in to Oxford just after 5 p.m. and so would probably arrive home about the same time she and Noah got back from nursery. She could manage that, couldn't she?

'Yes, Mum. What d'you take me for? Of course I can manage to pick up my own son from nursery. You should trust me a bit more, you know.'

I rang her from the train just as it pulled out of Birmingham at about half past three. She should have just been leaving college. Her phone rang, but she didn't answer. I tried three more times. On the fifth attempt, she did answer, but it was just a stream of filthy abuse. She was completely off her head. I was in despair; not only was she clearly back with Mohammed, but there was no one to collect Noah from nursery.

In panic I rang Jean, the childminder and our cleaner, but none of them could collect Noah. I tried to call the nursery to warn them, but the signal went as I was dialling. The phone signal on the railway line disappeared for most of the journey. I spent the time in a cold sweat. I knew Noah would be OK: the nursery would have a procedure for what happened if a parent or carer hadn't turned up before they closed. I didn't suppose he would be handed over to social services immediately, but I didn't want to expose any weakness in how we were coping. We hadn't had any social services involvement in our lives for over a year and I wanted to keep it that way. But my main concern was what had happened to Lara. She had been entrusted with the responsibility of picking up her child from nursery, and she knew there was no one else to do it, so what could have made her let Noah down?

The train got to Oxford at 5.20 p.m. I was first off and ran up the stairs through the ticket barriers, out of the station, over the bridge and into the car park, and roared off. I made it with one minute to spare. Noah was the last child there.

'Wretched trains,' I grimaced at the carer as I snatched him up.

We didn't see Lara until the next evening. She came home dirty and sullen and refused to talk, threatening to go off again when I raised the issue of Noah and the nursery.

And then a month later, just before Christmas, our dear friend Mary, one of my closest friends and colleagues of many years standing, and Lara's frequent saviour in London, was given just weeks to live. She had been feeling unwell for some time and was due for tests in hospital a few days after staying with us in Oxford in early December. They diagnosed inoperable pancreatic cancer. I needed to get up to London to see her. Lara would have to cope for a day, and, thankfully, she did. She had to cope for a day at New Year as well, as my mother fell in her flat in Wales on New Year's Eve and I had to go rushing down to A & E.

Mary died in mid-January, barely a month after being diagnosed. We could scarcely believe it; it was all so sudden and shocking. The three of us went to her funeral in London, at which I was to speak, and Noah, along with several other children whom she knew well, painted a picture to go on the side of her coffin. I was bereft; it felt as though life was just nothing but worry, fear and loss.

The next day I was in the kitchen emptying the dishwasher when Lara came in.

'Mum, can you stop doing that for a moment? I have something important to say.'

I turned round to look at her. I had never heard her sound so grown-up and serious.

'Mum, I need to get out of Oxford. They're turning me into a drug addict, and now they're threatening to kill Noah as well as you and me if I try to pull away from them.'

'Lara, who are they?'

'Mohammed and his gang. They're everywhere, all over Oxford. There's no getting away from them. One of the bosses even turns up at college.'

I had on many occasions over the years suggested that we move to start a fresh life, but Lara had always refused. This time she was desperate to go. And she was confirming what I had always suspected, that there *was* a gang of people. We reported the threats to the police, and they talked about getting a restraining order against Mohammed, but Lara didn't want to say anything else.

Our house went on the market two days later.

We decided to move to Wales, somewhere within an easy drive of my brother and sister-in-law, my mother and my other brother, who had recently moved there too. It had always been Lara's safe haven; it was the obvious place. I would have loved a country cottage, but rural life can be very limiting for children and teenagers, and Lara had always lived in an urban area, so we settled for a small town with good communication links and started house-hunting. You get more bang for your buck in Wales than you do in Oxford, so I knew if we were lucky, we could end up with a bigger house, no mortgage and still have some cash in hand. Within a couple of weeks we found an eight-year-old six-bedroom house and made an offer. It was right on the edge of the town, looking out onto open countryside, so we would have the best of both worlds. Lara was so excited; she was going to have a bedroom, bathroom and small living room all to herself.

I was relieved that we would be getting away from the source of so much worry and grief, but I was going to miss Oxford. It was my ideal place. I loved it, and I had so many friends, a lovely house and fantastic neighbours. We would also be leaving behind Lara's new boyfriend, and I worried about Kelly and Will and who would give them supper in future. It was so hard to leave, but Oxford was toxic to Lara; we had to go.

With ten days to go to the anticipated exchange of contracts, the sellers of the house we were buying pulled out, leaving us devastated. The sale of our Oxford house was, after a couple of setbacks and a price drop, looking pretty solid, so I decided we would look for somewhere to rent until we could find another house to buy.

'Don't waste money on renting,' my brother Michael said when I told him we had lost the house. 'We can put you up for a bit.'

'What, all of us? An adult, a teenager, a toddler, two dogs, a cat and a budgie?'

'Well, maybe Mum could look after the budgie.' They were wonderful, my brother and sister-in-law. I don't know what I would have done without them.

So I arranged that our furniture would go into storage and set about sorting and clearing out stuff. You accumulate a lot of possessions when you live somewhere for twenty-one years; I must have done a dozen runs to the dump.

It was at this time, knowing we would soon be out of Oxford, that Lara agreed to talk to Lisa, a detective we had got to know during Ricky's trial. Lisa didn't fit any stereotype of a detective. She had hair dyed bright pink, a wardrobe of wacky T-shirts and a great concern about young girls being sexually exploited by older men, particularly one very vulnerable girl Lara and I both knew whom Lisa was convinced was being abused by Mohammed. She had asked if Lara could give her any information.

The removal men were in the house, so we sat in the back garden on a beautiful summer morning while Lara told Lisa about Mohammed's many phones full of pictures of young girls and phone numbers of older men, of the women who ran brothels full of underage girls in Oxford and of Mohammed's attempts to get Lara to recruit younger girls, white and preferably blonde, for him.

She turned to me and said, 'But don't worry, Mum – he never did anything to me,' and refused to say another word.

Oh, Lara, my love, I am not the fool you take me for.

The packing and crating of our belongings took two days, and on the second day, just as the last bits were being loaded onto the van and Lara and I were sitting outside the house watching, her phone went. Her face broke into a silent wail as she listened to a member of the gang telling her they were going to cut off her face, slit my throat and decapitate her son. Sitting right beside her, I could hear almost every spine-chilling word.

We picked Noah up from his childminder, headed down to the M4 and turned west. We were quite a carful, Lara, Noah, Meg and Alfie the dogs, Chippie the cat and the budgie (unnamed because in eight years we hadn't been able to work out what sex s/he was) and me. We sang our way through our entire repertoire of children's songs about five times before we crossed the Severn Bridge into Wales to start our new life. As we did, I felt a door close behind us. We would never again be going back to that life in Oxford.

19

Another Country

Lara and I found another house within a couple of weeks and, as cash buyers, were able to proceed quite quickly. Having been living out of suitcases for six weeks, the day we finally got the keys to our new home was very exciting. We opened the door and ran around the house marvelling at all the space. By Noah's second birthday, at the end of August 2010, we were fairly settled in our very different life. We had gone from a three-bedroom terraced house in a city centre to a six-bedroom house with loads of bathrooms and a huge double garage on the edge of a town. In Oxford, everything had been within walking distance, but here I had to get the car out just to buy some milk.

Lara had celebrated her eighteenth birthday the week after we left Oxford. With no local friends to celebrate with, it was a fairly tame affair, but my sister-in-law organized a birthday breakfast and then we all went out for a family lunch with champagne and finished off with cocktails in the garden.

Lara signed up for a public services course in a college in a town nearby with a view to becoming an ambulance technician. Such a career seemed made for her. She could use her extra-ordinary ability to rise to the occasion and her compassion for those in distress; no two hours would be the same, which would suit her low boredom threshold. Unfortunately, to get to the minimum educational requirements would mean at least three years in college, but she seemed reconciled to that.

My mother, who was becoming very frail, lived in the town where Lara's college was, so we were able to see her two or three times a week, and Lara would sometimes drop in during her lunch break. By the end of the year, though, it was becoming clear that my mother could not continue to live on her own. We certainly had plenty of room, and Lara was keen to have her with us, even offering to give up college to look after her. She told me then that she wasn't really enjoying the college course.

My mother came to us for Christmas, but on Boxing Day I had to call an ambulance as she was having difficulty breathing. She spent a miserable four weeks in a dreary old people's ward in a hospital twenty miles away. Lara came with me to visit most days and showed the most extraordinary compassion. She was able to do things for my mother that I found difficult. She would clean her teeth and fingernails, and comb her hair with such great care and sensitivity that my mother enjoyed the experience rather than feeling embarrassed that her granddaughter had to do these things for her.

My mother died on 16 January 2011, the day before the first anniversary of our friend Mary's death. It was yet another loss for Lara in a lifetime of losses; she was very fond of her grandmother, but this was a 'normal' loss of a frail and elderly person who had led a full life. She shared her grief with the rest of us and we all supported each other.

Lara struggled on at college until Easter and then dropped out. Because she had missed almost all her secondary schooling, she was at an educational level years below her actual age and intelligence. Nearing nineteen, she was in a group with fifteen- and sixteen-year-olds, who she found young and silly. Lara was now a very different young woman from the impulsive and reckless girl of even twelve months ago. She still had the occasional mad moment, but ironically my worries now for her were more that she was overly serious and anxious about life, and didn't go out and have fun nearly enough.

During the summer she made a new friend, the first since leaving Oxford twelve months earlier. Joe was a young gay man, and they became very close. Both feeling like misfits in their wider social circles, they gave each other a lot of support and companionship. Joe was in the middle of a catering course at a different college and he persuaded Lara to join him. I couldn't really see Lara pursuing a career in catering, but it was certainly a useful skill to learn, so I encouraged her. She took up driving lessons again, having dropped them before we left Oxford, and I bought her a small car.

Life ticked on. Noah was now three, bright, healthy and happy at nursery, learning to swim and attending a weekend soccer class, with an endless round of parties. I decided to fully retire in autumn 2011, not because I really wanted to – I was only sixty-one – but because I was finding that having to travel to London, Manchester and Birmingham was incompatible with looking after Lara and Noah, especially given the amount of chauffeuring that was needed even to get them to college or nursery. I found the stress of trying to be in at least two places at once very difficult, and the sense of never doing any job properly was very dispiriting. I would miss the income, but we could manage, and there were more things to life than money in the bank, especially now I had no mortgage to worry about. Having worked since I was sixteen, it was a wrench, but I had scaled down my career a lot since deciding to adopt a child, so it wasn't too life-changing to give it up altogether. Also, I was beginning to realize that life still had much to offer in other ways, not least seeing Lara grow into a young woman and Noah into a little boy.

Then in November 2011, out of the blue, I received a letter with an Oxford postmark. It was from a social worker who said it had come to the notice of the police and social services in Oxford that a number of young girls were going missing in similar circumstances and a special team had been formed to investigate, including historic cases. He said I would not be surprised to learn that Lara's name had come up. He asked if Lara would be prepared to talk to them and give them a bit more information.

I asked her. Her first reaction was horror and anger that her past wouldn't leave her alone.

'That's all over and done with. I have a new life now. I don't want to talk to anyone about what happened.'

'But it isn't really all done with, is it, not for you. You may have buried it a bit, but I can tell it's all still eating away at you. Why don't you at least meet this person, hear what he has got to say and then decide?'

She agreed.

Over the next few months the police visited often and with every visit took longer and longer statements from Lara. She had to return to Oxford twice to take part in identity parades. I didn't sit in on the interviews or go to Oxford with her, partly because Lara didn't want me to hear the details of the things she had been subjected to, partly because I didn't want to hear it and partly because I might be called as a witness in my own right.

What I did gather from Lara, the police and the media coverage was that Lara and several other girls had been groomed, drugged, raped and trafficked by an organized gang for many years. I had always known there had to be someone or more than one person behind most of her disappearances, but I didn't know there was a whole gang trafficking girls across the country, nor did I fully understand the degree of coercion and mind games involved to control the girls and keep them silent.

Lara was first approached by Mohammed when she was twelve, although the full exploitation and trafficking didn't start until she was thirteen. The gang had gone to great lengths to find and 'befriend' vulnerable girls, lavishing them with care and attention and gradually undermining their relationships with their parents and carers, persuading them that their families were not really where they belonged. It emerged that Egyptian Mo and Sam the Rapist were brothers, Mohammed and Bassam Karrar. Even Lara hadn't known that. Also in the gang was another set of brothers from a different family, Akhtar and Anjum Dogar, as well as a couple of cousins. Child exploitation was, it seemed, a family affair.

I was interviewed and my diaries taken in case they were needed as evidence. I was eventually asked to do an identity parade to see if I could pick out Mohammed Karrar.

Jane Crump, the PC who had run the Missing Persons Unit for most of the time Lara was one of their frequent flyers, had joined the investigation, which was known as Operation Bullfinch. She was our main point of contact and kept in regular touch with Lara. They got on really well. One cold March morning, just as we were returning from taking Noah to nursery, Jane's number came up on the screen of Lara's phone. Had we seen the news? There had been a series of dawn raids at addresses across Oxford and twenty-two arrests. We rushed indoors and turned on the radio and TV. The arrests were making headline news on the national stations.

So there it was – what had happened to Lara for all those years and been largely dismissed was finally being seen for what it was, a huge crime of national importance. We made coffee and found chocolate biscuits and spent the morning watching the news reports. I rang my brothers and a few close friends.

'You know that's Lara they're on about? She's one of the victims.'

'They were horrible, scary people,' Lara said, 'but somehow I feel it was my fault. I'm glad they've been caught, but I feel bad for them too. I thought they were my friends.'

Over the next few days nine men were charged, five of them for offences against Lara. They were refused bail and remanded in custody.

After the initial elation of the arrests and the media coverage, which showed Lara just how serious her abuse had been, she became terribly depressed. She dropped out of college, saying that she didn't want anyone to know what had happened to her but it would be impossible to keep it secret. She dropped her new boyfriend, a soldier just back from Afghanistan, who seemed very nice. She returned to the sofa and *Jeremy Kyle*.

I tried to talk to her, to persuade her not to give up on the new life she was beginning to have, but I could tell she was now starting to allow herself to experience the trauma of her past.

Platitudes from me were utterly inadequate; we needed some real professional help if Lara would accept it.

I took her to see the GP. We both sat there, and as I tried to explain what had happened, I burst into tears.

'Please look at Lara – she's falling apart. We need some help.'

The doctor prescribed antidepressants and gave us a telephone number for a rape and sexual violence counselling service. Lara started to see a counsellor called Nick every couple of weeks, but they were not allowed to discuss anything relating to the case until the trial was over, so they focused on her early childhood, which meant that she had to process all that trauma at the same time as getting ready for the trial. She was very agitated, but we quickly established that Nick would be able to come to the trial with her and support her, which greatly reassured her.

We booked ourselves two weeks in Greece in July and had a lovely time, but Lara found it hard to really enter into the spirit of it. Despite, or perhaps because of, surviving years of the most appalling violent crimes, she had become fearful of the smallest things. Bees, wasps, crabs, jellyfish, all the usual associates of a seaside holiday would send her screaming back to the hotel room. It was awful to see just what damage had been done. Those men had virtually destroyed her emotionally, and none of us had been able to stop it. I couldn't get my head round it.

At least Noah had a wonderful time in Greece; he still talks about it. He was what he called 'three and a half quarters' (three and three-quarters) and coming to the end of his time in a lovely nursery. In September, just six days after his fourth birthday, he would be starting school. He was lively, very articulate and seemed happy, confident and secure, if occasionally a bit of a handful, as he was probably too used to getting his own way. We stayed in a family resort with lots laid on for children, although the only thing he really wanted was the beach. We tried to shield him as much as we could from Lara's trauma and our shared anxieties about the impending trial and made a rule never to talk about it when he was in the house, but inevitably he must have picked up on some of it.

The year dragged on. The trial, which was to be in the Old Bailey, was expected to start in January 2013 and last a couple of months. We were invited to go to the Old Bailey on a familiarization visit in November 2012, where we were met by two women from witness support, a voluntary service who look after witnesses in court. One showed us round the witness suite where we would be when not giving evidence. She also took us into a typical courtroom and Lara was shown how she would be screened to hide her from the defendants and the public area of the court. Lara was terrified that somehow one of the defendants would break free and come and attack her. She was shown the locks on the dock and just how thick the glass was and seemed somewhat reassured.

Lara's evidence-giving was expected to last up to a week. The police had organized a safe house for all the victims who were witnesses to stay in while giving evidence and also personal police escorts for protection. We would be picked up from home and taken to London by the police, who would remain with Lara at all times, chauffeuring her to and from the court each day. If we had needed any confirmation about what a big case this was, the level of security laid on demonstrated that.

Victoria said she would look after Noah while we were in London, and Michael offered to be in London with us for extra support. All in all we did feel very looked after. But what to tell Noah?

In the end we simply told him that Mummy had to go to London to talk to a judge about some bad men. He digested that very calmly but didn't ask for more information. It was enough for him that he would be staying with his beloved 'granny Victoria'. We had invited my brother and sister-in-law to become honorary grandparents to Noah a couple of years before, putting a title on the role they were already playing.

Christmas and New Year had a slightly anxious edge to them this time round. The trial was due to start in the first week of January 2013 and it loomed over the festivities like the spectre at the feast.

20

Trial By Ordeal

The trial of nine men charged with a total of sixty-six offences began at the Old Bailey on Monday 14 January 2013. Over a period of eight years girls as young as eleven had been groomed, abused, tortured and trafficked around the UK for sex by a gang based in Oxford. Noel Lucas QC, the chief prosecuting counsel, told the court, 'The depravity of what was done to the complainants was extreme.' Over the eight years the nine men made the girls' lives a 'living hell', subjecting them to extreme physical and sexual violence. They were plied with drugs and drink, and raped, sometimes by several men and sometimes 'for days on end'.

The charges took over forty minutes to read out. They included nineteen counts of rape, seven of them with a child aged under thirteen, arranging or facilitating child prostitution, trafficking within the UK for sexual exploitation and using an instrument to procure a miscarriage.

Kamar Jamil, twenty-seven, Akhtar Dogar, thirty-two, Anjum Dogar, thirty, Assad Hussain, thirty-two, Mohammed Karrar, thirty-eight, Bassam Karrar, thirty-four, Mohammed Hussain, twenty-four, Zeeshan Ahmed, twenty-seven, and

Bilal Ahmed, twenty-six, denied the charges against them, thus forcing the girls to give evidence and ensuring that their abuse and attempts to control the girls would continue into the court-room. The police had told Lara that the gang didn't expect any of the girls to actually turn up to give evidence against them. Lara was determined to prove them wrong.

Noel Lucas QC told the jury that the men targeted children in care or from chaotic backgrounds, children who were unlikely to be believed and whose behaviour would be seen as delinquent. They groomed their victims with gifts, offers of friendship and protection, and got them addicted to alcohol and drugs.

Once groomed, the girls could then be sold for sex and used to recruit other children into the sex ring. Some of the girls, ranging in age from eleven to fifteen, were groomed to be child prostitutes, for whom punters from across the UK and beyond paid large amounts of money.

He told the jury that they would have to steel themselves to hear the evidence. 'The facts in this case will make you feel uncomfortable. Much of what the girls were forced to endure was perverted in the extreme.'

The children were taken to hotels and empty houses, thought to be kept for the abuse, and prevented from escaping. They were subjected to 'humiliating and degrading conduct', including biting, suffocation, burning and scratching. Weapons, including knives, baseball bats and meat cleavers were used during the torture, the court heard. The jury was told that sometimes men had urinated on the girls, who were raped vaginally, orally and anally.

Noel Lucas said the girls were also given 'so many drugs they were barely aware of what was going on – indeed, they say it was the only way they could cope with what was going on'.

The men gave the girls cannabis, cocaine, crack and sometimes heroin. The girls became addicted to certain of the drugs and felt unable to live without them. 'This made them even more dependent on the men,' he said. The men had complete power over the girls in their control. They were threatened 'that should they ever seek to free themselves from the grasp of the group, they and their families would suffer serious harm'.

At home in Wales, I listened to the details of the opening prosecution statements on the lunchtime radio. Lara didn't want to hear it and shut herself in her room. I had to sit down; I thought I was going to pass out. Suddenly there it was in a few hundred words, a summary of what had happened to Lara over those terrible six years, much of which I hadn't even guessed at. There was also an explanation, of sorts, of the reasons for her behaviour to me. The gang had, Noel Lucas said, used all kinds of tactics to turn the girls against their parents, families and friends.

How could I not have known exactly what was going on? Why hadn't she told anyone? How was it possible for all that to have gone on in a place like Oxford and no one know? How were we all so blind? Why hadn't I tried harder to rescue her?

I felt myself getting swept into a downward spiral of questions and self-recriminations. I knew I mustn't let that happen; I wasn't sure I'd be able to get out of it if I did. We had to survive this trial somehow, and I had to stay cool, calm and collected for Lara's sake. I drew upon the habits I had adopted during 'all the craziness', as I now paraphrased those six years: just survive, don't think forwards or backwards too much, just cope with the here and now.

We had been told we must not listen to or read reports of evidence of other victims, so we didn't, but I checked the progress of the trial each night on the blog of the *Oxford Mail* so we could get an idea of how it was progressing and when Lara might be called. The logistics of going up to London to give evidence were quite complicated. We knew we would be away for several days. Victoria was on standby to take time off work to look after Noah and our dogs, but she needed some notice. We also needed to pack and shut up the house, sorting out the cat, the bird and the fish before we left. And Nick and his colleague from the sexual violence counselling service who were to come with us needed notice too. But it was hard to get a feel of the progress of the trial from the reports in the press because so many of the days were not spent taking evidence but behind closed doors hearing legal arguments.

We knew Lara was to be referred to in court as Girl 3, so assumed she would follow Girl 2, but no. In the end, Girl 2 was the first victim to give evidence. When Girl 1 started her evidence, we decided it was time to prepare Noah for our impending disappearance, the first time I'd be away from him for more than a night.

'You remember we told you that Mummy was going to have to go to London to talk to a judge about some bad men?'

'Yes, the bad men that did spit at their mum and dad.'

'Um, yes, those bad men. Well, Mummy and I will be going to London on Sunday.'

'Yeah, and I'm going to stay with Granny Victoria. Yippee!'

At four years old the worst thing Noah could imagine a

person doing was spitting, so he had given himself that explanation. It suited him and it suited us, so we left it at that. Later we would probably have to tell him more, but not yet. Hopefully we could protect him from the horror of what had happened to his mother for a few more years.

On Sunday morning we took Noah and the dogs up to Michael and Victoria's house; then Lara and I came back home to pack. Nick came over to our house in the afternoon and we waited for the police. They turned up in a large people carrier with blacked-out windows. We all loaded the suitcases in the back and off we went. Lara was shaking and looking white as a sheet. The two police officers were part of Thames Valley Police's personal protection squad, and as such were used to looking after royalty, prime ministers and the like. They were articulate and funny and made us feel very well looked after; thanks to them, the tedious journey up the so-familiar M4 passed quite pleasantly.

I knew we were heading to a safe house in West Hampstead, which is an area of London I know fairly well, as I lived there for a couple of years in my early twenties. It hadn't changed much in the intervening forty-one years; the fish and chip shop that I had used regularly in my flat-sharing days was still there and seemed to be run by the same people. The safe house was round the corner from the house I had lived in all those years ago; we could even see my old bedroom window from the garden. While this was familiar territory for me, it was unknown to Lara and she looked terrified.

There were two other police officers in the house, who were expected to follow our every move. As the kitchen and living room were in one big split-level room, there was no privacy at all. Even if we had wanted to discuss the case, we couldn't. When we went to bed, there were two police officers sitting on the sofa watching TV, and when we got up, there was a different pair of police officers sitting on the sofa watching TV.

It had snowed overnight. Nowhere gets so transformed by snow as London does. At least for the couple of hours before it turns to slush. I looked out of the skylight in the bedroom Lara and I were sharing at the top of the house, over miles of white rooftops shimmering in the early morning moonlight. In the distance was Big Ben. It looked so beautiful, quite magical in fact, that it could have been a scene from *Peter Pan*, such a contrast to the dark and terrible reasons we were in London on that bitterly cold morning.

Lara was physically sick with anxiety when she woke up, but prepared for her first day in court. Then they broke it to us: she wouldn't after all be called that day, as the jury wouldn't be sitting. It was instead to be a day of legal arguments, which meant a day of the lawyers discussing in front of the judge just how they wanted to manage the trial. It was slowly dawning on me just how heavily choreographed these trials are. They are nothing like they are on TV dramas, in which one side or the other has a whole bag of surprises, brings up new evidence or witnesses, or simply springs the killer question on a witness.

Far from being relieved not to have to give evidence that day, Lara became stressed and unwell. By lunchtime she was running a temperature and had developed a terrible cough. I took her to a chemist, who felt she should see a doctor, so we called a taxi and went to a walk-in GP surgery in Cricklewood. I explained the situation to the doctor: somehow Lara had to get through several days in the witness box. He prescribed some fast-acting antibiotics and a very strong cough mixture. We went back to the safe house and dosed her up and waited. We tried to watch TV and read, but it was impossible to concentrate. We couldn't talk about the only thing we had on our minds, the trial, so we paced around, drank a lot of coffee and made inconsequential chit-chat with Nick. The legal arguments continued the next morning too, but we were assured Lara would start her evidence after lunch.

Our personal protection escort turned up at 11 a.m. and drove us across London to the Old Bailey. When we were about a mile away, they rang the court to announce our imminent arrival so that they could open the gates and allow us to drive into the bowels of the court. The dramatic nature of our entrance was slightly diminished by the fact that when we drove up to the gates, they didn't open. After a few toots on the horn and another phone call, the gates opened about eight inches and a head poked out and looked at us suspiciously and then very slowly and, it felt, reluctantly, the doors opened and in we drove. Lara looked absolutely petrified.

She was met by one of the volunteers from the witness support service, who took her off to the smoking area, and then we all crowded into a tiny lift for the journey up to the witness suite. Owing to the nature of the trial, we were given our own room to use for the duration of our evidence. Normally witnesses, including victims, have to wait in a public waiting room, which must be a terrifying experience. The two prosecuting counsel came to introduce themselves, and Lara was whisked down to the courtroom by the witness support volunteer. Nick went too to give her support, as I was not allowed to.

'Go sock it to them, love,' I said.

'I will.' She turned and blew me a kiss.

I waited in the room and Michael, who had just arrived from Wales, joined me. We sat and talked and made vague attempts to read or watch a film on the iPad, but it was impossible to concentrate.

Eventually, at about 4.30 p.m., Lara came into the room with Nick. After two and a half hours in the witness box it was over for the day. She was still just being taken through her evidence by the prosecution, so the afternoon hadn't been too bad, but she was very stressed and anxious, and her cough seemed no better.

We found a wonderful Italian restaurant that evening and cheered ourselves up with tricolore salad, freshly made pasta, some wine and live music. I had forgotten just what a fantastic range of food could be found more or less anywhere in London within a ten-minute walk. It felt like the best food I had eaten for years, but maybe that was in part just the contrast to the rest of the day. We couldn't discuss the trial, but in such a cheerful atmosphere we found plenty to laugh and joke about; it was a lovely relaxing evening. But then it was back to the house and the ever-present police presence. We went to bed, Lara still coughing her lungs out.

By Friday the defence barristers had started on Lara. As there were five men charged with offences against her, this meant that she had to be cross-examined by five different barristers. She was tired and upset as we drove out of London on Friday night, but the thought of seeing Noah again lifted her mood. When we arrived four hours later at Michael and Victoria's house, Noah and Granny Victoria had transformed it into a restaurant complete with welcome signs, illustrated menus and handmade place mats. It was a lovely homecoming.

Sadly the weekend was over all too soon. Sunday afternoon came round so quickly, and in no time at all Lara and Nick were at our house waiting in our living room to be picked up by the police. I stayed down in Wales for a day to look after Noah, as Victoria had some urgent work to do. I didn't like to see Lara go off without me, although I knew perfectly well that Nick and the police officers would take good care of her. In the end the Monday turned out to be another day of legal arguments, so she wasn't called and she and Nick amused themselves in Camden Town, Lara marking the occasion with a tattoo. I was horrified that she was going to spend the day where she had experienced such awful times and nearly been killed, but she said she wasn't worried and wanted to see why everyone said Camden Town was such an exciting place.

Michael and I joined Lara and Nick at the Old Bailey on the Tuesday. Although Lara was not allowed to tell me what had been said to her, she was clearly being mauled by some of the defence barristers. She was very agitated, alternating between tears and anger and shaking and feeling cold, but Nick was being a great comfort and support.

Later, when we had both given our evidence and were free to talk to each other and to others who had witnessed her cross-examination, particularly some of the journalists, I discovered how most of the defence barristers had been gratuitously unpleasant to her in their cross-examination, some more than others. The weaker their case, the more they tried to insult and humiliate the victim, it seemed. By far the worst was Mark Milliken-Smith, the barrister defending Sam the Rapist, real name Bassam Karrar, the man who had raped Lara in the Nanford Guest House. Milliken-Smith tried to suggest she had made the whole thing up, despite knowing, which Lara did not, that the next witness on the stand would corroborate her whole story. His manner was contemptuous, insulting and bullying. If he thought he would break her with that approach, he had picked the wrong person. Although she was devastated by what he was putting her through in open court, Lara became determined that he was not going to break her.

Lara finished her evidence at lunchtime on Wednesday 13 February 2013. She was so traumatized by her treatment by the last defence barrister that we persuaded her to let the police take her and Nick straight back to Wales rather than wait for me to finish my evidence. Wales was her safe place and I knew she'd feel better there. By going straight away they would miss the rush hour, and she might even be back in time for Noah coming out of school.

I was called to the witness box that afternoon. I had, of course, already seen the courtroom on our visit in November, but it had been empty then. Now it was packed to the rafters. There were a couple of dozen barristers in wigs – each defendant actually had three barristers and about the same number of solicitors. Then there were the prosecution lawyers, numerous police, court officials and reporters, but I still couldn't account for everyone crowding out the body of the courtroom. And then there was the public gallery, which I couldn't see, but I could hear coughs and shuffling noises from up above, so I knew there were people up there too. I knew that Michael was one of them, but who were all the others?

I was surprised at how nervous I felt. I had given evidence

in court before, had had a lifetime of public speaking and had done some work on radio and television, but I had never heard myself stutter before, never felt cold sweat run down the back of my neck as it did that afternoon.

Clearly some deal had been struck during legal arguments about what I would be asked. The prosecution counsel seemed to focus mainly on Lara's various abductions from the children's home in Devon when she was trafficked to London, which seemed to have no bearing at all on the case. The defence mainly wanted to know about my knowledge of the rape in the Nanford Guest House. I was also asked why I knew who Mohammed was, and I talked about the local neighbourhood campaign against drug dealing for which he was such a big target.

In stark contrast to the treatment they had meted out to Lara, the defence barristers who questioned me were revoltingly smarmy. They didn't try calling me a lying, deceitful piece of trash, presumably because they saw in me a middle-aged, middle-class professional woman, someone from a world they knew. I was finished in less than three hours.

Michael and I travelled back to Wales on the train. My evidence was over, but rather than relief I felt a sense of anticlimax. Lara had survived, just, and had certainly vindicated herself, but what price would she pay for that now in terms of her mental health? I felt utterly deflated. There was so much more evidence I could have given, which would have been backed up by my diaries, but it felt that I wasn't given the chance to say anything important.

Two days later, on 15 February, we celebrated ten years since Lara had come to live with me. What a decade! We marked it with a bottle of champagne. We reflected on the key moments, especially the good bits, of which there had been many, and it was good not to let them be obscured by all the crap. We had survived; we were now very definitely mother and daughter. Lara was a young woman, a mother, and I was a grandmother. Blimey, that was quite a lot to happen in just ten years.

It took a couple of weeks for us to get the adrenalin out of our systems. The trial continued and now, our evidence over, we could follow it in the press. We took enjoyment in reading about the discomfiture of the golf-playing forensic doctor in the witness box; he had clearly forgotten the whole thing, and even his notes didn't help him much. But the real triumph for Lara was the evidence that followed mine from a young man also staying in the Nanford Guest House the night she was raped by Bassam Karrar. He had heard the whole thing and had rung 999; they even played his 999 phone call in court.

While the evidence we heard vindicated what we had been saying for years, Lara was so down and also so angry and irritable that I became very worried about her. I realized it was inevitable after everything she had been through over the past year, but it was hard to live with, and I worried about the effect it might all have on Noah. I started working on her to look for a job now there was nothing looming in the future that would prevent her. Every time I raised it, there was a row, but I sensed she was beginning to come round to the idea, although she said she didn't think anyone would want to employ her. Her self-esteem was at rock bottom.

Michael and Victoria took the three of us to Disneyland Paris for some post-trial R & R. We spent four days in the realms of fantasy and had an amazing time, on our feet from virtually dawn to dusk and we still didn't cover everything. It was the perfect antidote to the all-too-real world of sleaze and violence we had been occupying for so long. Noah and Lara had a whale of a time doing things together. I had taken her to Disneyland soon after she moved to Oxford and she thoroughly enjoyed sharing with her son the things she remembered as a ten-year-old.

The trial dragged on, with more victims giving evidence. On Good Friday we were having a family lunch party in our house when there was a knock on the door; Lara and I both went to answer it. It was a reporter from the *Daily Mail*: would Lara give them an exclusive interview? Lara ran off crying in shock at this intrusion, and I sent the reporter packing. We had been warned the press might try and contact us, but we hadn't expected them on the doorstep on Good Friday. Clearly we had to work out a strategy for handling the media.

The following week the press officer from Thames Valley Police came to see us and the other victims to discuss how they were handling the media interest in the case. Knowing that the press, TV and radio would be seeking interviews from the victims in the event of guilty verdicts, they had asked the journalists to send their requests via the press office and under no circumstances to contact any of the victims directly. Most had gone along with that and there was quite a pile of requests in the folder the press officer handed us.

The requests were by and large informed and respectful. Both Lara and I saw an opportunity to tell the story more in our words than had been possible in court. But we wanted to try and keep some control over how it would be used and to limit the number of individual interviews we would have to do. Victoria had senior contacts in BBC News and so via them we were put in touch with Naresh Puri, a news producer working in both radio and TV. We agreed to let her come down to our house with a crew to record interviews with both of us. They would then be used across the BBC TV and radio networks, killing many birds with one stone, so to speak.

Naresh came with Alison Holt, the BBC's social affairs correspondent, who was a familiar face from TV for us. They spent the best part of a day filming carefully anonymized interviews with us. We also spoke to BBC Oxford and agreed to take part in a *Panorama* programme about the failings of children's homes in cases like this. Esella Hawkey, a *Panorama* producer, had heard my evidence in court about the care home in Devon allowing Lara to be repeatedly trafficked up to London. One of the BBC journalists who visited us made a point of saying how appalled she was at the way Lara had been treated in the witness box by Mark Milliken-Smith. She said she left the court in tears over it and would be writing something to go on the BBC website about it. I also spoke over the phone several times to Andrew Norfolk of *The Times*, who had been following the trial closely and had heard both Lara's and my evidence. He had followed and reported on many other similar cases on the targeting, grooming and sexual exploitation of teenage girls. We also gave an interview to the *Guardian*, but that was plenty, and the rest of the requests we declined.

Although Lara wasn't at first sure she wanted to do any interviews, she grew more and more confident with each one and found the experience of telling her story in her own words very helpful. The reporters and producers were all so impressed

with her and gave her such positive feedback and encouragement that the interviews gave her back a lot of the self-respect
that the court process had stripped away.

Saying no wasn't enough for the *Sun*, though. One morning
Lara and Kirsten, who was staying with us at the time, left the
house to walk to the dentist. A few seconds later Kirsten came
flying back through the front door shouting for me. There were
journalists from the *Sun* pursuing Lara up the road and they
wouldn't leave her alone. I rushed out. There were two men, one
driving a car slowly along behind his colleague who was on the
pavement shouting, 'Lara, Lara, we're from the *Sun*. We want to
talk to you about the trial.' Lara was running up and down the
road trying to get away from them.

It turned out they had also been knocking on neighbours'
doors, completely undermining the life-long anonymity Lara
was entitled to as a victim of a violent sexual crime. I chased
them off, saying the *Sun* in particular, with its habitual exploitation of young women on page 3, was in no moral position
to cover a story like this. We should have made a formal complaint, but there were so many things going on at that time that
I never got round to it.

April passed quite quickly with all our media activities and
the enjoyment of reading how some of the defendants were
making fools of themselves in the witness box. Mohammed
Karrar took the stand to say how, as a thirty-something man,
he was hounded by eleven- and twelve-year-old girls chasing
him around Oxford and trying to sell him drugs and sex. His
evidence was clearly so compelling that the judge had to ask
the jury to try and compose themselves and stop laughing.
Meanwhile as we also had Kirsten living with us and in crisis,

having become homeless, there was plenty of distraction for Lara, who threw herself into trying to help her sister sort out her life.

Lara was beginning to make plans for her own life too, and on 9 May she had an interview for a job as a care assistant in a local residential home for frail elderly people, including some with dementia. She had often said it was the sort of work she would love to do, and having seen her with both my parents when they were dying, I knew she had the perfect combination of skills and compassion for such work. I also knew it was difficult, heart-rending work for a young person who had already had more than her fair share of the hard sadnesses of life. I would have wished for her a job that was potentially a bit jollier and more life-enhancing, but Lara was determined that this was what she wanted to do.

Two phone calls came in quick succession that evening, the first from the police to tell us that the jury had finally gone out to consider their verdict, and the second from the home to offer her the job. We spent the rest of the evening in a strange state of apprehension and celebration.

We had tried to estimate how long the jury would take. Various people had told us that the evidence was pretty overwhelming, but there were still over fifty charges for them to consider (some had been dropped in the course of the trial) and they would, I assumed, have to consider each one separately. I thought it might take a week, and obviously every day we listened out for news on the radio. By around 3 p.m. each day we would say to each other, 'Well, it won't be today, as the courts are about to close for the day.' It always felt like a bit of an anticlimax.

We tried and I think largely succeeded to keep things fairly relaxed and normal at home for Noah's sake. We would allow ourselves to discuss and speculate on the trial's outcome while he was at school, but come half past three and the school pick-up, life reverted to how his day had gone, would we be late for his swimming lesson, what would we have for supper, and had he found his lost football boot? He didn't seem to have picked up on any of our anxiety, though on some level he must have done: he had grown up in a home with more than its fair share of anxieties, so I suppose he had long since adapted to a certain amount.

On the afternoon of Tuesday 14 May I persuaded Lara and Kirsten to walk the dogs. As it was past 3.30 p.m., we'd decided we wouldn't hear anything that day. 'I don't think we'll hear anything before Friday at the earliest,' I told the girls.

As it was pouring with rain when they went out, I assumed they would be back within a few minutes. I looked at the phone and noticed I had missed a call from Jane Crump of Thames Valley Police. I rang her, but she was engaged, so I went on the *Oxford Mail* website, heart thumping. The verdicts were in. I couldn't get my brain or my eyes to focus properly, but from what I could make out the verdicts seemed to be guilty. I paced up and down the kitchen.

Oh yes, oh thank God. Oh my goodness, it's finally over. They believed her. I thought my head was going to explode.

But where on earth was Lara? She hadn't taken her mobile, so I couldn't ring her. I walked up and down the road for a bit, but there was no sign of her. Where were they? Surely nothing could have happened to them. Back in the house, the phone started to ring – Michael and Victoria had heard the news on the radio while driving. Finally, Jane rang back. Yes – they'd been found guilty of all the offences against Lara. She sounded ecstatic.

Eventually Lara and Kirsten, and the dogs, fell through the front door giggling hysterically and soaking wet.

'Lovey, have you heard the news?'

'No.'

'The jury is back. It's guilty.'

We danced a crazy jig up and down the hallway. We had known the police were quietly confident about the outcome of the trial, but nothing is certain until the verdicts are in, and I think we had both prepared ourselves for the possibility of not getting the verdicts we'd hoped for.

We had been advised by the police not to be in the house for a day or two after the verdicts because they were sure we would be door-stepped again by the media. We rushed around like mad things packing overnight bags, the dogs and ourselves into the car. We told Noah the bad men had been found guilty by something called a jury. He nodded, but he must have thought it was a lot of fuss for a bit of spitting.

We headed to our refuge at Michael and Victoria's, stopping at a shop on our way to buy some celebratory wine. As we walked in, we could hear one of Lara's pre-recorded interviews being played on the radio on the five o'clock news.

'You better let me do the talking in case they recognize your voice,' I said. It was surreal.

It was the main story that night and the next day on TV, the radio and in the newspapers. We got tired of hearing our voices everywhere. We received loads of phone calls, texts and emails from friends, including many who we had never told of our involvement in the case but who had recognized Lara's story.

A couple of weeks before the verdicts the chief constable of Thames Valley Police had come to see us at home. She had wanted to know more about what we had both experienced during all the years Lara was being exploited so that she could understand how the police could work better to protect children in the future. It was an open and friendly meeting in which we were able to speak freely. During our meeting she suggested that it might be helpful if Lara went to court for the sentencing, which would be a few weeks after the verdicts were in. Some of the other victims were going to go, and if we wanted to, she would make sure that we were taken and collected.

To start with, we didn't think we wanted to be there, but after the verdicts and in view of the overwhelmingly positive and sympathetic treatment given to the victims by the media, we decided it might be a positive experience for Lara. It wouldn't in itself achieve 'closure', that horrible word, but it might be the end of a chapter. I wanted Lara to go back to the place of all that torment and humiliation as a triumphant and vindicated victim and to realize that she was not only entitled to justice but deserved it for at least some of the awful things that had been done to her in her life.

So we said yes to the chief constable and on 27 June 2013 Lara, my brother Michael and I waited at our house for the police to arrive to take us back to the Old Bailey for the sentencing of five men who had abused, tortured and come close to killing my daughter, and had so nearly wrecked our lives.

But the gang didn't succeed in wrecking our lives or in breaking up our relationship, despite their best endeavours to claim Lara as their own. If anything, it's had the reverse effect. Because Lara and the other victims stood up to them and gave evidence against them, they will be in prison now for a very long time, while our lives will continue and our relationship go from strength to strength. Reliving those awful years through the trial, talking to the media and giving evidence to the serious case review that is looking at how the services responded to what was happening to the girls has given both of us an insight into what went on for each other during those dark times and an opportunity to process at least some of it.

What happened to Lara at the hands of those men and all her other abusers before them is so astronomically terrible I don't suppose she will ever be able to process it all, but somehow she has accommodated it and not let it corrupt her fundamental goodness and integrity or her sense of what matters in life, what is right and wrong. She is very cautious about relationships, particularly with men, but is open and loving with those she knows and trusts, with Noah and me, and our family and close friends. She is a woman now and our relationship is reciprocal. She supports and cares for me as much as I do her.

We have shared a rather unusual eleven years, and I have no idea how things might have been between us if those years had been rather more ordinary, or if she had been my birth child. What I do know is that Lara has immeasurably enriched my life and that we are at last properly mother and daughter.

Postscript

July 2014

I am just back from buying tiny-size baby clothes for the second time, girl's ones this time. Lara's daughter, Olivia Rose, was delivered by emergency C-section three days ago. Olivia is now out of the incubator, but will remain in the SCBU for a week or so more. She is doing fine, but being five weeks early, she hasn't got the hang of feeding properly. She is tiny and exquisite. Without the trauma of a normal birth, she is not at all pulled about, just round and pink, like a little, soft, gently breathing doll. She is a mini-me Lara.

Lara, the consummate survivor, is doing remarkably well too after having a serious haemorrhage and a placental abruption. Fortunately she was already in hospital with pregnancy complications when it happened and could be rushed into theatre and operated on immediately. If she had been at home, we might have lost them both. It doesn't bear thinking about. Noah and I can't wait to have them safely at home with us.

Noah is now a big brother and, at nearly six, old enough to relish the wonder of this tiny new life. He has just brought home an excellent end-of-year school report. He loves school and seems to have lots of friends. He plays in an under-six football team, has just received his twenty-metre swimming badge and has mastered a two-wheeler bike. He asks us from time to time about his dad, who and where he is and why he doesn't see him. We have tried to be honest with him in a way that is appropriate to his age.

I overheard another child at school asking him in the playground the other day why he didn't have a dad.

'I do have a dad,' he retorted firmly. 'It's just that he isn't very nice. He hurt Mummy when she was very young and we don't want to know him. But I do have a dad – everyone does.'

Olivia Rose has a dad, too, of course, again someone much older who isn't very nice and took advantage of a vulnerable young woman on virtually her first night out after she had just about got over the trauma of the trial. She didn't want to mix socially with anyone for months after we came back from the Old Bailey and then one night decided to go into town with some friends.

It's over a year now since the end of the trial. As well as the baby, a lot has happened, especially Lara finding through her job working with frail old people a real sense of purpose, maturity and self-worth. She has blossomed. She is on maternity leave now, of course, but plans to go back and eventually get day release to start training to work in the ambulance service. Her ultimate ambition is still to be a paramedic. She is also already showing what a wonderful, loving, natural mother she is. I won't need to do the baby care this time.

I have spent a long time thinking about all those dreadful years, trying to work out how it happened, whether and how it could have been prevented and why no one could or would help us. All my beliefs and prejudices were turned on their head by those terrible times.

I had thought social services would have the knowledge and experience to help a twelve-year-old child going into meltdown after years of abuse. Instead they blamed the victim, which facilitated further abuse, and in the end I discovered that a couple of serious offenders just out of jail had more instinct about how to offer care and protection to a vulnerable girl than costly children's homes and any number of professionals.

I thought the police would have intelligence about areas of organized gang crime rather than studiously turning a blind eye to offences too big and sensitive to get a grip on. There are more trials to come, but even with those the police have barely scratched the surface.

I didn't expect there to be, in a small place like Oxford, large numbers of people living quite beyond the reach of the law like in the Wild West or the Australian outback in the nineteenth century.

I hadn't fully appreciated how our justice system accepts as a legitimate tactic attempts to bully and break an innocent victim by the defence counsel so that a guilty abuser has the chance to go free.

I thought education was a right, not a treat to be withdrawn as a punishment by services frustrated and unable to cope with complex and challenging children, just to show they have the upper hand.

In short I hadn't realized just what a chocolate teapot our public sector is. It is simply not fit for purpose; it does not do what it says on the tin.

Whatever the conclusion of the long-overdue serious case review, and I won't hold my breath, my confidence in the system has been irrevocably shattered. We did encounter some good committed individuals, Jane Crump from the police and members of the Attach Team, but they were overwhelmed by organizations that stifle individual initiative and are founded on inertia, procedural rules and looking the other way.

I will, of course, encourage my grandchildren to respect the law and our public services, but I would say to them never, ever trust or rely on any of them. If you can cope without them, do, for they are very likely to make the situation worse. Only use them as an absolute last resort and be prepared for it all to back-fire on you. At the ripe old age of sixty-four, my latent anarchism, dormant since school, has been well and truly reawakened.

However, despite all that the gang and the system could throw at us, somehow we survived, came out the other side, and life is now really pretty fantastic.

ACKNOWLEDGEMENTS

As a completely inexperienced writer I am indebted to the guidance and support of Ingrid Connell and Zennor Compton at Pan Macmillan in helping me turn my diaries, notes and memories into something approaching a coherent description of some tumultuous times.

While for most of these awful years we received nothing but disinterest or condemnation from the statutory services in Oxfordshire, there were some people who tried to understand and support us and I would like to express my appreciation for the humanity and insight of PC Jane Crump of Thames Valley Police's Missing Persons Unit, Professor Anne Stewart at Oxfordshire Mental Health NHS Trust, and Gillian Burr and the rest of the Attach Team at Oxfordshire County Council.

But what really mattered and gave me the strength to keep going was the unconditional love and support of family and friends and in particular Michael, Victoria, Jean and Sue.

Note: Most names have been changed in the text to protect the anonymity of Lara and her children and of other vulnerable young people.